Working-Class Raj

Focusing on the military men, railway workers, and wives and children of the British working class who went to India after the Rebellion of 1857, *Working-Class Raj* explores the experiences of these working-class men and women in their own words. Drawing on a diverse collection of previously unused letters and diaries, it allows us to hear directly from these people for the first time. Working-class Brits in India enjoyed enormous privilege, reliant on native Indian labor and living, as one put it, "like gentlemen." But within the hierarchies of the Army and the rail yard, they remained working class, a potentially disruptive population that needed to be contained. Working in India and other parts of the empire, emigrating to settler colonies, often returning to Britain, and all the while attempting to maintain family ties across imperial distances, the British working class in the nineteenth century was a globalized population. This book reveals how working-class men and women were not atomized individuals, but part of communities that spanned the empire and were fundamentally shaped by it. This title is part of the Flip it Open Programme and may also be available Open Access. Check our website Cambridge Core for details.

Alexandra Lindgren-Gibson is Assistant Professor of History at the University of Mississippi. Her work has been published in the *Journal of Colonialism and Colonial History* and has been supported by the Charlotte W. Newcombe Foundation, the International Association for the Study of Sexuality, Culture, and Society, and the University of Rochester's Humanities Center.

Modern British Histories

Series Editors:

Deborah Cohen, *Northwestern University*
Margot Finn, *University College London*
Peter Mandler, *University of Cambridge*

'Modern British Histories' publishes original research monographs drawn from the full spectrum of a large and lively community of modern historians of Britain. Its goal is to keep metropolitan and national histories of Britain fresh and vital in an intellectual atmosphere increasingly attuned to, and enriched by, the transnational, the international and the comparative. It will include books that focus on British histories within the UK and that tackle the subject of Britain and the world inside and outside the boundaries of formal empire from 1750 to the present. An indicative – not exclusive – list of approaches and topics that the series welcomes includes material culture studies, modern intellectual history, gender, race and class histories, histories of modern science and histories of British capitalism within a global framework. Open and wide-ranging, the series will publish books by authoritative scholars, at all stages of their career, with something genuinely new to say.

A complete list of titles in the series can be found at:
www.cambridge.org/modernbritishhistories

Working-Class Raj

Colonialism and the Making of Class in British India

Alexandra Lindgren-Gibson

University of Mississippi

CAMBRIDGE
UNIVERSITY PRESS

CAMBRIDGE UNIVERSITY PRESS

Shaftesbury Road, Cambridge CB2 8EA, United Kingdom

One Liberty Plaza, 20th Floor, New York, NY 10006, USA

477 Williamstown Road, Port Melbourne, VIC 3207, Australia

314–321, 3rd Floor, Plot 3, Splendor Forum, Jasola District Centre, New Delhi – 110025, India

103 Penang Road, #05-06/07, Visioncrest Commercial, Singapore 238467

Cambridge University Press is part of Cambridge University Press & Assessment, a department of the University of Cambridge.

We share the University's mission to contribute to society through the pursuit of education, learning and research at the highest international levels of excellence.

www.cambridge.org
Information on this title: www.cambridge.org/9781009356589

DOI: 10.1017/9781009356565

First published 2024

A catalogue record for this publication is available from the British Library.

Library of Congress Cataloging-in-Publication Data
Names: Lindgren-Gibson, Alexandra, 1982- author.
Title: Working-class Raj : colonialism and the making of class in British India / Alexandra Lindgren-Gibson, University of Mississippi.
Description: Cambridge, United Kingdom ; New York, NY, USA : Cambridge University Press, 2023. | Series: Modern British histories | Includes bibliographical references and index.
Identifiers: LCCN 2023022926 (print) | LCCN 2023022927 (ebook) | ISBN 9781009356589 (hardback) | ISBN 9781009356572 (paperback) | ISBN 9781009356565 (epub)
Subjects: LCSH: Working class–India–History. | English–India–History. | Emigration and immigration–India–History. | Great Britain–Colonies. | Families–India–History.
Classification: LCC HD8684 .L563 2023 (print) | LCC HD8684 (ebook) | DDC 305.5/620954–dc23/eng/20230714
LC record available at https://lccn.loc.gov/2023022926
LC ebook record available at https://lccn.loc.gov/2023022927

ISBN 978-1-009-35658-9 Hardback

Contents

Acknowledgments

When I was growing up, my mom worked as an archivist at the Minnesota Historical Society. She occasionally would have to work on Saturdays and would take me along with her to the reading room. Between grumblings about having to thread the umpteenth microfilm for weekend genealogists, she would pull folders for me to look at. Sitting in a corner of the reading room, I read 1890s farmers' daybooks (very dull, mostly weather), news clippings, and letters. The letters were my favorites. Written by settlers, farmers, and immigrants, even if they didn't have much to say, they still carried with them the illicit thrill of reading someone else's mail and the magic of reaching back into the past. It was memories of these Saturdays that came back to me sitting in the Asia, Pacific, and Africa Collections reading room (whose staff deserves an enormous thanks) at the British Library, reading shelf lists in search of working-class histories. The letters I found there were in so many ways similar to those I had looked at as a child. These were once again the records of people of no particular note, who wrote about the immediate things that mattered to them, and who left their histories behind, even if what remained was fragmented and seldom seen. It never occurred to me that these records would be difficult to find, because I had spent my childhood reading ones just like them. So I would first like to acknowledge and dedicate this book to my mom, Dallas Lindgren, for teaching me to find delight in histories of the ordinary and everyday and that these histories exist if you take the time to look for them.

This book would not have been possible without the generous support of the following organizations: the University of Rochester's Humanities Center and Joanie Rubin for having me as a fellow for the 2019–20 academic year; the University of Mississippi's Sarah Isom Center for Women and Gender Studies, College of Liberal Arts, and the History Department; the Charlotte W. Newcombe Foundation; the International Association for the Study of Sexuality, Culture, and Society; the Sexualities Project at Northwestern, Northwestern University's Buffett Institute, History Department; Chabraja Center for Historical Studies;

and the Graduate School. These organizations' funding and faith in my work have made all the difference.

If I have learned anything over the course of the years I have spent working on this project, it is that no academic work is done alone. Whether excitedly writing home about how I stumbled upon a perfect and perfectly unlikely discovery in the archive, commiserating about my struggle through a chapter that would simply not come together, or realizing that the idea I had been joking about was actually kind of great, my work has been enormously enriched by the help, knowledge, and love of my friends, colleagues, mentors, and family. The research and writing of the book has taken me all over the world, and I want to acknowledge the people who have made the places I have lived, whether for months or years, into homes. Enormous thanks to the friends who I have met and who have taken me in while on research and conference trips and made them greatly enjoyable: Carol Gold, Marianna Potterton, Trang Tran, Ellen Filor (who, along with her family, also falls into the former category and put me up for three fantastic weeks in Edinburgh), Sabrina Rahman, Hilary Ingram. Arunima Datta, and Elizabeth Prevost. In Rochester, New York, thank you to Daniel Rinn, Jean Pedersen, Brianna Theobald, Stewart Weaver, Kate Phillips, and the writing group at the Susan B Anthony Institute. In Chicago and Evanston, Illinois, thank you to Tessie Liu, Ed Muir, Rajeev Kinra, Deborah Cohen, Alex Owen, Blake Smith, Sam Kling, Ian Saxine, Emma Goldsmith, Beth Healey, Rachel Taylor, Marlous Van Waijenburg, Sarah Roth, Ashley Johnson Bavery, Don Johnson, Sally Olson, Sara Jatcko, Rob Winkeler, Katie Gustafson, and especially to Kevin Baker for his brilliant and very last-minute guidance. In Oxford, MS, thank you to Mikaela Adams, Becky Marchiel, Peter Thilly, Eva Payne, Zack Kagan-Guthrie, Frances Kneupper, Theresa Levitt, Marc Lerner, Emily Fransee, Susan Stearns, Anne Twitty, Jared Pack, Jacqueline DiBiasie-Sammons, Kyle G. Fritz, Jonathan Klingler, Miles T. Armaly, Carolyn Freiwald for her Midwestern beers and friendship, Sudeshna Roy for being willing to book a flight at the drop of a hat, and to Tori Brown for forest bathing, gossip, and friendship. And thank you to Michelle Pusari, Karla Hurtley, Jen Coleman, Caroline Manning, and Dave Gibson for being in my life much longer than this book has.

Introduction

This book begins with a family that does not fit. Pollie Keen was born to a Buckinghamshire washerwoman. She spent her teenage years as a servant, married a farm laborer-turned-soldier, and lived out her late twenties as a lady of leisure, flitting between tea parties, carriage rides, and dances that lasted into the early hours of the morning. In 1889, Pollie, her three children, and her husband Dick, by then a sergeant with the Royal Horse Artillery, went to India. It was once the family had settled in Sialkot in Punjab that Pollie's social status and material world changed so dramatically. Dick wrote to his brother that the family was enjoying the "fine country" and enumerated the servants at their disposal. "I am same [*sic*] like gentleman. We are both in bed when the cook comes in to light the fire, lay the breakfast and all ready before we get up, and the barber taps at the door to shave me and man is waiting to clean the boots and clothes for all of us."[1] Having fires laid, shoes polished, breakfast made, and a barber at the ready were luxuries Dick and Pollie could never reasonably have hoped for in Britain. Pollie bragged to her mother that, after a lifetime of domestic labor, her only duties were dusting and changing the bed linens.[2]

For the Keens and many families like them, India was indeed a fine country. Racial hierarchies, combined with the vast supply of native labor, allowed members of the British working class to live in relative leisure and to hold management positions that would have been inaccessible in Britain. But the Keens were still officially classified among the enlisted men and camp followers, they were subject to weekly inspection of their quarters, and their children attended the inadequate schools provided for the offspring of soldiers. Moreover, once the family returned to England, they lost the lofty status and material comforts they enjoyed in India. The Keen family's precipitous climb up, and unstable position upon, the social ladder was a product of Britain's imperialism.

[1] Dick Keen to Arthur Keen, December 22, 1889, IOR MSS Eur. F528/8.   [2] Ibid.

1

The Keens' story was not unusual, though it is one that is seldom told in the histories of both empire and the British working class.

Starting at the end of the Indian Rebellion in 1858 and extending into the early twentieth century, *Working-Class Raj* uncovers the histories of individuals and families like the Keens to make three major, interconnected arguments. First, the Victorian British working class should be understood as a global population. By the end of the nineteenth century, British non-elites made up half of the British residents of India, 75,000 of 150,000 total.[3] Most of this population was drawn from the British working classes at home, and the vast majority came to India with the Army. Some came to build and manage the railways that began to carve up the Subcontinent in the middle of the nineteenth century. Men came to India because they were weary of life in factories or mines or unable to find employment in Britain. They joined the Army because military service was one of the few avenues for adventure available to men of their class. Most of these men came to India on their own. Some brought wives and children with them; others met and married or formed alliances with British, Indian, or Eurasian women while in India. Once there, they joined communities in which the class structure of Britain was at once replicated and refracted by race.

Second, though the British working class in India lived within the spaces of British imperialism and was governed by its institutions, they were neither successfully regulated nor contained by them. In the aftermath of the Indian Rebellion, military and civilian leaders increased the numbers of British soldiers and workers in India, hoping to create loyal, easy-to-manage fighting and labor forces. Civil servants, military officials, and reforming elites put some of the same techniques used to contain and manage a native population to work corralling a large and potentially unruly subordinate British working class. Presidency governments conducted large-scale population surveys to quantify and define the poor European population. Private charity schools, funded in part by government grants, struggled to determine what combination of racial make-up, class background, and education could produce a salvageable British subject. Military cantonments placed strict controls on where, with whom, and under what conditions people could live.

And yet, none of these plans managed the people brought in to prop up British rule or anticipated the effects of decades lived in India on this

---

[3] David Arnold, who was the first to call for a larger study of the non-elite population of India, estimated this population at 75,000 in 1900. "European Orphans and Vagrants in India in the Nineteenth Century," *The Journal of Imperial and Commonwealth History* 7, no. 2 (1979): 104.

population. Demographers despaired of accurately distinguishing between the poor white and mixed-race populations. Schools turned out students trained for jobs that existed only in England. Military regulation of intimate life in cantonments limited certain types of sexual immorality while creating the conditions for others to flourish. In response to these failures of official imagination, British non-elites created their own social worlds within the institutions of British imperialism. With no rubric to understand the changes in social status produced by the intersection of race and class in empire, imperial administrators governed India without ever finding a way of successfully managing the population they had helped to create.

Third, this study asks how members of the British working class understood themselves in empire and argues that family histories are key to answering that question. The Raj's working-class subjects did not sever their roots in Britain once in India. They frequently left extended families at home and spent a great deal of time, energy, and money corresponding, exchanging material goods, and anticipating reunions with their friends and relations. As a result, being part of the British working class meant being part of global networks. These networks spread information and helped those embedded within them to maintain affective ties. It was through these networks that the Raj's working-class British residents passed, disseminated, and managed information about empire and social mobility. Families at home eagerly awaited "exotic" tales of Indian life. Along with the anticipated accounts of wild animals and Mughal palaces came stories of Indian servants, leisurely afternoons with nothing to do, and summers in the hills. Imagery that has been both historically and historiographically associated with British elites also formed part of the working-class world. These stories linked Britain and India while providing first-hand evidence of just how malleable status could be. For working-class Britons in India, class and status in India were fluid categories, fluctuating to allow for shifts in place, occupation, family, race, and knowledge. By surveying the archival records and remnants these people left behind, we see that class in the British Empire was neither given nor static, but instead informed by British preoccupations, constructed and constantly renegotiated on the ground in global sites.

Working-Class Raj unites histories of the soldier with histories of the family and the British working class in empire. The men and women of working-class origin who went to India came from a wide range of occupational backgrounds and from locations spanning the British Isles. Once in India, however, they fell into two primary occupation groups, which overlapped at times – the Army and the railways. Most of the non-elite British population of India was connected with the British Army at some point in their lives. Fully one-third of all troops enlisted in the British Army passed through India during their term of service, making Indian service a characteristic, rather than extraordinary, component of a military career.[4] Military service was an element of many working-class lives – it was one of a number of avenues working-class men pursued in a search for employment, mobility, and adventure. While the enlisted men of the British Army came almost exclusively from working-class or rural backgrounds, they have occupied a peripheral role in working-class histories. Nick Mansfield's *Soldiers as Workers* has challenged this narrative, writing the enlisted men of the East India Company armies into the labor history of the British working class.[5] Carolyn Stedman's account of a British soldier's Indian political awakening likewise understands soldiers' histories to form part of working-class histories.[6] In the Indian context, Philippa Levine and Erica Wald have analyzed the ways in which elite concerns over working-class morality shaped imperial policy.[7] And Robert Bickers has traced the social rise and fall of a British soldier-turned-Shanghai police officer.[8] Building on this previous scholarship, *Working-Class Raj* treats imperial soldiering as a particular and disputed type of labor and considers its place in a post-Rebellion, largely peacetime India. Rethinking soldiering as work and soldiers as part of an expansive British working class helps to bring together the histories of the British working class in empire and at home.

Family and domestic culture became central to British identity in the Victorian era, with a well-run nuclear family defining what it meant to be middle class and, in the empire, what it meant to be British.[9] Families acted as information networks to spread information about Indian

---

[4] T. A. Heathcote, *The Military in British India: The Development of British Land Forces in South Asia, 1600–1947* (Manchester: Manchester University Press, 1995), 127.

[5] Nick Mansfield, *Soldiers as Workers: Class, Employment, Conflict and the Nineteenth-Century Military* (Oxford: Oxford University Press, 2016).

[6] Carolyn Steedman, *The Radical Soldier's Tale John Pearman 1819–1908* (London: Routledge, 1988).

[7] Philippa Levine, *Prostitution, Race, and Politics: Policing Venereal Disease in the British Empire* (New York: Routledge, 2003); Erica Wald, *Vice in the Barracks: Medicine, the Military and the Making of Colonial India, 1780–1868* (London: Palgrave Macmillan, 2014).

[8] Robert A. Bickers, *Empire Made Me: An Englishman Adrift in Shanghai* (Columbia University Press, 2003).

[9] Leonore Davidoff and Catherine Hall, *Family Fortunes: Men and Women of the English Middle Class, 1780–1850* (Chicago: University of Chicago Press, 1991); Anna Clark, *The Struggle for the Breeches: Gender and the Making of the British Working Class* (Berkeley: University of California Press, 1995) on the working class. This familial view of class has not been universally convincing – Dror Wahrman argues that changing political formations at the turn of the eighteenth century shaped class and made middle-class

experiences. They changed in structure in response to absences, money gained and lost, and relationships broken as a result of Indian military service and employment. And they were subject to critique and regulation from above. This book builds on recent studies that have unsettled the middle-class subject as the logical point from which to start thinking about empire and instead argues for the family as a useful category of analysis.[10] Scholars studying the connections between race and identity argue that imperial policy played a major role in shaping what family meant on the ground in empire.[11] These histories demonstrate the significance of family formation to the empire and the role empire played in shaping British family life in colony and metropole. In a metropolitan context, scholars studying working-class families have returned to classic questions of social history through a cultural lens, delving into the histories of working-class fathers, the lives of illegitimate children, the family wage, and the history of the marital bed to better understand working-class marriages and families.[12] Historians are likewise embracing genealogical methods to tell working-class histories through Census records, passenger lists, and enlistment papers.[13] *Working-Class Raj* seeks

identity the British default. *Imagining the Middle Class: The Political Representation of Class in Britain, c.1780–1840* (Cambridge: Cambridge University Press, 1995).

[10] Margot Finn, "The Barlow Bastards: Romance Comes Home from the Empire," in Margot Finn, Michael Lobban, and Jenny Bourne Taylor, eds., *Legitimacy and Illegitimacy in Nineteenth-Century Law, Literature and History* (London: Palgrave Macmillan, 2010), 25–47; Catherine Hall, *Macaulay and Son: Architects of Imperial Britain* (New Haven: Yale University Press, 2012); Emma Rothschild, *The Inner Life of Empires: An Eighteenth-Century History* (Princeton: Princeton University Press, 2011); and Erika Rappaport, "'The Bombay Debt': Letter Writing, Domestic Economies and Family Conflict in Colonial India," *Gender & History* 16, no. 2 (August 2004): 223–60.

[11] Durba Ghosh, *Sex and the Family in Colonial India: The Making of Empire* (Cambridge: Cambridge University Press, 2006); Elizabeth Buettner, *Empire Families: Britons and Late Imperial India* (Oxford: Oxford University Press, 2004); Esme Cleall, *Missionary Discourse: Negotiating Difference in the British Empire, c. 1840–95* (London: Palgrave Macmillan, 2012); Ann Laura Stoler, *Carnal Knowledge and Imperial Power: Race and the Intimate in Colonial Rule* (Berkeley: University of California Press, 2002).

[12] Julie-Marie Strange, *Fatherhood and the British Working Class, 1865–1914* (Cambridge: Cambridge University Press, 2015); Ginger S. Frost, *Illegitimacy in English Law and Society, 1860–1930* (Oxford: Oxford University Press, 2016); Emma Griffin, *Bread Winner: An Intimate History of the Victorian Economy* (New Haven: Yale University Press, 2020), Vicky Holmes, *In Bed with the Victorians: The Life-Cycle of Working-Class Marriage* (London: Springer, 2017).

[13] Alison Light uses this technique to moving effect in both a history of her own family *Common People: In Pursuit of My Ancestors* (Chicago: University of Chicago Press, 2015) and *Mrs. Woolf and the Servants: An Intimate History of Domestic Life in Bloomsbury* (London: Penguin, 2007).

to draw together these types of studies, bringing the insights of working-class histories of family to bear on family histories of empire.[14]

The question of how the British working class came to learn about, understand, and incorporate empire into their own worldviews has prompted plentiful historical work. John MacKenzie's Studies in Imperialism Series first grappled with the question of how the British came to understand and be affected by their own empire in the mid-1980s and continues, now under the editorship of Andrew Thompson, to argue for the essential role of empire in British history and vice versa.[15] Bernard Porters' *Absent-Minded Imperialists* took on a contrary position.[16] While that book inspired lengthy debates and plentiful critiques, Porter's dismissal of empire as a relevant part of British working-class experience was not prominent among them. It has been easy to ignore the working class as imperial actors because of the relatively small number of men and women who lived in imperial space. But doing so perpetuates the notion that once in India, members of the British working class ceased to have any connections to the working class in Britain and became solely imperial instead. What has seemed to some historians to be a working-class indifference to empire is, *Working-Class Raj* argues, an assimilation of it into everyday life.

Through working-class correspondence, we can reframe these questions to ask how being a part of empire became such an unexceptional part of life for working-class British families and communities. Empire mattered; it was not peripheral, nor did it only capture attention in moments of great violence or drama. Though working-class experiences of British imperialism might be fraught with anxiety or families separated by imperial distances struggle to maintain connections, these affective responses were an ordinary part of what it meant to be working class in the second half of the nineteenth century. The effects of a single letter, material object, social connection, or shared experience reached far.

---

[14] Among many others, John McKenzie and the historians of the Manchester Studies in Imperialism Series, Frederick Cooper and Ann Laura Stoler, eds., *Tensions of Empire: Colonial Cultures in a Bourgeois World* (Berkeley: University of California Press, 1997), Tony Ballantyne and Antoinette M. Burton, eds., *Moving Subjects: Gender, Mobility, and Intimacy in an Age of Global Empire* (Urbana: University of Illinois Press, 2009) and *Empires and the Reach of the Global, 1870–1945* (Cambridge, MA: The Belknap Press of Harvard University Press, 2012).

[15] *Propaganda and Empire* inaugurated the collection, which now runs to hundreds of volumes. John M. MacKenzie, *Propaganda and Empire: The Manipulation of British Public Opinion, 1880–1960* (1986; repr., Manchester: Manchester University Press, 2003).

[16] Bernard Porter, *The Absent-Minded Imperialists: Empire, Society, and Culture in Britain* (Oxford: Oxford University Press, 2004).

Much like their elite counterparts, the numerically insignificant proportion of British working-class men and women who directly participated in the Raj had an outsized effect on life in British India and their working-class communities of origin.

Where Do Their Stories Come From?

At the core of this book are the textual remnants that working-class correspondents and memoirists left behind. This written record not only preserved histories of the working-class Raj for the present day but also formed the sinews that bound together communities across great distances. Correspondence between far-flung members of working-class families and friend groups is scattered throughout the India Office Collections at the British Library and the National Libraries of Scotland and Ireland. These papers reveal not only individual correspondents' subjectivities but also how they managed, and sometimes damaged, family relationships through the act of writing.

Working-Class Raj focuses primarily on the correspondence of those who came from Britain to India. Domiciled Europeans, who spent generations in the country, and Eurasians, of European and Indian descent, likewise formed a part of this imperial Indian non-elite, but they tended to maintain correspondence links with British friends and family less. How people communicated across physical and experiential distance, why that communication lapsed, and how those lapses affect knowledge and memory of Indian experience in Britain are among the central questions this book seeks to answer. Because non-elites in India had no choice but to write to one another to communicate, they produced a significant volume of correspondence. Soldiers paid penny post rates to send mail to Britain, suggesting that correspondence was both accessible to enlisted men and their families and understood as important across classes by elite officials.[17] Those who could not write themselves enlisted friends or family members or paid an amanuensis to write for them.[18] And because working-class correspondence across empire was bound up in systems of colonial governance, it was more likely to be

---

[17] Nigel Hall, "The Materiality of Letter Writing: A Nineteenth Century Perspective," in David Barton and Nigel Hall, eds., *Letter Writing as a Social Practice* (Philadelphia: John Benjamins, 1999), 88.

[18] In the 1860s, the English literacy rate hovered around 60 percent according to David Vincent's calculations in *Literacy and Popular Culture: England 1750–1914* (Cambridge: Cambridge University Press, 1993), 24–25. The rate for working-class women was slightly lower; see Robert Woods, *The Demography of Victorian England and Wales* (Cambridge: Cambridge University Press, 2000), 148.

preserved for the archive than were the letters of a working-class family in Britain. Combining these papers with elite accounts – including the official reports of the India Office Records held at the British Library, the records of charity schools in India and elite institutions in England, the papers of anti-prostitution investigators, and the British Indian press – allows me to access the perspectives of working-class Britons.

The British Library contains the private papers of hundreds of non-elites who were involved with the military, railways, charity schools, and civil service in some way. Among these scores of letter collections, some, like the letters of Jim Jones of the 1st Bengal Light Cavalry, comprised only two letters, an inquiry from a friend and Jim's response, still unsent when he died.[19] Others, like the Keen family papers, span decades and contain correspondence, photographs, sketches, family jokes, and family arguments shared between India and Britain. Many of these papers came through family donations, but many more arrived at the archive through a combination of happenstance and exhaustive imperial record-keeping. The collections that came to the archive by chance provide something closer to a view of non-elite life unfiltered by archival bias.

These documents of working-class life in empire likewise appear concealed in projects asking a different set of questions. The interview subjects of the "Family Life and Work Experience before 1918" oral history collection, for example, recalled fathers in imperial service and early childhoods spent in India. The interviewers, looking for evidence of social and political change in Britain, did little to follow up on these empire stories.[20] Though ex-soldiers' memoirs focus primarily on histories of military service, they also contain tales of life before and after joining the Army. These writers reveal the motivations that led them to travel across the globe, the economic pressures that shaped their decisions, and what they made of their lives in Britain after decades abroad. Radio 4's *Plain Tales from the Raj* series, first broadcast in the 1970s, helped kick-start Britain's imperial nostalgia culture industry with first-hand accounts of life in India. The interview subjects came from a wide range of backgrounds. Many of the interviewees recalled working-class childhoods and the novelty of improved material conditions and social standing in India. These individual stories were broadcast with audio clips spliced together, homogenizing the speakers and creating the impression of an elite Raj. By returning to the raw material of the oral interviews, a more granular view of British Indian life comes into view.

---

[19] James Jones collection, 1860, IOR MSS Eur. F133/83.
[20] Family Life and Work Experience before 1918, C707.

The most notable of the correspondence collections are filed under IOR Mss Eur F133, originating in the files of India House and now housed in the British Library. The letters in this collection came to the archive by a haphazard route. The circumstances of their survival can tell us as much about how working-class imperial experience was valued and remembered as the letters can about the lives and emotional worlds of their authors. These papers are what is left of the estates of East Indian Railway Company workers and members of the Indian Medical Service who died in India.[21] When a soldier or worker died, his personal effects were gathered together and sold, with the proceeds going to pay off any debts and the remainder going to his next of kin. Items of no monetary value should have been returned to the next of kin, but the papers in this collection were never returned, either because family could not be located or because the papers themselves were lost. Their journey to the archive was born out of the missed connections and miscommunications endemic to working-class lives – unstable housing, poor access to administrative or legal aid, and indifference from people in power.

Any texts that have made their way into the archive have already gone through a selection process that is both biased and arbitrary, subject as much to structures of power as to chance.[22] This selection process has not only preserved elite histories in far greater numbers but also made them more visible and available. Working-class letters are infrequently found in the archives, then, not because they were infrequently written but because there was no real archival interest in retaining the histories of such an obscure population until it was too late to preserve them in large numbers.[23] Because the letters in the F133 collection came to the archive by historical accident, rather than through purposeful donation, they

---

[21] Collections information from catalog note, Oliver Wooller, September 1995, MSS Eur. F133. The Indian Medical Service (or Establishment) was a civilian service that provided surgeons and other medical officers attached to the military to India. Though the Indian Railways have been known as a key employer for India's Eurasian population, in the first decades of their operation, they imported a significant proportion of their labor from Britain.

[22] Ann Laura Stoler and Antoinette Burton have looked at the archive in a specifically colonial context, while Carolyn Steedman has examined the archive and the histories it produces in the context of modernity. See Ann Laura Stoler, *Along the Archival Grain: Epistemic Anxieties and Colonial Common Sense* (Princeton, NJ: Princeton University Press, 2009); Antoinette M. Burton, *Archive Stories: Facts, Fictions, and the Writing of History* (Durham, NC: Duke University Press, 2005) and *Dwelling in the Archive: Women Writing House, Home, and History in Late Colonial India* (New York: Oxford University Press, 2003); and Carolyn Steedman, *Dust: The Archive and Cultural History* (New Brunswick, NJ: Rutgers University Press, 2002).

[23] For example, the interviews in the British Library's British in India Oral Archive were not conducted until the mid-1970s, prompted by a new interest in the experiences of ordinary people during the late years of the empire and decolonization.

sidestep this archival tendency. The F133 collection contains a much higher proportion of letters from poor and uneducated correspondents, and from correspondents whose experience in empire ended abruptly in displacement and loss.

Gender plays a role in the ways in which imperial experiences were recorded and entered into the archive. In the case of the F133 letters, this is an artifact of their history; men who died in India would have their wives' and sisters' letters in their possession rather than their own. But even in the case of donated collections, women's letters, written as events unfolded, predominate. Men, spurred by the late-century popularity of military memoirs, tended to record their experiences once they returned to Britain and after the fact.[24] This gender division in writing style can give us insight into the ways in which working-class correspondents transmitted information about India to their respective audiences. Women were the bearers of class in Victorian thought and, entangled in that role, maintainers of moral standards.[25] Because men were loath to write about their own sexual experiences, dominant ideas about what was moral, how society was or should be structured in British India, and the role of the Army in shaping family life and social relationships can be read in accounts about and by women.

These letters have much in common with immigrant correspondence – one of the few types of archival materials produced by non-elites that have been preserved in large numbers. These commonalities are more than just stylistic; they reveal the continuities between these groups. Drawing for the most part from the holdings of North American archives, historians like Laura Ishiguro and David Gerber have discussed the effects of form and style on settler and migrant epistolary practices in the Canadian and US contexts, respectively.[26] The similarities between working-class imperial and migrant letters are striking – and for good

---

[24] Edward Gosling, "'A Soldier's Life Is a Merry One', or, 'A Certain Cure for Gout and Rheumatism': The Shift in Popular Perceptions of the Common Soldier in Late Victorian Britain, 1870–c.1910," in Kevin Linch and Matthew Lord, eds., *Redcoats to Tommies: The Experience of the British Soldier from the Eighteenth Century* (Boydell & Brewer, 2021), 187.

[25] Leonore Davidoff and Catherine Hall make the argument that women create and bear middle-class status. Davidoff and Hall, *Family Fortunes*, 30.

[26] Laura Ishiguro, *Nothing to Write Home About: British Family Correspondence and the Settler Colonial Everyday in British Columbia* (Vancouver: University of British Columbia Press, 2019); David A. Gerber, *Authors of Their Lives: The Personal Correspondence of British Immigrants to North America in the Nineteenth Century* (New York: New York University Press, 2008). Marina Carter has shown similar community-making tendencies in the even scarcer traces left by forced migrants in the Indian Ocean world. Marina Carter, *Voices from Indenture: Experiences of Indian Migrants in the British Empire* (London: Leicester University Press, 1996).

reason. The correspondents come from similar class backgrounds, and the correspondence shares many of the hallmarks of the migrant letter. Letters passed from hand to hand, stream-of-consciousness style, references to local gossip rendered at once irrelevant and precious by vast distance – are stylistically replicated in the Indian correspondence. As in the case of immigrant letters, correspondence played an integral, if uneven, role in the creation of family and community networks. While imperial experience itself was not widespread, either among elites or the working class, letters granted access and information about empire to a far larger group and a more diverse range of people than can be suggested by merely tallying up those involved in imperial service. And letters from home served to maintain community between individual members of the working class separated by distance and experience.

But not all information was shared equally among these correspondents. Details about imperial experiences that further emphasized the separation between correspondents infrequently found their way into letters. Again, these silences are characteristic of imperial correspondents; Ishiguro has found similar elisions among settlers in British Columbia, where leaving Indigenous Canadians unrecorded allowed settlers to present an uninhabited and untouched landscape to their correspondents.[27] Britain-based letter writers were preoccupied with the world of South Asians, but British writers in India offered little information in response to queries. James Commack's sister and brother-in-law wrote him to be wary of offending the people he encountered as they were known to be "vicious and spiteful."[28] India-based correspondents gained little from discussing the things that made them different and stood to lose much if they no longer had a common basis of experience with their families. As a result of this self-censoring, members of imperial working-class families based in Britain might gain a working understanding of life in India for European railway workers or soldiers, but they had little sense of the larger contexts in which their correspondents lived. These silences make the few instances in which information about native India life or critiques of British rule break through all the more striking.

A White Working-Class Raj?

A working-class Raj is a seeming contradiction in terms. British rule was predicated not only on the fact of British military and political power, but

---

[27] Ishiguro, *Nothing to Write Home About*, 6.
[28] Fanny and Fred Winter to James Commack, November 24, 1861, IOR MSS Eur. F133/ 43.

also on British claims to superiority – racial, moral, and administrative. One of the ironies of British imperialism was that this rule was carried out by members of the British working class, people who were rhetorically deraced in Britain and India alike, whose morality failed to align with middle-class notions of propriety, and who could not govern – either the colony or themselves.[29] And yet, men and women of working-class origin went to India in thousands to support British rule, whether by their labor – as in the case of railway workers – or their mere presence, in the case of the British Army in India.

If members of the British working class held an ambiguous position to rule in India, they also held an ambiguous position to work. Once in India, the British working class no longer worked, at least not in the same way they had at home. Men who had labored building rail lines across Britain became managers of teams of laborers. Women who had earned a living in domestic service directed servants of their own. After 1858, there was relatively little for British soldiers to do in India apart from being there, representing the threat of British military might. Some were involved in the infrequent "small wars" on the borders, but the vast majority spent much of their time in cantonments and on marches, engaging in little fighting. Failure to work became a defining feature of British non-elites in India and underlies elite anxieties about class instability. The relationship to labor was made even more ambiguous by the simultaneous presence of another, much larger, Indian working-class, servant, and peasant population. The lowest rungs of society in the Raj, the positions usually taken by the working class in Britain, were relegated to grossly underpaid Indian workers.

That working-class Britons in India did not appear to do that much work was a constant source of concern for elites. But idle soldiers were not shirking their duty; they were idle by design; their leisure was a necessary by-product of maintaining a standing Army in India. Likewise, railway workers in managerial positions traded hard physical labor for more money and more leisure, at the expense of separation from family in Britain. This mass of people thus was defined by elites and the state in the negative. They rejected British moral codes, they did not uphold British claims to racial superiority, they were not educated to British standards, they stayed in India, and they lived among Indians. In short, they did everything that a respectable, middle-class member of British Indian society was not meant to do. Ultimately, British elites in India defined those of working-class origin by their culturally and racially

---

[29] This of course mirrors the other great irony of British rule, that many of the troops enforcing imperial authority were natives of the colony in question.

suspect connections to South Asians and the colony itself.[30] But this is not how they understood themselves. One of the goals of this book is to uncover how British men and women of working-class origin saw their own relation to imperial rule and developed private lives and public worlds in response to and in spite of regulation and rule from above.

For British people who went to India, class became a fluid category, much like a life-stage.[31] One might start a young adult life single, marry, be widowed, and marry again. In a similar process, one might be working class in London, non-elite in India, and working class again in London. These shifts did not mean that these class categories cannot be used to understand social life, relationships among individuals, and individuals' relationships to the state and politics, but rather that they must be understood as conditional. And that people might choose to ally themselves with one category regardless of their material circumstances, relationships to power, or position as an employer or worker. These movements did not happen smoothly; they are identifiable in the frictions they create between families, classes, and races. These men and women did not belong solely to an Indian world; they comprised a significant and long-ignored segment of the British working class as a whole. Working class became not an all-encompassing category, but one that subjects could move into and out of. Indian service did not create strictly upward or downward mobility, but instead created the conditions for non-elites to live in a state of social flux. In order to locate this change, it is necessary to think differently – to shift focus to the ties that bind the British working class in India to their counterparts at home. This enables us to reintegrate the experience of working-class Britons in India back into the history of the working class in Britain.

Terminology and Identity

Defining who made up this population and what to call it has been a problem since the colonial period. Because the social organization of

---

[30] Elizabeth Buettner argues that British racial and class identity was at stake in maintaining a middle and upper class in early twentieth-century India – through racial and geographic separation. Elite British families sent their children to Britain to be educated out of any habits that may have connected them to India. See Buettner, *Empire Families*, 2004.

[31] This discussion relies on E. P. Thompson's classic formulation of class in Britain as a relationship resulting out of shared experience as well as Joanna Bourke's familial and cultural insight that people might call themselves working class based on family histories and upbringing, regardless of their current position in society. E. P. Thompson, *The Making of the English Working Class* (New York: Vintage, 1966), 9 and Joanna Bourke, *Working Class Cultures in Britain, 1890–1960: Gender, Class, and Ethnicity* (London: Routledge, 1994), 25.

British Indian society was in such flux, because one of the common results of Indian service was social mobility in either direction, and because British non-elites in India felt little allegiance to the vast population of laboring South Asians, "working class" does not fully encompass the position British non-elites occupied in India.[32] But, at the same time, these men and women were treated by their social superiors in much the same way they would have been in Britain. To manage these inconsistencies, I use the terms "working-class," "of working-class origin," and "non-elite" where relevant. Non-elite is a capacious term that can contain downwardly mobile members of the middle class, elites who chose to abandon their class position, mixed-race Eurasians who aligned themselves with British society, but were proscribed from participating fully in it, and men and women who were born into the British working class in Britain. On the other hand, "working-class" and "of working-class origin" indicate class position in Britain. Even as these men and women experienced changes in status in India, they remained part of working-class communities rendered global in scope by family and communication networks. When I refer to the "working-class Raj," I mean to suggest this very phenomenon, a Raj populated in part by members of the British working classes, which was a result shaped by them.

Ideas about race and the status of mixed-race people further complicate the definition and enumeration of this group in the Raj.[33] Though clearly not Indian, the racial status of British non-elites was uncertain, and ideas surrounding status and race changed over time. In the eighteenth century, official anxieties circled around the interracial offspring of British military men and Indian women; their nationality and racial standing were yet to be determined at that point.[34] As a result, the British non-elite population was conceived of as hybrid, composed of soldiers, poor whites, and interracial families. Although this description remained fairly stable throughout the nineteenth century, the moral

---

[32] For this dynamic in Britain, see Andrew S. Thompson, *The Empire Strikes Back?: The Impact of Imperialism on Britain from the Mid-Nineteenth Century* (London: Routledge, 2014), Chapter 3. See also Anthony Cox, *Empire, Industry and Class: The Imperial Nexus of Jute, 1840–1940* (London: Routledge, 2012), and Jim Tomlinson, *Dundee and the Empire: "Juteopolis" 1850–1939* (Edinburgh: Edinburgh University Press, 2014).

[33] Since Ann Laura Stoler called for scholars to further investigate the relationship between the imperial state and intimate life, historians have responded with histories of relationships and childhoods shaped by racial hierarchies. Harald Fischer-Tiné, *Low and Licentious Europeans: Race, Class, and White 'Subalternity' in Colonial India* (New Delhi: Orient BlackSwan, 2009); Satoshi Mizutani, *The Meaning of White: Race, Class, and the "Domiciled Community" in British India 1858–1930* (Oxford: Oxford University Press, 2011); Laura Bear, *Lines of the Nation: Indian Railway Workers, Bureaucracy, and the Intimate Historical Self* (New York: Columbia University Press, 2007).

[34] See Ghosh, *Sex and the Family in Colonial India*.

implications of such a hybrid community did not. Racially mixed relationships and offspring were no longer the necessary results of an occupying army, but signs of moral decay and signifiers of failure to understand or live up to middle-class ideals. In the mid-nineteenth century, low-ranking soldiers and their families drew concern, as intersecting discourses of scientific racism, medicine, and hygiene united to make the poor soldier both an object of charity and a vector of British national disintegration.[35]

"Eurasian," "Anglo-Indian," and "domiciled European" all recur in contemporary accounts and historiography. In the eighteenth and much of the nineteenth century, "Eurasian" was the official term used to refer to people of mixed European and Indian heritage. The European component was usually either British or Portuguese or a combination of both.[36] In the early years of East India Company rule, it was expected that British men stationed in India would enter into sexual relationships, sometimes marry, and have children with Indian women.[37] The offspring of these relationships, for the most part, were treated with the same sort of limited and idiosyncratic acceptance as illegitimate children were in Britain. The combined forces of rising British evangelicalism, the reactionary, scandal-averse governors who followed Warren Hastings' notoriously decadent rule, and the increasing numbers of British women encouraged to join husbands in India meant that by the 1840s, such relationships were no longer tolerated.[38]

Eurasians were prohibited from rising in either the East India Company Army or the covenanted civil service, limiting them to low-level clerkships.[39] Railway employment became a popular and, in many cases, the only option as rail lines expanded across the country in the 1860s and 1870s. In response to these prohibitions, the Eurasian

---

[35] David Arnold, *Colonizing the Body: State Medicine and Epidemic Disease in Nineteenth-Century India* (Berkeley: University of California Press, 1993), 36–40, and "Race, Place and Bodily Difference in Early Nineteenth-Century India," *Historical Research* 77, no. 196 (May 2004): 254–73; Dane Kennedy, *The Magic Mountains: Hill Stations and the British Raj* (Berkeley: University of California Press, 1996); Philippa Levine, *Prostitution, Race, and Politics: Policing Venereal Disease in the British Empire* (New York: Routledge, 2003).

[36] C. J. Hawes, *Poor Relations: The Making of a Eurasian Community in British India, 1773–1833* (Richmond, Surrey: Curzon Press, 1996), 2.

[37] William Dalrymple, *White Mughals: Love and Betrayal in Eighteenth-Century India*, reprint edition (New York: Penguin Books, 2004); Ghosh, *Sex and the Family in Colonial India*; Finn, "The Barlow Bastards," 25–47; Deborah Cohen, *Family Secrets: Shame and Privacy in Modern Britain* (Oxford: Oxford University Press, 2013); Valerie Anderson, *Race and Power in British India: Anglo-Indians, Class and Identity in the Nineteenth Century* (London: Tauris, 2015).

[38] Ghosh, *Sex and the Family in Colonial India*, 8–10.   [39] Hawes, *Poor Relations*, 124–26.

community began to organize politically in the 1880s and 1890s and renamed itself Anglo-Indian, emphasizing their connections to the Anglo world.[40] This is the term the community continues to use to this day. It is also the term that British people living temporarily in India for the majority of the Victorian period used to refer to themselves, as well as the term used by most historians for this temporary British population. (To avoid confusion, I refer to the mixed-race population as Eurasian, except when directly discussing the Anglo-Indian political movement.)

The term "domiciled European" refers to the predominantly British group of largely lower-class men and women who settled in India. Settlement was a fraught proposition, as British rule in India was predicated on the idea that the British population was only temporarily in India. Remaining on the Subcontinent meant running the risk of being deraced – Europeans made great financial and emotional sacrifices to avoid this fate, sending their India-born children "home" to a Britain they had never seen for schooling.[41] Those among the domiciled population who could not afford to send their children to Britain attempted to replicate British domestic ideals to further their claims to respectability and whiteness.[42] Domiciled Europeans were often clumped together with Eurasians – Census officials despaired of successfully enumerating either group. In his report on the 1881 Census, Census Commissioner J.A. Baines concluded, "the Eurasian community is, I believe, much more numerous than here represented, as in Bombay and elsewhere, there is great confusion between this class and the European ... either intentionally or through negligence, the words 'British subject' alone, or with the clipped prefix of 'Eur', were entered in many cases in which the persons concerned were of distinctly mixed race."[43] In fact there was a good deal of crossover between the two groups. And because Eurasians who could successfully pass as domiciled Europeans did so, the domiciled population was thought of as racially ambiguous and treated accordingly.

As we can see from the confusion surrounding racial and national categories in the Census, coming up with reliable numbers for the

---

[40] Ibid., 97, Elizabeth Buettner, "Problematic Spaces, Problematic Races: Defining 'Europeans' in Late Colonial India," *Women's History Review* 9, no. 2 (2000): 277–78.

[41] Buettner, *Empire Families*, 83.

[42] Lionel Caplan, "Iconographies of Anglo-Indian Women: Gender Constructs and Contrasts in a Changing Society," *Modern Asian Studies* 34, no. 4 (2000): 863–92; Alison Blunt, *Domicile and Diaspora: Anglo-Indian Women and the Spatial Politics of Home* (Malden, MA: Blackwell Publishing, 2005).

[43] William Chichele Plowden, *Report on the Census of British India*, vol. 1 (London: Eyre and Spottiswoode, 1883), 38.

non-elite British population of India at any given time is difficult. The first full Census of India was not conducted until 1871. The 1881 Census listed the numerical distribution of the male British population by profession. Extrapolating a non-elite population from these numbers can only take us so far, as they leave out anyone who was not employed, fail to disambiguate between military ranks or managerial and labor roles in the professions, and leave women and children completely unaccounted for. Sorting through these many variables to come up with reliable numbers for each of the Census years is beyond the scope of this project. David Arnold has come the closest to estimating what he calls the poor European population of India in 1900 at 75,000.[44] He includes three large categories of people in this group: military men and their families, low-level managers and service workers, and the least powerful members of the European population, including orphans, vagrants, and the mentally ill. This book is most concerned with the first two segments of that population, those who might have been labeled "respectable working class" in Victorian Britain.[45] Arnold's full list includes "Soldiers and sailors, along with their families ... skilled and semiskilled workers, intermediaries in government departments and private enterprises, and those employed in special service relations with the dominant white community ... in the police, the railways and public works, and some jails, factories, and engineering works, or as domestic servants, clerks, nurses, midwives, teachers, and shop assistants for European employers ... and orphans (mainly the children of soldiers and railwaymen), vagrants (ex-soldiers, sailors, and horse-grooms from Australia), prostitutes (many of them from Eastern Europe), lunatics, and convicts."[46] Arnold does not specify how many or to what extent Eurasians were included in these numbers. Harald Fischer-Tiné and Clare Anderson, among others, have taken up the study of this population, drawing on legal records as well as government reports and correspondence to tell their stories.[47] This population is similar enough to the population I call non-elites that I can rely on these numbers for 1900.

---

[44] Arnold, "European Orphans and Vagrants in India in the Nineteenth Century," 104.

[45] See Gareth Stedman Jones for a discussion of this concept and its fungibility. Gareth Stedman Jones, *Outcast London: A Study in the Relationship between Classes in Victorian Society* (Oxford: Clarendon Press, 1971); "Working-Class Culture and Working-Class Politics in London, 1870–1900; Notes on the Remaking of a Working Class," *Journal of Social History* 7, no. 4 (1974): 460–508.

[46] David Arnold, "Poor Europeans in India, 1750–1947," *Current Anthropology* 20, no. 2 (1979): 454–55.

[47] Fischer-Tiné, *Low and Licentious Europeans*; Mizutani, *The Meaning of White;* Clare Anderson, *Subaltern Lives: Biographies of Colonialism in the Indian Ocean World, 1790–1920* (Cambridge: Cambridge University Press, 2012).

Because the European population in India remained relatively stable in the years after the Indian Rebellion, I feel comfortable using Arnold's figure, placing the non-elite population at half the total British population throughout the period.

More significant than counting the precise proportion of the population of India constituted by British non-elites, though, is remembering how tiny that population was compared to the working-class population of Britain. In 1900, around 27 million Britons could be considered working class.[48] The vast disparity between these two numbers might suggest that the British working class in India was too small a proportion of the total population to merit extended scholarly attention. But imperial elites in India were similarly outnumbered by their counterparts in Britain. The effects of imperial non-elites on the British working class at home should be just as worthy of study. As we have seen in the case of elites, the effects of imperial service multiplied exponentially through material exchange, letter writing, and the spread of information through social networks that extended far beyond the original correspondents.[49]

Working-Class Raj begins roughly at the end of the Indian Rebellion in 1858 and ends in 1914, before the start of the First World War. By 1858, certain ideas about race and sexuality had shifted from the forms they had taken at the start of East India Company rule. Interracial sexuality went from being an accepted and openly acknowledged aspect of imperial life to an object of social opprobrium.[50] This shift in sexual mores affected non-elites in particular, as interracial unions, which still existed in spite of official interdictions, became yet another marker of class and racial difference. At the same time, views on race in Britain and the empire hardened. Scientific racism lent authority to claims about innate hierarchies of race and provided a justification for British imperial expansion. These ideas were complicated in the Indian context by caste and religion, and by Orientalist understandings of India's history, which held that Mughal invasions had ended a lost golden age and caused Indian decline.[51] In response to the Rebellion, British ideas about race and

---

[48] Clapson, Mark, *The Routledge Companion to Britain in the Twentieth Century* (London: Routledge, 2009), 10.

[49] Buettner, *Empire Families*, 2; Finn, "Anglo-Indian Lives in the Later Eighteenth and Early Nineteenth Centuries," 49–65; Rappaport, "'The Bombay Debt'," 246–248.

[50] Dalrymple, *White Mughals*, 405–406, n 3.

[51] David Arnold, "Race, Place and Bodily Difference in Early Nineteenth-Century India," *Historical Research* 77, no. 196 (May 2004): 254–73; Thomas Metcalf, *Ideologies of the Raj: The New Cambridge History of India* (Cambridge: Cambridge University Press, 1997), 84–85; Clare Anderson, *Legible Bodies: Race, Criminality, and Colonialism in South Asia* (Oxford: Oxford University Press, 2004), 7–10.

sexuality calcified into forms that favored the segregation of British and Indian populations.

With the transition to Crown rule after the rupture of the Rebellion and the dissolution of the East India Company, the British military presence on the Subcontinent grew. The British Crown increased the number of troops directly imported from Britain, with the aim of maintaining a military population capable of subduing any future rebellions.[52] The British military presence in India in the years following the Indian Rebellion was divided into two entities. The Indian Army consisted of Indian sepoys and British officers. The British men serving in the Indian Army were elites; even subalterns were drawn from the middle and upper classes and were essentially serving an apprenticeship period before climbing the ranks to take on higher positions in the military hierarchy. Within both British and Indian society and with few exceptions, the sepoys of the Indian Army held a higher status than the British recruits.[53] The British Army in India, on the other hand, was drawn from across classes in Britain and employed South Asians not as soldiers, but in support capacities. This new military population required housing and a speedy means of transportation around the country.[54] British railway companies exported skilled workers to take on management roles and build the massive rail infrastructure.[55] These changes increased the British working-class population of India and put that population in more privileged and managerial positions.

Though enlisted men had, to a certain extent, shrugged off their "scum of the earth" designation by the late nineteenth century, enlisted service was still seen as vaguely disreputable, even among the working classes.[56] This all changed decisively in 1914 as the Tommy Atkins figure gained national and imperial prominence and came to represent a new kind of non-elite British ideal to be beloved across classes.[57] The start of the First World War massively disrupted India's military population. Troops, both British and Indian, were transported around the world in support

---

[52] T. A. Heathcote, *The Military in British India*, 127.

[53] On the Indian Army, race, and status, see David Omissi, *The Sepoy and the Raj: The Indian Army, 1860–1940* (Basingstoke, Hampshire: Palgrave, 1993), and Gavin Rand and Kim A. Wagner, "Recruiting the 'Martial Races': Identities and Military Service in Colonial India," *Patterns of Prejudice* 46, no. 3–4 (July 1, 2012): 232–54, https://doi.org/10.1080/0031322X.2012.701495.

[54] Bear, *Lines of the Nation*, 27.   [55] Ibid., 65–70.

[56] See Erica Wald on "scum of the earth" in *Vice in the Barracks*, 16–17; see Jonathan Rose on working-class ideas about soldiers in *The Intellectual Life of the British Working Classes*, 2nd ed. (New Haven: Yale University Press, 2010), 337.

[57] Nicoletta Gullace, *The Blood of Our Sons: Men, Women, and the Renegotiation of British Citizenship during the Great War* (New York: Palgrave Macmillan, 2002), 36.

of the war effort. And ideas about soldiers changed dramatically. The year 1915 also marked the height of a decade of nationalist violence in India. Regulating the behavior of the newly lionized British soldier was no longer a priority for an empire engaged in a global conflict and struggling to retain control of an increasingly politicized and organized Indian populace.

What Comes Next?

In the first chapter, we meet five families whose histories each exemplify parts of the British non-elite experience of India. The Keens, whose story started this introduction, and the Wonnacotts represent opposing forms of social mobility. Dick and Pollie Keen ascended the social ladder, while Emily and William Wonnacott, working as schoolmistress and master, respectively, descended it. Both of these families had been stationed with the Army in other parts of the world, but it was only with their journey to India that their social status, bolstered by the presence of native labor and constrained by the strictures of military hierarchy, changed so dramatically. John Brand and Ned Crawford came to India as single men, working for the Army and the railway. Their stories are accessible to us because they maintained correspondence with friends and family. John Brand related tales of stasis and sickness, confined first to cantonments as his regiment waited for an imperial conflict to fight in and then to a series of hospitals and convalescent depots as his health failed. Ned Crawford, who came to India as his search for work along the east coast of Britain failed and expanded into the empire, sought to maintain connections to both his brother and British political culture. And George and Lucy Cole, whose marriage suffered with George's choice (as Lucy saw it) to abandon the family to seek employment with the railroad in India, reveal the effects Indian service could have on family units across imperial distance. These themes of upward and downward mobility, attempts to create community, both local and intraimperial, and the fallout of Indian and imperial separation on intimate relationships recur throughout the book.

The second and third chapters consider how working-class subjects and families created community – both across imperial distances and on the ground in India. Chapter 2 explores the form and practice of correspondence between Britain and India, uncovering the social and affective worlds of British non-elite families. Because many of these correspondents had low levels of literacy, they did not write for private audiences, but relied on friends, neighbors, and children to read and transcribe their correspondence. Intimate details of private lives became family – and public – knowledge. Letters transported information about India back to Britain and spread it throughout communities of origin, far beyond the reach of a single letter. Correspondents based in India maintained ties to their communities at home as they consumed everything from family gossip to political news. And correspondence was central to maintaining the economic health of a family – demands for money and goods from absent husbands or their employers supported working-class households in Britain. But the same mechanisms that sustained families and communities could disrupt them as well. Scorned spouses shared their grievances with neighbors, marshaling the condemnation of the community to corral wayward husbands. Mothers relied on daughters to convey their intimate feelings to their husbands, upending familial relationships. The form of correspondence and the practicalities of writing across long distances determined how relationships were sustained or disrupted, how information about empire was disseminated, and how empire shaped the lives of children and parents.

Following on from this discussion of community across the empire, Chapter 3 focuses on the army cantonment of Rawalpindi and its associated hill station of Murree, where we see working-class and elite ideas about family, respectability, sexuality, and race collide. Across British India, men, women, and children of different classes and races were thrown together in army cantonments. Military policy coded the physical spaces that comprised the cantonment – the Army barracks and civil lines, mess halls and married soldiers' quarters, bazaars and red-light districts – as sites of potential dissolution, destructive to British prestige. Thousands of soldiers, officers, camp followers, and army wives passed through these installations. As they did so, they created domestic worlds within militarized spaces. Domestication of military space did not, however, assuage official fears about the destructive potential of a population of non-elite whites, but rather expanded those fears to encompass not only single men but families and children as well.

Chapter 4 takes up the discussion of domesticity to examine the relationships between domestic service of working-class women born in Britain and their India-raised daughters. The slipperiness of status in India was most visible in the presence of servants in the homes of military men and women and in the workspaces of British of all classes. Working-class women, many of whom had worked as servants themselves before coming to India, found themselves transformed into mistresses upon arrival in the country. Women could assign their domestic duties to servants, take them up again when they chose, and even take on roles as servants themselves. These changes in relationship to service came about not just as the result of changing financial circumstances, but in response to causes as disparate as the birth of a child, clashes of person-alities, or a change in the season. Working-class women born in Britain tended to see their status as employers as unstable, but that instability did not necessarily provoke anxieties over racial degeneration. Their daugh-ters, in contrast, saw service differently. Girls raised, educated, and remaining in India balked at the notion of going into domestic service, even as the schools designed to educate them attempted to train this second generation for that purpose.

Chapter 5 considers the relationship between colonial knowledge, imperial education, and class mobility. British working-class children were not educated for empire, and British soldiers received almost no country-specific training. Once in India, enlisted men were actively discouraged from developing more than the most basic of language skills. But in spite of gaining no material benefits from learning about India, some non-elite Brits did devote themselves to learning native languages, local religious practices, and further understanding the social world of British India. To do so, they at times crossed boundaries of class and race, developing relationships with South Asians and elite British in the process. The remnants of these educational endeavors include poetry, exam results, scrapbooks, and hand-illustrated glossaries through which non-elites constructed their own forms of colonial knowledge. But autodidacts failed to translate this learning or these new relationships into material gain because the governing institutions of the Raj could not conceive of the utility of colonial knowledge for this class.

Chapter 6 revisits some of the individuals and families we have encountered throughout the text. The documentary traces of working-class lives that inform this study capture only a narrow window of time within the lives of their authors. Using genealogical records to open that window further, I follow these families past their time in India. Who remained, who returned to Britain, and who went on to other parts of the empire? Thinking about the forces that compelled families and individ-uals to make these choices, or foreclosed possibilities, provides an answer to the question of what happened to popular and historical memory of the working-class Raj. Back in Britain, men and women who had enjoyed an elevated social status could find it difficult to reintegrate into their communities of origin, which reinforced conformity rather than differ-ence. As a result, returning Brits purposefully forgot tales of Indian service and elite pretensions in efforts to manage family relations. In contrast, those men and women who settled with their families in India or other parts of the empire – or who chose to abandon their families of origin – had a greater incentive to embrace a new class status and create family histories celebrating their climb up the social ranks of the British

Empire. This study of how families developed and responded to new political, economic, and social contexts helps to tell the story of how imperial service impacted class and identity over time in Britain, India, and the settler colonies. Taken together, these chapters can help us rethink how class functioned in the British Empire and how imperial experience became a naturalized part of British working-class life.

1   Family Histories and Remaking Class in British India

In the first pages of *Kim*, Rudyard Kipling enumerates his titular character's sparse inheritance: "O'Hara … died as poor whites die in India. His estate at death consisted of three papers."[1] As Teresa Hubel has suggested, Kim O'Hara is the paradigmatic poor white in Victorian India.[2] Born to a mother in domestic service and a father in military service, followed by a stint on the railways, his childhood was shaped by a family history of disease and dissipation, leading to orphanhood. The existence of the O'Hara family is recorded in little more than a page of text and a few scraps of paper. When historians have attempted to trace these poor white subjects in the past, they have accordingly relied on court cases, settlement reports, and other scant government and company records left behind.[3] These records reflect official interests, but leave the interior lives and intimate concerns of these men and women elusive, to be filled in by novelists rather than historians.[4] A private's enlistment papers may offer some clues to suggest why he left Britain behind, but cannot help us understand how he thought about the people he encountered in India or how he managed the dissonance of being at once subordinate and invader. A railway worker's contract might suggest the financial benefits of employment in India, but cannot reveal the emotional toll on his marriage or how his wife forged support networks in his absence.

The publication of *Kim* helped to solidify Late-Victorian discourses around poor whites in India and transmit them to readers who would have otherwise given the group little thought. Among the most powerful of these was that white soldiers and workers were alone in the world.

---

[1] Rudyard Kipling, *Kim* (New York: Doubleday, 1901), 2.

[2] Teresa Hubel, "In Search of the British Indian in British India: White Orphans, Kipling's Kim, and Class in Colonial India," *Modern Asian Studies* 38, no. 1 (2004): 227–51.

[3] Arnold, "European Orphans and Vagrants in India in the Nineteenth Century," 104–27. See also Bear, *Lines of the Nation*; Fischer-Tiné, *Low and Licentious Europeans*; Mizutani, *The Meaning of White*.

[4] For literary examples, see Kipling, *Kim*; Paul Scott, *The Raj Quartet* (London: Penguin Books, 1966–1975).

24

They were either without family altogether or separated from distant and unhelpful relatives in Britain by the vast empire. They might even have formed alliances and started families with Indian women, thus definitively sundering themselves from the European world. These ideas had real effects on the lives of mixed-race and white lower-class imperial subjects, the most notable of which was the separation of generations of children from their parents, with varying degrees of familial consent, to be either worked or educated into good imperial subjects.[5] Historians in turn inherited this atomized notion of working-class Europeans in India and have as a result generally studied them apart from their families. But these men and women were not isolated individuals, and many of them left behind much more than the scarce textual fragments of the O'Hara family. This chapter introduces five families, each selected because they break with this narrative in their own way. Some, such as the Keens and Wonnacotts, left behind reams of documents that allow me to reconstruct years of family histories. For others, such as the Coles and the Crawford brothers, the remnants that remain did not amount to much more than the O'Hara family's fictional legacy. But even the existence of a few pieces of correspondence can open up the possibility of exploring emotional worlds of the past.

Each of the families featured in this chapter represents a certain facet of the lower-class experience in British India. George and Lucy Cole, whom we will encounter again as part of a larger exploration of the affective and material aspects of love and marriage in Chapter 3, here represent the experiences of railway families. George was drawn to India by the higher wages offered there, and Lucy was left behind to raise their children and attempt to maintain both her own financial position and her marriage. John Brand, a soldier whose military experience was marked by the common elements of disease and monotony, seems at first glance to be one of those atomized individuals – with few blood relations – who became subjects of concern to the government and do-gooders in India and Britain alike. But he maintained connections with his sister in Scotland and, after her death, with her husband and his family. Emily and William Wonnacott would have been surprised and chagrined to find themselves referred to as lower class – they both came from middle-class families, and he was a schoolteacher with well-connected brothers –

---

[5] See Jane McCabe, *Race, Tea and Colonial Resettlement: Imperial Families, Interrupted* (London: Bloomsbury Academic, 2017); Andrew J. May, "Exiles from the Children's City: Archives, Imperial Identities and the Juvenile Emigration of Anglo-Indians from Kalimpong to Australasia," *Journal of Colonialism and Colonial History* 14, no. 1 (2013) http://doi:10.1353/cch.2013.0016; Satadru Sen, *Colonial Childhoods: The Juvenile Periphery of India, 1850–1945* (London: Anthem Press, 2005).

but, through a quirk of military rank, they spent their time in India grappling with downward mobility. The Wonnacotts' efforts to maintain their class position amid the disruption of life in India are echoed in the history of the Keen family. Dick and Pollie Keen, who started their working lives as a farmhand and servant, respectively, found themselves climbing the social ladder in India. One of the ways in which Pollie took advantage of her ample leisure time was by writing weekly letters home to her mother, an activity she would not have been able to do (nor have had cause to do) if she had remained in England. And finally, Ned Crawford and his brother George demonstrate how working-class men in Britain might think of India as just one option for improving their lot in life – alongside others, including internal migration, military service, and trade unionism. The Crawford brothers give us a sense of the class politics – and sometimes lack thereof – existing beneath the surface of non-elite imperial experience.

George and Lucy Cole: A Family in Crisis

In the early 1860s, working men in Britain rushed to join the East Indian Railway Company (EIR). The Indian railways gained a reputation by the end of the nineteenth century as a key employer for India's Eurasian population, but in the first decades of their operation, they hired a significant proportion of their labor from Britain. Laura Bear suggests that the EIR imported British workers not only out of a sense of their superiority over native labor but also as part of abortive attempts in the late 1850s to create a British settler class in India.[6] With the Indian Rebellion stoking British fears of Indian disloyalty, bringing over British workers seemed a justified expense to railway management. George Cole was just one of many men who turned to the EIR for work. In 1863, John Anthony wrote to the EIR from Cardiff on behalf of his brother and himself seeking employment. "We … intend to go to India for five years one as a stoker and the other as a mason that have been use to Railways for many years."[7] Henry Higglesworth wrote that his brother-in-law had gone out "before crismiss," adding, "if you cud give me A gob out thear as A fiter I shud be very glad."[8] The phonetic spelling sprinkled throughout Henry's letter gives some indication of the great

---

[6] Bear, *Lines of the Nation*, 27, 68–70.

[7] Railway Home Correspondence – C. Letters to and from Railway Companies, etc.: Register IX – Miscellaneous (1863–65), /IOR/L/PWD/2/169: IX 6/63. When quoting from manuscript sources, all errors in spelling and punctuation have been transcribed from the originals. [*sic*] is only indicated when required for clarification.

[8] Railway Home Correspondence – C. IOR/L/PWD/2/169: IX 11/63.

effort he must put into contacting the company. George Hewett wrote from Surrey, saying that he had been persuaded by a friend already employed in India to apply.[9] Edward Harper wrote from Dundalk in the north of Ireland, having heard the company was thinking of sending ten under-engineers to India in the summer of 1864. Harper was looking for steady work and assured the company that, though currently residing in Ireland and working for the Dublin and Belfast Junction Railway, he was in fact an Englishman and a "thorerly good and Sober Steddey workman."[10] John O'Connell, writing from County Cork, gave his credentials as a chainman or observer, noting that he had worked on the railways in America and promising the "most respectable references."[11]

Common threads run through these accounts. Working in India was frequently a social endeavor – the Anthony brothers planned to travel together, Henry Higglesworth had heard promising stories from his brother-in-law, and John O'Connell was following a friend. Seeking work in India could reinforce family bonds or strengthen friendships as men were drawn together into unfamiliar territory. Nor was traveling to India for employment a major break with established labor-seeking practices. Edward Harper had left England for Ireland; John O'Connell had left Ireland for America. Moving on to India was simply the next available step in a series of moves these men were prepared to make. The ease with which working men decided to travel halfway around the world for employment suggests that these men saw the British Empire and, as James Bellich suggests, the Anglo World, as an extension of their own world of work – not as a fundamentally different or separate space.[12]

George Cole was one of the men flooding the EIR office with letters in the early 1860s. George came from a working-class London family – his father drove a coach and his mother took in laundry. Railway work should have provided him with a stable income, but George had trouble finding a job in the early months of 1860. George signed his contract with the EIR in late July of 1860 and spent the months leading to his departure in an unending argument with his wife. Lucy begged him to stay, but George was determined to leave England behind and threatened to enlist

---

[9] Ibid.: IX 4/64.   [10] Ibid.: IX 59/63.   [11] Ibid.: IX 41/64.

[12] James Bellich, *Replenishing the Earth: The Settler Revolution and the Rise of the Anglo-World 1783–1939* (Oxford: Oxford University Press, 2009). On migration around the empire and beyond, see also Marjory Harper and Stephen Constantine, *Migration and Empire* (Oxford: Oxford University Press, 2010); Marjory Harper, *Emigrant Homecomings: The Return Movements of Emigrants, 1600–2000* (Manchester: Manchester University Press, 2005); David Lambert and Alan Lester, eds., *Colonial Lives across the British Empire: Imperial Careering in the Long Nineteenth Century* (Cambridge: Cambridge University Press, 2006).

as a private in the Army if Lucy prevented him from taking up his job with the railway. George's four-year contract would ensure the family an income almost three times more than he could ever have hoped to attain working in Britain.[13] George would make about £14 a month as an engine driver based out of Howrah Railway Station, on the outskirts of Calcutta.[14] Half of this sum was supposed to be paid directly to Lucy from the EIR's London offices. But it also meant at least four years of loneliness and uncertainty for Lucy. She was left caring for three small children in rented rooms on the outskirts of London.

The extended Cole family was a peripatetic group. Lucy's sister Elinor discussed leaving for America, while George's sister Mary Anne and brother-in-law Patrick Hanley were planning a permanent move to Argentina in the same year that George left for India. Argentina housed a growing population of British settlers in the mid-nineteenth century, working as sheep ranchers and railway workers.[15] Like many of his fellow migrants, Patrick Hanley may have used his income from railway work to fund a farm. The Hanleys acquired a flock of 2,000 sheep after only a few months in the country, suggesting long-term plans to settle and a significant investment.[16] Migration as a means of self-improvement was not out of the ordinary in the Coles' community or family circle, but it had to be done in the right way and for the right reasons. Abandoning his wife and family soon after the birth of his youngest child numbered among the wrong ways to migrate. George Cole's family knew him to be an "unsteady" character and flooded Lucy with sympathy in the weeks after his abrupt departure. She was careful to forward on any critical letters to her husband. Living in a hotel near Howrah Station and running up bills for brandy and sodas, George received piles of mail questioning his character and defending his poor, deserted wife. His sister Mary Anne wrote from Buenos Aires to condemn George's move to India as the "crowning point to his mad Pranks had he have been single I should have said nothing about it, but to go an leave a dear kind wife and dear children and such a nice house."[17] George's misstep was not the act of

---

[13] Jeffrey G. Williamson, "Earnings Inequality in Nineteenth-Century Britain," *The Journal of Economic History* 40, no. 3 (1980): 474; Dale H. Porter, *The Thames Embankment: Environment, Technology, and Society in Victorian London* (Akron, OH: University of Akron Press, 1998), 176.

[14] Alphabetical List of European and East-Indians in the Company's Service East Indian Railway Company 1862. IOR/L/AG/46/11/138.

[15] David Rock, "The British of Argentina," in Robert Bickers, ed., *Settlers and Expatriates: Britons over the Seas* (Oxford: Oxford University Press, 2010), 22, 26.

[16] The description of the Hanleys' flock suggests Mary Anne married a man of significantly greater means than her family of origin.

[17] Mary Anne Hanley to Lucy Cole, January 12, 1862, IOR MSS Eur. F133/42.

leaving itself, but leaving behind a wife, children, and home – all the markers of the type of successful life one might migrate to obtain.

Lucy was not the only wife of a railway worker to have trouble corralling a recalcitrant husband. Railway workers could bring along their wives and children to India, but most did not, instead relying on the EIR to disburse their pay to their dependents in Britain.[18] The EIR correspondence files are filled with requests from worried wives writing to the company's directors asking for news of husbands working in India who provided no means of support for their families or who stopped sending the money they had previously promised. An 1863 complaint from a Mrs. Gibbs, whose husband had left her and her six children with no income, prompted the Board of Directors to consider "whether they will not make it a condition of engagement that when men of this class leave their families in this country they shall be bound to make an allowance for their support payable through this office."[19] The wives of railway workers in India considered their husbands' employers to be part of the network of aid upon which they could draw for support in securing their families' financial stability. The EIR's response established the company's role as a replacement for disintegrating families, providing direct financial support and disciplining irresponsible husbands and fathers.

By the end of 1861, months after George Cole had arrived in Calcutta, the EIR did reorganize its budget to allocate more funds for fares for wives and children to join their husbands in India. The company feared they would not be able to get or retain good employees if the men were separated from their wives. Lucy herself considered following George to India once he had time to get settled. Mary Anne, with her own experience of moving across the ocean, dissuaded her. "I could not advice [sic] you [to follow George]," Mary Anne wrote.[20] "With 3 young children you have no idea of what one has to suffer and put up with in a foreign country."[21] Unwilling to risk the voyage to India with young children in tow and an uncertain reception on arrival, Lucy turned for help to the family networks still available to her in person and through correspondence.

In response to George's abandonment, Lucy restructured her family, substituting uncles and cousins as needed to fill caretaking roles.

---

[18] Railway Home Correspondence – C. IOR/L/PWD/2/77 – 1861. See also Bear, *Lines of the Nation*, 69–70.
[19] Letter to Agent, no. 811, August 3, 1863, Railway Home Correspondence – C. IOR/L/PWD/2/79.
[20] Mary Anne Hanley to Lucy Cole, January 12, 1862, IOR MSS Eur. F133/42.
[21] Ibid.

George's own brother wrote to inform him of various childhood illnesses passing through Lucy's household.[22] He also noted that "a single life seems to agree with [Lucy] she looks remarkably well lately."[23] He need not have bothered writing; Lucy had reported the compliment in an earlier letter. By engaging the extended family in her campaign, Lucy accomplished twin goals. She secured the practical help required to look after two small children and an infant. And she ensured that George remained enmeshed in the social world of their suburban community even after leaving for India. While middle- and upper-class men saw Indian service as a means of fulfilling their role as head of the household by supporting the family and potentially increasing their wealth, the working-class Coles viewed leaving the family in terms of neglect and abandonment.[24] In the Coles' social circles, the domestic disruption occasioned by running off to work the railways in India could not be glorified as part of an imperial mission. A middle-class father's absence might strengthen his authority in the family, but George, away from home, could not exert his own authority in domestic affairs. Instead, Lucy became the point around which new familial relations coalesced, uniting far-flung family members in opposition to George's imperial adventure.

Lucy quickly realized that family pressure and emotional appeals were not sufficient and turned to other strategies. In late October 1861, Lucy took in a pair of male lodgers. While rent from David Drake and William Bailey certainly helped Lucy support her family, the presence of two single men in the house also gave her more ammunition in her war with George.[25] Having strange men in the house would not have been unusual – one in nine English working-class households included lodgers among their numbers at mid-century.[26] The Coles had a lodger living with them in the spring of 1861 when George was still at home.[27]

---

[22] Thomas Cole to George Cole, October 20, 1861, IOR MSS Eur. F133/42.   [23] Ibid.

[24] Buettner, *Empire Families*, chapter 3.

[25] David Drake probably worked on the railways. Later census records (1871 and 1881) for a David Drake, who would have been in his early twenties around 1861 and thus a likely lodger, list a David Drake living in Stratford and working as an engine driver. William Bailey's name was too common to usefully locate, and the 1861 Census was completed while George Cole was still at home with Lucy and his children. "David Drake," *Census Returns of England and Wales 1871* (The National Archives: Public Record Office RG 10/1626/156:66).

[26] Eric Hopkins, *Childhood Transformed: Working-Class Children in Nineteenth-Century England* (Manchester: Manchester University Press, 1994), 102.

[27] "George Cole," *Census Returns of England and Wales 1861* (The National Archives: Public Record Office RG 9/1056/253:42).

However, David Drake and William Bailey featured prominently in Lucy's letters and soon took on a larger role in the household. "Drake sometimes tryes to make little Lucy believe he is her father but she says no you are not my father my father is in India."[28] Lucy was particularly fond of this story and repeated it in two subsequent letters, playing on what she hoped were George's fears of threats to his paternity and the integrity of his home. "Mr Drake is very fond of the Chirldren he brings them home some sweets tow [sic] or three times a week. I think it seems so kind of him ... Mr Bailey plays the violin I try to make my self as happy as I can ... I could not live without men lodgers I should go melancholy."[29] Lucy's (pointedly male) lodgers offered emotional comfort that George, in his absence, could not. She did not mention the financial benefit. In Lucy's mind, George was far from the idealized Victorian *pater familias*. He had failed to provide for his family, so lodgers and family friends took over his financial, parental, and companionate roles. George relinquished his place as head of the household, and Lucy responded by creating a piecemeal family structure that turned the domestic ideal on its head.

The Coles' story, which I will pick back up in Chapter 3, brings up a number of issues that will be explored throughout the rest of this volume. The far-flung Cole family offers a key example of what a working-class family in empire could look like. George and Lucy's attempts to work out their conflicts through correspondence networks drew together family and friends spread throughout the formal and informal British Empire. Instead of coming apart across vast distances, the family reformed itself. Lucy baptized the months-old infant who George had left behind Mary Anne, after the sister-in-law who provided her with vital, if distant, support. Brothers-in-law drew together to help Lucy and her children. The crisis of George Cole's abandonment helped to create and consolidate new ties. Working-class epistolary culture played a foundational role in this process. While the majority of the surviving Cole letters were written by Lucy, they suggest a much larger, lost correspondence. Sharing knowledge through correspondence reshaped families' understandings of their relationships to one another and their understandings of themselves as social entities. Framing the analysis around the extended Cole family, rather than George or Lucy as individuals, reveals not disunity but continuities and connections that demonstrate the global spread of the British working-class population.

---

[28] Lucy Cole to George Cole, November 19, 1861, IOR MSS Eur. F133/42.   [29] Ibid.

John Brand and the Gardiners: Time Hangs Heavy

John Brand joined the British Army at twenty-two in the summer of 1865, leaving his lodgings in a tenement on the outskirts of Edinburgh for the life of a private with the 10th Hussars.[30] He had spent his childhood and early adult years in the Canongate, a burgh wedged between Edinburgh proper and the Salisbury Crags. By the time Brand turned eighteen, he had made enough money working as a hairdresser to afford a room of his own in a block of close-packed flats.[31] His letters do not indicate why he chose to abandon his life in Scotland for the Army, but they do suggest a romance gone awry. His closest correspondents were his sister, Jessie, and brother-in-law, Peter Gardiner. John and Peter maintained their correspondence even after Jessie's death, their connection perhaps strengthened by the tragedy. Brand stayed relatively close to home in the first years of his service – with little conflict to draw them east, the 10th Hussars were posted in Ireland and the Home Counties until 1873, when the regiment embarked for Muttra (present-day Mathura, Uttar Pradesh).

John Brand identified the central problems of Indian military service for enlisted men just days after he got settled in the cantonment in Muttra. They were hot. And they were bored. Enlisted men like Brand had few tasks to occupy them on a day-to-day basis. Troops occasionally fought in the wars endemic to the borders of the North-West Frontier and the Punjab after the Indian Rebellion. But these wars required little manpower and tended to mobilize those men stationed closest to the conflict. Military officers were worried about the effects of unfilled time on soldiers. Writing to his sister, Brand noted that the troops had to stay out of the hot sun not just at noon, but for the majority of the day, doing military drills and other duties only in the very earliest and latest hours of daylight.

We have all our work done by the natives. In fact soldiering out here is a Gentlemans life to what it is in England, but of course all owing to the Climate – it is lightsome enough at first as it is a change, but I expect the novelty will wear of [sic] very soon there is no Society out here only among ourselves.[32]

Brand found the company in Muttra dull and grasped at every opportunity for entertainment or profit. Located on the road from Agra,

---

[30] Army record book in Papers of John Brand, NLS Acc. 6386.
[31] "John Brand," *Census of Scotland 1861* (National Records of Scotland: Census 685/3/61/17).
[32] John Brand to Mrs. Peter Gardiner, March 2, 1873, NLS Acc. 6386.

Muttra served as a way station for people traveling between Delhi and the former Mughal capital. When the Governor General Lord Northbrook stopped at the cantonment on his journey from Agra, Brand was delighted to have an opportunity to revisit his former profession: "I had the honour," Brand wrote, "of cutting his hair, for which I got 10 Rupees not a bad half an hours work. I wish he would come every day, & want his hair cut."[33] Brand must have gained a reputation among his fellow soldiers for his skills as a barber and been brought out specially to serve Northbrook. It was not uncommon for soldiers to pass the time and make some extra money in this way, drawing on skills from their former lives. Dick Keen, a noncommissioned officer skilled at making tack for horses, put his needle to use in his off hours piercing the ears of military wives.[34]

Brand's description of a typical summer day on the plains is one of enforced idleness:

Life is so very wretched out here in the summer months, especially when you have nothing to do; confined to your Bungalow from morning till night you can't lay down from the heat as it is much hoter laying about than walking about & you can't read all the day & can assure you that time hangs very heavy on our hands there is a old saying that "time flies" but it seem rather tardy here.[35]

Brand's account of his time leaves him free from around eight in the morning until a quarter past five in the afternoon. Idle soldiers were not shirking their duty; their leisure was a necessary by-product of maintaining a standing army in India. But at the same time, the notion that the British working class in India did not appear to do much work was a constant source of concern for military and civilian leadership. Clubs, reading rooms, and institutes opened in an effort to provide wholesome entertainment for troops who, according to dominant notions of working-class morality, could not be expected to control themselves. The Allahabad-based newspaper *The Pioneer* argued for the development of soldiers' workshops in language that prefigured Brand's complaints: "The men are driven into habits of dissipation and immorality by having nothing to occupy their attention with, and with no means of getting through the hours that daily hang idly on their hands. The State would be the gainer in the improved moral condition of its soldiers."[36] Calcutta's Outram Institute, which offered reading and recreation rooms, a museum, and a lecture hall, along with sewing circles for military wives,

---

[33] John Brand to Peter Gardiner, January 9, 1874, NLS Acc. 6386.
[34] Pollie Keen to Mary Holloway, January 26, 1891, IOR MSS Eur. F528/10.
[35] John Brand to Peter Gardiner, May 11, 1875, NLS Acc. 6386.
[36] "Soldiers' Workshops," *The Pioneer*, May 1, 1865, 1.

opened in the early 1860s as a model soldiers' institute. Another *Pioneer* article discussed plans for soldiers' recreation rooms and compared them to working men's clubs in Britain, assuring readers that "such provisions for rational and innocent recreation cannot fail to prove a formidable rival to the grog-shop, and all its debasing accompaniments, which has hitherto been the soldier's almost only resort in the hours of leisure and sociality."[37] And when all else failed, the Army provided ample alcohol provisions and state-sponsored prostitution to manage, if not curtail, the immoral activities of the troops. The military provided access to these vices in hopes of preventing the public drunkenness, venereal disease, rape, and sodomy they feared would ensue if men had to seek out liquor and sexual companionship on their own.[38]

Enlisted men like Brand and military leadership alike expressed anxieties over the fluidity of class markers in India. These worries came to a head in debates around leisure time and ran in two directions. First, having accepted the notion that maintaining control in India required a standing Army manifesting British power and, post-Rebellion, populated by British bodies, the British Army then had to manage many thousands of working-class men brought to India and left with little to occupy their time. Working-class soldiers, the argument went, lacked the self-control to manage their own leisure time and were bound to misuse it. Colonial officials feared bad behavior, including excessive drinking, sexual profligacy, and casual violence among the men, would reflect poorly on the British Army as a whole. These behaviors would cause chaos and reveal British claims to moral and racial superiority to be spurious. In the logic of imperial rule, the behavior of one Briton represented the moral success or failure of the entire group.

Second, leisure time suggested class privilege. An excess of unfilled time afflicted the British in India, regardless of class origin. Middle-class wives complained of their circumscribed lives; civilians in the Indian Civil Service (ICS) and officers in the British Army suffered from medicalized malaise that could only be treated by retreating to the hills.[39] A working class that did not work destabilized both middle-class and British identities. If soldiers and their families shared with middle-class Britons in India the experience of directing servants and whiling the summer day away, then the distinctions between them began to melt

---

[37] "Education in the Army," *The Pioneer*, Allahabad, May 26, 1865, 6. Originally published in *The Scotsman*, Edinburgh.

[38] Levine, *Prostitution, Race, and Politics*.

[39] Jeffrey A. Auerbach, *Imperial Boredom: Monotony and the British Empire* (Oxford, United Kingdom: Oxford University Press, 2018), 109, and Kennedy, *The Magic Mountains*, 30, have discussed this malaise among the British upper classes.

away/Not working may have undermined social identities around class, but it strengthened those identities around race, establishing even lower-class whites as superior to the vast majority of the native population, whose labor made possible their leisure.

It was evident to many working-class soldiers that racial hierarchies in India provided them with possibilities that would have been unthinkable at home. An East India Company gunner called Luck wrote to his mother that "we live beter than many Gentlemen in England we have nothing to do only our will the blacks clean our boots."[40] Mauger Monk, a one-time lawyer hiding out in the East India Company artillery under an assumed name after his own troubles with the law, wrote that "soldiering in this country is very different from what it is at home our clothes & linen are most beautifully washed by the native dhobis, even our arms, & great guns are cleaned by natives. All the Europeans have to do is to serve them."[41] Differing ideas about service play off one another in these accounts. For Luck, gentlemanliness was defined by being able to follow your pleasure. For Monk, who would have already experienced the agency afforded by leisure back at home, soldiering in empire was an ironic trade – with white military service purchasing the equivalent of domestic service from native laborers. Luck and Monk, though from vastly different backgrounds, each found themselves occupying a class position in India that defied their expectations and confused class markers, and they used racial difference to describe this class change. Neither Monk nor Luck seem to have found the extra time as onerous as John Brand did.

By the autumn of 1878, Brand's regiment had moved on from sleepy Muttra to Rawalpindi, the largest military cantonment in the Punjab. There, they joined scores of other regiments preparing to stage an invasion of Afghanistan that would become the Second Anglo-Afghan War. But John Brand was sick in bed. He had been sent some forty miles up the road to convalesce in the cooler climate of the hill station at Murree. By this time, Brand had served with his regiment for nearly a decade, and military living conditions had been hard on his health. He was suffering from a liver complaint, a catch-all diagnosis that could refer to anything from excessive alcohol consumption to what we would now understand to be a water-borne parasitic infection.[42] Long-term sufferers were

---

[40] Letters of Gunner Luck, June 29, 1840, IOR MSS Eur. E339.
[41] Mauger Monk to Sarah Magrath, July 1, 1839, IOR MSS Eur. C575/1. Monk gave the surname Fitzhugh when he enlisted.
[42] Arnold, *Colonizing the Body*.

prescribed a period of rest in the hills, a treatment that often worked by separating the patient from whatever sort of liquid was causing the problem. Convalescing required rest in a quiet, well-ventilated, and ideally rural setting with time set aside for contemplation to slowly introduce the patient back into the world of the healthy.[43] It was above all else a dull experience, and one that gave Brand ample time to write to friends and family in Scotland and other parts of India. From his sickbed, he provided a running commentary on Anglo-Afghan relations, the British elections, and military life in the Punjab.

Enforced idleness differentiated soldiers from working-class friends and family at home, but it also provided the time necessary to maintain relationships through correspondence. Brand acknowledged that he had "plenty of spare time" and did not expect his correspondent Peter to waste the occasional hour he had to himself in writing; merely having someone read the letters was enough.[44] Though he was kept from the field by his illness, Brand had plenty of opinions to share about Britain's first major military excursion into Afghanistan since their disastrous defeat in 1842. He was skeptical about the war, weighing British claims that victory was essential and his own doubts about the wisdom of the invasion. "I do not have the slightest doubt that we will prove their masters in the end," Brand wrote to Peter,

> although I think it would have been better if we had left them alone in the first place as they will be only a source of annoyance to us always as there is some of the tribes only a lot of robbers ... better anything than loss [sic] prestige in this country especially where they are more impressed by the strong hand than moral power which they don't seem to understand so well as physical.[45]

Brand did not appear to have had any real contact with the Afghan tribes he wrote about, but he nevertheless provided his own perspective on British Afghan policy. While the British Army made many of their decisions in hopes of maintaining the appearance of morality, Brand understood power in India to derive from violence – an irony given how little time he spent doing any actual fighting. Brand experienced military service in India in terms of stasis, unfilled time, and convalescence. But those responsible for governance and military administration would have regarded Brand's experience differently, as potentially disruptive to the stability of British rule.

---

[43] Maria H. Frawley, *Invalidism and Identity in Nineteenth-Century Britain* (Chicago: University of Chicago Press, 2010), 39–41.
[44] John Brand to Peter Gardiner, October 17, 1879, NLS Acc. 6386.   [45] Ibid.

Emily and William Wonnacott: Downwardly Mobile

William Wonnacott spent his first night aboard the *Floriana* listening to the skittering of "numerous and immense" cockroaches across the deck. William and his family were leaving Malta, where he had spent two years as an Army schoolmaster, for a new posting in India.[46] On the journey to Malta, William and Emily had been newlyweds and enjoyed their private cabin and daily feasts cooked up by the officers' mess. Now, with a small child and newborn infant in tow, Emily was given the courtesy of a cabin, while William was ordered to sleep among the other NCOs and enlisted men. The men slung hammocks overnight, but William, "not caring to risk [his] neck by a tumble," made a hard bed on the floor, before escaping from the encroaching insects to a nearby table. He eventually managed to smuggle a mattress out of Emily's cabin and create an ersatz bed for himself with the help of his orderly. William's situation aboard ship was an early clue that the Wonnacotts' status in India would be different from the one they had enjoyed in Malta. William may have had a servant, but he put the man to work sneaking around the ship to secure for his master what little comfort was available. Emily could rest in relative comfort, but only because she had very recently given birth.

William and Emily Wonnacott both came from middle-class backgrounds, but by the time they departed for India in 1868, they had started on a course of downward mobility. William was an Army schoolteacher, a career choice that precluded the type of future advancement to which an officer could aspire. He was the only member of his family who did not earn a BA, choosing instead to stop his schooling with teacher training, a choice he would regret and attempt to remedy later in his life. Both of his brothers had professional careers and went on to distinguish themselves. Thomas became an architect, and John, a Fellow of the Royal Geographical Society.[47] Emily's family, the Shorts, was less affluent or educated; Emily went to work at thirteen. The Shorts had sufficient money to provide their daughter with some of the hallmarks of a middle-class life – a writing desk to mark the start of her pupil teacher training and a generous marriage settlement – but not enough to protect her finely honed sense of respectability.[48] Emily's family lost a good deal of money in a bank failure in 1868, during the Wonnacotts' first year in India, and was forced to sell furniture and take in lodgers to support

[46] William Wonnacott to parents, November 7, 1868, IOR MSS Eur. C376/2.
[47] William Wonnacott to mother, March 28, 1873, IOR MSS Eur. 6376/4.
[48] Emily Wonnacott to parents, April 1871, IOR MSS Eur. C376/3.

themselves. Perhaps because her family's financial position was more precarious, Emily felt threats to her status acutely.

William and Emily married in February of 1866, and shortly after they departed for Malta, where William took up a position as schoolmaster with his regiment.[49] Emily taught a small class of young children. The Wonnacotts found Malta charming. The couple enjoyed large, private quarters and had two sons in the two years they lived on the island. Emily wrote that their eldest boy, Ernest, had acquired a number of Maltese habits, including a taste for olives and garlic and the tendency to cross himself "like the Catholics do."[50] But the Wonnacotts were not posted in Malta for long – in May of 1868, they learned the regiment would move on to India, a prospect Emily greeted with a "presentiment of evil [which] I trust is only fancy."[51] The next few years proved Emily's worries to be justified, as the Wonnacott family suffered a series of losses.

The first among these was a loss of status, made evident by the sleeping arrangements on the *Floriana*. The confusion that existed around status on board the ship was to be repeated many times once the family landed in India. Both Wonnacotts came to understand that William's noncommissioned rank, which had little effect on their lives in Malta, was to dictate the social world they could inhabit in India. There were a number of reasons for this change. The military community in Malta was transient, the island itself was a way station, and the Maltese, under British rule in the wake of Napoleon and plague and seen by the British as a willingly subjected people, posed no threat to British self-concept or rule. Perhaps because the British Army felt little need in the mid-nineteenth century to justify its Maltese presence, social strictures were lax. For the Wonnacotts, Malta provided the comforts of a British setting within a foreign context. The Wonnacott family's various postings around the western districts of India, however, presented a series of accumulating threats to status.

During their first years in India, William was far less concerned about being grouped with social inferiors than Emily. As schoolmaster, he was supposed to mix socially with people of all classes. William led regimental singing groups, participated in theatricals, and joined art classes that included men of all ranks. Emily, in contrast, had little to do but police the family's social connections. As the Wonnacotts settled into their new

---

[49] The British Army used Malta as a way station on the sea route to India. They also maintained a military presence on the island – the Wonnacotts lived on Malta for two years while William's regiment (the 8th King's Regiment of Foot) was stationed on the island. The Keens also stopped for a short time on Malta, where their daughter Nell died of whopping cough and bronchitis.

[50] Emily Wonnacott to parents, November 13, 1867, IOR MSS Eur. C376/1.   [51] Ibid.

quarters in Nusseerabad, Emily worried they were too close to the native dwellings.[52] Living so close to South Asians suggested that the Wonnacotts were not deserving of the distance that supposedly kept upright and upper-class British officers and their families safe from the moral and physical contaminants of the native town. Bored, and no doubt in need of funds, Emily worked as a regimental schoolmistress. Returning to the profession she held before marriage did little to cement Emily's status; regimental schoolmistresses were usually culled from the better-educated wives of NCOs. And it did little to relieve her boredom – the work amounted to very little real instruction, and the school was only open four hours a day and frequently closed when the weather was too hot. As a result, Emily spent long stretches of time with nothing but social calls to occupy her.[53]

Finding her place in the world of the regiment only furthered Emily's sense of social displacement. She complained frequently in letters home about the regimental culture, unruly women, and the native population. In Emily's view, these complaints served to distinguish the Wonnacotts from the working-class soldiers surrounding them. "There are a few, & only a few, nice women in the regiment," Emily wrote to her parents. "Not one I would like to make a friend of. They are very illiterate and very fond of fighting & drinking which leads to worse."[54] By the time Emily began to navigate the social hierarchies of Nusseerabad, the Army was in the midst of a cautious liberalization of its marriage policies. Until the early 1880s, most British enlisted men were forbidden from marrying while in the Army. The families of men who married without the approval of their commanding officer would not be acknowledged, housed, or financially supported on "the strength of the regiment."[55] A soldier could marry without permission and consign his wife and children to precarious lives as camp followers, making money through casual work as washerwomen, cooks, or market women, and leaving them without any financial support should the soldier die. The move to increase the number of officially sanctioned marriages turned camp followers into semirespectable Army wives, but Emily would likely have still thought of these enlisted men's wives as tainted by unsanctioned marriages or illicit liaisons.

---

[52] Emily Wonnacott to parents, June 16, 1872 and April 1871, IOR MSS Eur. C376/4.
[53] Emily Wonnacott to mother, April 8, 1870, IOR MSS Eur. C376/2.
[54] Emily Wonnacott to parents, January 12, 1871, IOR MSS Eur. C376/3.
[55] Soldier's documents of Pte William Randall, 1st Battalion Wiltshire Regiment, 1889–1907; includes pay book and discharge certificate, National Army Museum 9703–34.

Emily clung hardest to her role as the respectable mother of a middle-class family when that family was under threat. By the autumn of 1870, the premonitions that worried her in Malta started to seem less fanciful as Emily learned that her brother Tom had died at the Mhow Cantonment. Soon after, she suffered a miscarriage, which Emily attributed to her grief over Tom's death. And in the same month, the Wonnacotts lost their seven-month-old son Bertie, the first of their children to be born in India. Tragic in their own right, these losses underscored the instability of Emily's position. She derived her respectability from her status as a wife and mother. If William should die, she would be left with no pension, reliant on the kindness of the regiment to buy passage for her and her children back to England. Emily saw many widows of the regiment hastily remarry, a practice she bemoaned as "a disgusting custom" and for which she could muster little sympathy.[56] But she, too, might have been left with few alternatives in the absence of William's support. Subject to a military hierarchy that did not respect Emily's pretensions to status and posted too far from home to speedily call on family help, the Wonnacotts had unwittingly gotten themselves into a precarious social and economic position. Without access to either the status of the officer class or the informal support systems of the enlisted men, schoolmasters and their families had few sure resources to rely on in times of trouble.

Ultimately it was not Emily who was left to fend for herself in India, but William. Still in mourning over her losses and sniping with her parents over her brother's personal effects, Emily died in childbirth in September of 1871. While Emily was alive, William had been unconcerned by the threats of downward mobility that occupied so much space in her mind. Only after Emily's death did he begin to become disenchanted with India and the life of the Army. Unnerved by a cholera outbreak in May of 1872, William sent his surviving children – Willie and Nellie – home to Emily's parents.

Paradoxically, it was this move that caused William to realize how poorly he ranked in the military hierarchy. Middle-class British in India, among whom William still numbered himself, insured their respectability by sending their children to be educated in England.[57] But by sending his children away, William lost his last remaining claim to be treated as a respectable head of household. In 1874, he was kicked out of his schoolmaster's bungalow and replaced by the quartermaster sergeant, who wanted the "pretty garden attached [and argued] he ought

[56] Emily Wonnacott to parents, January 24, 1871, IOR MSS Eur. C376/3.
[57] Buettner, *Empire Families*.

to have them because he is a married man, and his wife is with him."[58]
The family home and the peaceful garden were no longer accessible to
the widowed and effectively childless William. While Emily had worried
about the family's position, her presence itself protected it. With Emily
gone and the children in England, William was demoted, in practice to
the position of a lone NCO, with no claim to the more generous living
standards provided for a married man. Through the Wonnacotts' experience, we can see how military rank, gender, and marital status worked
together in imperial spaces to destabilize class hierarchies and create new
social statuses. While the Wonnacotts may have considered themselves
victims of the social hierarchies produced by a British military concerned
with race, status, and respectability on Indian land, such confusion
around status could and often did work to the benefit of enlisted men
and their families.

The Keen Family: "Same Like Gentleman"

Coming to India from a background of domestic service and farm labor,
Dick and Pollie relished the social and leisure opportunities afforded by
their new position. The Keen family occupied the same social position
within the military ranks as the Wonnacotts, but for the Keens it was a
promotion. The Keens would have been in the class of people Emily
found to be such trying social companions. But, unlike Emily, Pollie
benefited from her improved social and financial position as an NCO's
wife in India. The Keens were among the first generation of Army
families to be able to take advantage of more generous marriage allowances for men in the ranks. By the time Richard and Pollie married in
1884, marriage allowances per regiment had increased to include half of
all sergeants over the age of 24, transforming being a soldier's wife from a
financially risky to a more respectable position.[59]

The Keens threw themselves into the social life of the cantonment.
Eight-year-old Dorothy breathlessly informed her grandmother by letter
that she had "been to the dances two or three times a week mother takes
us for an hour and then she takes us home and puts us to bed and I mind
baby till mother comes home and father comes home to see if we are all

---

[58] William Wonnacott to parents, April 24, 1874, IOR MSS Eur. C376/4.
[59] David French, *Military Identities: The Regimental System, the British Army, and the British People, c. 1870–2000* (Oxford: Oxford University Press, 2005), 129.

right."[60] The Keens also attended band concerts alongside officers. Like John Brand, Pollie needed to fill her unaccustomed leisure hours. With none of the endless work that would have accompanied working-class housekeeping in England, Pollie's newfound free time indicated the vast gulf between the family's former status as workers at home and their current, if temporary, role as employers in India.

The Keens understood the impermanence of class categories in the military. Because Dick had been promoted up the ranks to sergeant, he could be demoted for relatively minor bad behavior. Pollie had a cook and other servants to direct and ample leisure time to bemoan her boredom and miss home – echoing the complaints of many a bored ICS wife before her – but she left no record of experiencing any social pressure to maintain the façade of a lady. Pollie might rely on servants one day and be a lady, or do her own cooking and be a soldier's wife the next. Pollie was not unique in doing her own cooking. A Mrs. Lee, the wife of a coronet player stationed in Mooltan, recalled her own attitude toward domestic servants in an oral history interview for the Plain Tales of the Raj radio series. "More often than not," Mrs. Lee recalled, "I didn't keep a cook because I was a bit fussy with my cooking."[61] When it grew too hot to cook, Pollie wrote to her mother, "I have started being a lady again and got a cook as we think of stopping on the Plains."[62] Though Pollie's use of the term "lady" was playful, her usage reveals the instability of the category in India – "lady" to Pollie and Mrs. Lee was a role one could pick up and put down again. For the Keens, and others like them, having servants and leisure time in India did more to destabilize class categories than to offer a sense of any permanent chance of upward mobility.

This became all the clearer when the British class system intersected with military hierarchies. "Yesterday we had the Major come round to visit the quarters," Pollie wrote to her mother. "We knew he was coming so the dusting was all finished and we were all tidy. He…said I had my place very pretty with the pictures and flowers. Dick was standing to attention up against the wall."[63] Pollie was raised in a military environment and knew the Major's visit was an inspection, not a social call. In her narrative of the incident, she gratefully accepted the Major's praise for her decorating skills, playing up her domestic achievements, rather

---

[60] Pollie Keen to Mary Holloway, undated 1893, IOR MSS Eur. F528/12.
[61] Mrs. Lee transcript, Plain Tales from the Raj, IOR MSS Eur. T40.   [62] Ibid.
[63] Pollie Keen to Mary Holloway, February 16, 1890, IOR MSS Eur. F528/9.

than the intrusion into her home. Pollie's domestic role allowed her to cloak the inspection in the language of a house tour, while Dick, more firmly embedded in military hierarchies, could only remain standing to attention against the wall, in an unmistakably subservient position. The Keens knew any improvement in status was fleeting.

In England, Pollie would no longer enjoy the boost in status afforded by her position as a white woman in a country where racial hierarchies could subsume class concerns. British people of working-class origin were at once elevated by having power over South Asians, while at the same time knowing that certain Indians held social positions far superior to theirs. The Keens' situational affluence was derived from the Army, but was also located within the Army's hierarchy. As a result, the Keens were subject to higher levels of scheduled paternalist intervention than a comparable family at home, while at the same time the family mixed with a wider range of social classes in India than they would have in the Army in Britain. Pollie could access the domestic ideal of a higher class, complete with servants, parties, and lazy afternoons, only by departing for India with the Army and living within the racial hierarchies of the Raj.

The Crawford Brothers: To Strike or Strike out for India

Before Ned Crawford made the decision to leave for India, he had traveled along the east coast of England and Scotland, seeking better wages. Ned did not find long-term employment in Dundee, but he did meet a woman named Nell who he "knocked about with" for a time.[64] In Tyneside, he tried for a job running a hauling engine in a coal mine.[65] By 1892, Ned had decided to try his luck in India and secured a job as an engineer with the EIR in Bengal. He left friends and family behind in hopes of higher wages and more secure employment. Ned was unmarried, but he maintained close ties with his brother Martin in Durham and with Nell, with whom he kept up a playful and gossipy correspondence. Nell and Martin were both eager to maintain their connections with Ned while he was in India. Their letters embedded Ned in a shared community stretching from Dundee to Durham to Asansol, a railway station some 120 miles northwest of Calcutta.

---

[64] Nell to Ned Crawford, late July 1893, IOR MSS Eur. F133/46.
[65] Memorandum to Edward Crawford acknowledging receipt of his application for the job of Hawling [sic] Engineman, Horton Colliery, South Shields, September 18, 1890, IOR MSS Eur. F133/45.

Along with family news, Martin's letters included talk of strikes, wages, and employment prospects. By the early 1890s, working-class politics were becoming impossible for the Crawfords to ignore. Coal prices in Britain fell, leading to a corresponding drop in miners' wages. This unstable labor situation may have been what ultimately drove Ned to leave for India. The Durham Miners' Association (DMA), of which Martin was a member, went on strike in 1892, managing only to mitigate the decrease in their wages, and debated striking again a year later.[66] In July 1893, Martin wrote to Ned: "We are expecting a national strike here very soon as the Midland Counties have got notice for a 25 percent reduction [in wages] and the Durham miners are federated with them so we might have to come out too."[67] Martin does not seem to have been an enthusiastic advocate of the strike – "have to" suggests a degree of reluctance. His position aligned with that of the DMA, which was loath to join the national strike so soon after securing concessions for themselves.[68] By August, the Midlands miners were on strike, the DMA was on the verge of being ejected from the national union for their failure to join, and Martin reported that "trade is brisk in Durham" as a result.[69]

Martin seems to have been a trade unionist by default rather than by political inclination. Solidarity was useful to the extent that it kept wages up and prevented serious abuses, but Martin's letters gave no indication that he wished to join in the general strike out of a philosophical devotion toward trade unionism. In fact, he celebrated the economic benefit to Durham as a result of stoppages in the rest of the country. Martin's approach to membership in the DMA had much in common with Ned's attitude toward working in the British Empire – neither brother was driven by ideological devotion. Rather, necessity led Martin to ally himself with the DMA, much as it brought Ned out to India.

While Martin relied on the DMA to secure a decent wage, Ned turned elsewhere. The East Indian Railway posted him to Asansol, a town northwest of Calcutta that had much in common with Durham. Located in Bengal's coal country, Asansol was experiencing its own

---

[66] Carolyn Baylies, *The History of the Yorkshire Miners 1881–1918* (London: Routledge, 1993), 95.

[67] Martin Crawford to Edward Crawford, July 21, 1893, IOR MSS Eur. F133/46.

[68] Baylies, *The History of the Yorkshire Miners*, 100. The DMA was a bit of an outlier tactically, as it operated on a sliding scale wage system. Wages could drop with the price of coal – but they could not drop too far. The sliding scale was a concession the DMA leaders used (effectively) to bargain with management, but it alienated them from many of the other mining unions, who insisted on a wage divorced from the price of coal. This conflict led to the split that kept the DMA from joining the MFGB strike and eventually ended with the DMA ejected from the Federation.

[69] Martin Crawford to Edward Crawford, August 9, 1893, IOR MSS Eur. F133/46.

boom in business, as the EIR increased coal exports and needed to run more trains with larger loads.[70] Ned, like George Cole, was lured to India by the promise of a substantial increase in wages – to £18 a month – more than twice as much as his brother would have made in a Durham colliery.[71] In reality, Ned brought in somewhat less than £18, but not so little that he was dissatisfied with his choice. Ned wrote to Nell that he was happy in Bengal and "beginning to like his work," but noted that the other men he worked with complained about the climate and the country.[72] Such complaints were ubiquitous among British in India regardless of class or gender, but they seldom led to anyone leaving their post early.

Ned's success in India prompted Martin to consider joining his brother. Many in the Crawford brothers' circle saw migration as an option. Nell had friends in the United States; she noted her delight in spotting the Indian stamp on Ned's envelope, having assumed at first glance that the letter came from America.[73] Billy Black, an acquaintance of the Crawfords, heartily approved of Ned's choice, saying upon hearing of his move that Ned "ought to have gone long since."[74] Martin wrote that a mutual friend had returned discouraged from his own venture into the colonies: "Billy Elliot has come back again from Africa and he gives a very bad account of it. He says there are hundreds of men out of work and cannot get a job nowhere."[75] Elliot's African failure made India seem like a brighter option. "I was thinking," Martin wrote, "that if you liked the country very well and there was any prospect for me I could come out to fire [stoke engine boilers] as I will never be no better where I am."[76] Decamping to India was a safer prospect for Martin with Ned already in the country, able to act as a guide and make connections for his brother.

Ultimately, the Crawford brothers took diverging routes to economic security. Ned joined the EIR, traveling a great distance in search of better prospects. Martin remained in Durham, trusting the DMA to ensure him a living wage. Both Martin and Ned drew on the resources available to them as working-class men in the late nineteenth-century British world. As the political and bargaining power of trade unions grew, men like Martin might be able to rely on unions to keep wages high and working conditions

---

[70] George Huddleston, *History of the East Indian Railway* (Calcutta: Thacker, Spink & Co., 1906), 161.

[71] Arthur Lyon Bowley, *Wages in the United Kingdom in the Nineteenth Century* (Cambridge: Cambridge University Press, 1900), 106. Martin Crawford to Edward Crawford, July 21, 1893, IOR MSS Eur. F133/46.

[72] Nell to Ned Crawford, late July 1893, IOR MSS Eur. F133/46.   [73] Ibid.

[74] Martin Crawford to Ned Crawford, August 9, 1893, IOR MSS Eur. F133/46.

[75] Ibid.   [76] Ibid.

acceptable. However, rank-and-file members remained subject to the decisions of both management and union leadership. Martin began to consider leaving for India at the same time as the Durham miners bowed out of the national strike. Martin would have observed the contradictory policy of the DMA alongside the hardships facing striking workers, especially as the national press reported on the miners' plight in great detail.[77] This instability may have forced Martin to consider the prospect of India more seriously. Ned, whose travels around the northeast suggest a history of patchy employment and who would have benefited only indirectly from trade unionism, turned to another field of opportunity open to men of his class – employment in the empire. With a limited set of options and driven by a desire for stable employment and higher wages, the two brothers made different choices. In a history of the British working class confined to Britain's borders, Ned's story would disappear. And in a history of empire, Martin's story would be peripheral at best. Looking at the brothers' stories together demonstrates that Martin's choices cannot be understood solely through the lens of working-class political organization, nor Ned's through that of imperial expansion.

Conclusion

Unlike the fictional Kim, whose family ties must fade away for his story to begin, the imperial histories of the Cole, Crawford, Keen, Brand, and Wonnacott families can only be made sense of within their larger networks of kinship, friendship, and community. George and Lucy Cole experienced George's imperial work as a disruption of their marriage, and their marital troubles drew family and acquaintances into the couple's conflict. For George, distance provoked fears of Lucy's infidelity. For Lucy, George's abandonment of the nuclear family prompted the formation of a new family structure. The damage to the Coles' relationship was not simply the result of distance, but of communications and miscommunications, both willful and accidental, mediated through the correspondence networks that bound together the Coles' extended families.

For the Wonnacott and Keen families, the intersection of racial hierarchies and military rule in India created status instability over which they had little control. For Emily Wonnacott, this came in a loss of purpose and identity experienced as she failed, or refused, to find a sense

---

[77] Andy Croll, "Starving Strikers and the Limits of the 'Humanitarian Discovery of Hunger' in Late Victorian Britain," *International Review of Social History* 56, no. 01 (April 2011): 103–31.

of place and a new community in the Indian cantonments. But for some, with disruption came possibility. For women like Pollie Keen, traveling to India as an Army wife provided a respite from the life of labor she had lived up until that point. The alteration in status that Emily Wonnacott felt as a loss was for Pollie a chance to try on different personae and a different relationship to work. In its most extreme form, though, disruption meant loss of life and purpose. For William Wonnacott, Emily's death caused immense grief, destabilized his own sense of self, and altered the material conditions under which he and his children lived.

Both Ned Crawford and John Brand were single and remained so throughout their time in India. For these unmarried men, John Brand in particular, the risk (or possibility) of Indian service causing a drastic disruption or a permanent severing of ties was greater than for those who had families of blood and marriage to return to and provide for. But the experience of the Crawfords and John Brand demonstrates the importance and persistence of these seemingly looser ties for single men. The Crawford brothers were bound together by family ties, but John Brand had to work to create and maintain connections of his own. While Brand experienced his own time in the Army as one of boredom and illness, that unfilled time gave him the chance to maintain connections with his extended family and friends. These relationships reformed through distance, with Brand's letter-writing strengthening and sustaining ties that might have fallen to the wayside had he not had the time and leisure to maintain them.

Thus far, I have suggested that stories of families like these have not made their mark on the historical record because it was difficult to find a place for them in histories of British elite rule, and as a result of a persistent mischaracterization at the time of the British working-class in India as male and unattached. But this is not the whole story. These stories have remained hidden in part because the subjects themselves had little interest in or ability to promote or preserve their own imperial histories. Working-class families did not tend to weave their tales of Indian life into their own family histories. Instead, upon returning to Britain, empire stories either faded away or bled into army tales. The family stories we have seen here are accessible not because they have been passed down through generations through oral and family tradition, but because they were preserved in correspondence collections.

Correspondence knit these men and women together across great distances in their own time and preserved histories of their relationships in the archive. While letter-writing was a common practice for British in India regardless of class, working-class correspondents had their own distinctive version of the practice. The next chapter explores in greater detail what it meant to maintain family connections through correspondence. Though correspondents wrote about the physical distance that separated them from one another, they also worried about the wide gap that grew as families split between India and Britain, rendering experience mutually incomprehensible. Working-class letter writers sought to strengthen connections, rather than emphasize difference, and in so doing, they shaped what the archive of working-class Indian experiences contains. Delving into the letters of these families, we can see the techniques deployed – some successful, others not – to manage financial needs and nurture relationships across imperial distance. And we can see how, in the long term, these methods obscured as much about Indian experiences as they revealed.

2   Writing Family Together across Imperial Distances

It was the autumn of 1861, and Ann Palmer missed her husband. James Palmer had left the family's home in Huntingdon for railway work in Bengal earlier that year. The Palmers worried over money and housing, separation and health, and the daunting prospect of reuniting a family spread across such vast distances. Ann wanted to send James news of their children and friends, to gently suggest that he stay away from drinking, and to beg him to return safely home to her. But Ann Palmer could not write. This would not have been terribly unusual – Ann was among the 40–50 percent of early Victorian women who could not write.[1] Instead, she drew on local networks of readers and writers to help her communicate with her husband. At first, Ann called upon friends and neighbors who would write out her letters to her dictation, however poor their spelling and rendering of names and places may have been. As her eldest daughter, also named Ann, progressed in school, Ann Palmer came to rely on her child's growing expertise to compose letters to James.[2] This put the younger Ann in a challenging position. She was eager to write to her father and often did put her own thoughts and stories down on paper. But her mother was the one dictating the correspondence, and as the period of separation grew longer, the elder Ann became increasingly irritated at what she perceived as her husband's profligate drinking and his refusal to send home a decent amount of money to his wife and children. She was distraught, too, at the thought that she might never see him again. Whether out of frugality or convenience, Ann Palmer's sometimes very personal thoughts were filtered through her daughter's pen, where they intermingled with childish pleas for a new frock or news of Christmas presents and accounts of schoolwork.

---

[1] Woods, *The Demography of Victorian England and Wales*, 148. Woods determines literacy by the imperfect measure of those who could sign their own wedding registries. There is nothing in the Palmer family correspondent to suggest whether or not Ann could read.
[2] For the sake of clarity, I will refer to Ann the mother as "Ann Palmer" or "Ann" and Ann the daughter as "young Ann."

The content of working-class correspondence was not too different from that featured in the correspondence of elites.[3] People of all classes wrote about money and material things, about children and family, and about love and jealousy. They wrote about distance and how to bridge it, offering up pressed flowers and locks of hair, valentines and news clippings, sketches, and, as the century drew on, photographs in lieu of their physical presence. What makes working-class letters distinctive is the collective nature of their production. Many working-class correspondents in the middle of the nineteenth century did not themselves do the physical act of letter-writing (or reading). Instead, they relied on friends, relatives, and neighbors, and hired writers and readers. While it was not unusual, whatever your class, to write with the expectation that your letter would be passed around by its recipient, writers with the luxury of literacy could, in theory, pick and choose which personal concerns would become public knowledge, demarcating certain information as "strictly private." For working-class writers, correspondence was necessarily a communal project. As a result, information – whether about the imperial experiences or emotional states of the writers – became public property. Letter writers did not necessarily see the public nature of private letters as a problem, but instead shaped their communication around this fact. Correspondence played an integral, if uneven, role in the creation of family and community networks based on shared imperial experience. While imperial experience itself was not widespread, either among elites or the working class, letters granted access and information about empire to a far larger group and a more diverse range of people than can be suggested by merely tallying up those involved in imperial service. Because correspondence held this productive potential and played a major role in shaping imperial experience, the letter, as a material artifact, formal object, and means of communication, became an essential force in creating non-elite cultures of empire.

For illiterate correspondents, getting a letter together represented an act of trust in those they relied on to do the work of writing. This practice could sometimes lead to changes in content. William Wilkie, who planned to depart with his regiment without informing his mother of his whereabouts, bowed to the scolding of an older woman staying in his lodging house in Edinburgh. Recounting his youthful indifference in his memoir, Wilkie recalled the woman admonishing him to "'Write her and

---

[3] Rebecca Earle, ed., *Epistolary Selves: Letters and Letter-Writers, 1600–1945* (Aldershot, Hampshire: Ashgate Publishing Ltd., 1999); Sarah Pearsall, *Atlantic Families: Lives and Letters in the Later Eighteenth Century* (Oxford: Oxford University Press, 2008); and Rothschild, *The Inner Life of Empires.*

let her know then you scoundral [*sic*]' said she. I said I could not write but she said that was no excuse if I got paper she would write for me."[4] The trust Ann Palmer had to put in her own daughter was of a different sort. Ann Palmer relied on young Ann to relay information and to keep the family intact by doing so. Young Ann wrote not only to her father but also to her aunts and uncles as well. This may have led Ann Palmer to censor herself in hopes of keeping some of her marital disputes and worries from young Ann.

These letters are not just a record of the experience of a specific working-class family in empire, but have much to tell us about the lives, emotional regimes, and lengths to which such families would go to maintain connections across vast distances. Drawing on an archive of letters from non-elite correspondents, this chapter closely examines the personal relationships and power dynamics at play in the correspondence of such families split between Britain and India. Ann and James' letters, and others like them, help us uncover how working families managed imperial lives and how their experiences of marriage, childhood, and family were altered by immediate or distant contact with empire.

Access and Education

Letter-writing became more accessible to the working class as literacy rates grew throughout the nineteenth century and postal rates decreased.[5] Penny post rates, introduced for the populace in the 1840s and for the military as early as the 1790s, meant that correspondence was not limited by financial considerations. Correspondents sent nearly a million more letters around the country in the year after the introduction of the penny post than they had the previous year. Corresponding had become so commonplace that even in communities with a large illiterate population, there was someone willing to read and write as a favor or for pay.[6] In these circumstances, letters did not represent a straight backward and forward exchange of information, a phenomenon that was exacerbated in the empire. Though the time frame shortened dramatically with the opening of the Suez Canal in 1869, when the Palmers were

---

[4] William Wilkie's Reminiscences during his sojourn in Crimea and during the Indian Mutiny was written from memory while night watchman in the Angus Jute Works, Dundee, 1890–91, IOR MSS Eur. B221, 1.

[5] Nigel Hall, "The Materiality of Letter Writing," in Barton and Hall, eds., *Letter Writing as Social Practice*, 88.

[6] Gerber, *Authors of Their Lives*, 74; Mark R. Frost, "Pandora's Post Box: Empire and Information in India, 1854–1914," *The English Historical Review* 131, no. 552 (October 1, 2016): 1043–73, https://doi.org/10.1093/ehr/cew270.

corresponding in the early 1860s, a letter going to or from India took about three months to reach its recipient. In unusually poor circumstances, years could elapse between sending and receipt. Once the letter was read, it might be sent on to another recipient, meaning that the news contained in private correspondence was both outdated and public. Letters traveled between metropole and colony, to outposts of informal empire, and back to the capital. When their recipients could not be located, bureaucracies swallowed them up or they were simply thrown away. The act of writing represented a gesture of trust in a massive system of imperial infrastructure, transit, and communications, which, as we see in the case of the misplaced East Indian Railway (EIR) records, could fail.

In common with many letters and journals from working-class writers in this period, there is little or no regular punctuation in the letters from EIR workers' families in the IOR F133 collection, which as we saw in the introduction was comprised largely of letters from correspondents with minimal formal education. Words are capitalized at random (a practice that by the 1860s had fallen out of favor with most educated correspondents), and there are no paragraph or sentence breaks. The Palmer mother and daughter's writing style was meandering and the spelling irregular. The writers jumped from subject to subject – Ann Commack, the wife of another EIR worker, covered her husband's infidelity, her poverty, her love for her child, and requests for news in one sentence alone. In the Palmer letters, this tendency was likely exacerbated by Ann Palmer breaking into her daughter's composition with "one more thing to tell father." Ann did not have a standardized spelling for either of her daughters' names, and her own name was spelled sometimes with an "e" and sometimes without. Ann's second daughter Diana is rendered in a number of different ways, including "Dianha" and "Diehannah," depending on the writer.[7] In spite of these difficulties, the Palmer family expected to correspond with one another – young Ann complained to her father, "I have rite servil letters for I have had a heavy task this week I have rote to aunt Diehannah and to uncle Joe and to Mrs Murden."[8]

Letter-writing as a skill did not enter the curriculum for working-class children until the educational reforms of the 1870s that made elementary education compulsory and started to take working-class children

---

[7] Ann the younger seems to prefer Anne with an "e" and the violent spelling of her little sister's name as "Diehannah," though sometimes different spellings appear in the same hand and on the same page, as in Ann's December 11, 1861, letter. Ann to James Palmer, December 11, 1861, IOR MSS Eur. F133/112.

[8] Ann to James Palmer, January 19, 1862, IOR MSS Eur. F133/112.

seriously as learners, rather than rote repeaters.[9] Unconstrained by a formal writing style, letters like the Palmers' (and Coles' and Commacks') allow the reader to "hear," or at least to form the impression of hearing, the cadence and accent of the writer. Martha Hanna and Carolyn Steedman have both pointed to the sense of immediacy practices like these lend to writing from people with little formal education.[10]

The effects of these educational reforms can be seen in Pollie Keen's correspondence. Pollie had a similar background to Lucy Cole and Ann Palmer – she was the daughter of a laundress and she went into service at a young age – but she was some twenty-five years younger. Pollie would have been born around the same time as the Cole and Palmer children, too early to benefit from the 1870 Elementary Education Act, but late enough to have greater access to formal schooling. Literacy rates illuminate the stark difference between her writing style and that of the women writing in the early 1860s. While just over half of women in Lucy and Ann's time could write, by the 1890s, 90 percent of the British population was considered literate.[11] As a result, Pollie's letters are far more polished than Lucy's or Ann's. Though they are still plagued with punctuation errors and spelling mistakes, they are coherent narratives, moving smoothly from one subject to the next and following proper letter-writing practice, making their format, if not their content, almost indistinguishable from the correspondence of elites.[12] Pollie was even able to pick and choose who would receive her news. She wrote in detail about the physical discomforts of her pregnancy to her sister Carrie, noting that she had not told their mother "any particulars in my letters because of the boys."[13] So while the Keens still shared news within their family circle, there were enough people who could read and write on their own that certain information could be kept private.

Neither Ann Palmer nor her daughter disciplined their thoughts into a traditional letter format, likely because they had never been taught to do so. Though the Palmer letters were a communal product, the differences between Ann Palmer and young Ann's contributions are clear. The one gesture toward structuring the letter according to the conventions of

---

[9] Vincent, *Literacy and Popular Culture*, 89.
[10] Martha Hanna, "A Republic of Letters: The Epistolary Tradition in France during World War I," *AHR* 108, no. 5 (2003), Carolyn Steedman, *The Tidy House: Little Girls Writing* (London: Virago, 1982).
[11] Woods, *The Demography of Victorian England and Wales*, 148.
[12] Martyn Lyons, "New Readers in the Nineteenth Century: Women, Children, Workers," in Guglielmo Cavallo and Roger Chartier, eds., *A History of Reading in the West* (Cambridge: Polity Press, 1999), 313.
[13] Pollie Keen to Carrie, March 26, 1890, IOR MSS Eur. F528/9.

written, rather than spoken, language is the phrase "my Dear father" or "my Dear husband." Both are scattered liberally throughout the text, in part to differentiate between the speakers when the letters are written in one hand. The voices are clearly those of two distinct people. In a joint letter, young Ann begins:

Dear father … I wish I could see you as often as I could see your letter I was very glad that I made most of your last letter out Dear father I would kiss you now if I could see you Dear father, you know what you promised me the first letter I rote a new frock but I hope if you are sparred to come home I hope you will buy me a silk one.[14]

Young Ann used her father's letter as a substitute for his presence. While middle-class writers might contemplate the significance of seeing their loved one's hand, as if penmanship itself could transport the essence of a person across distance, young Ann was more concerned with her access to the contents of the letter – her ability to read and comprehend her father's words brought them closer together. In contrast, Emily Wonnacott, who came from an educated family, attached great importance to the physical act of writing. Shortly after her son Ernest was born in Malta in 1866, she placed a pen in the baby's fist and held her own hand around his to scribble out the lines, "Dear grandma, I love you very much & my dear grandad. Accept my best love. Your loving baby."[15] Such play was not accessible to the Palmers and would not have had much meaning to correspondents who relied on others to write for them.

Love and Money

Love, money, and letters were closely linked for these correspondents. Wives of EIR workers at home in England did not differentiate between husbands' failures to correspond and to send additional money. For families waiting for financial support to come in the mail, emotional neglect and material neglect were functionally one and the same. Ann Commack's husband James was among the men working for the EIR. In the autumn of 1861, Ann Commack wrote to James castigating him for being a poor correspondent and provider. "i have received 2 leters from you since you been in india and in Each one expecting the money you promised me but was disapounted but my Dear husband i hope you dont forget you got a Wife and dear child but i think you do."[16] Ann used

---

[14] Ann to James Palmer, January 19, 1862, IOR MSS Eur. F133/112.
[15] Emily Wonnacott to Mother, October 1866, IOR MSS Eur. 376/1.
[16] Ann Commack to James Commack, October 31, 1861, IOR MSS Eur. F133/43.

similar techniques to those employed by Lucy Cole to spark a response from James. She emphasized her child's helplessness, her own maternal status, and his absence. Ann signed herself as "Bentey's mother" and described herself looking at her daughter and thinking "you might has well have no father and she points up to your likeness and says dad Dad and makes me shed many tears."[17]

Ann was in desperate financial circumstances. She had been forced to pawn most of her clothing and her ring to pay rent after James left for India and the family's two lodgers moved out. She was heavily pregnant and had no means to pay the doctor.[18] Ann wrote to James that she expected to give birth "by the time you get this leter," accounting for the passage of time in relation to when the mail was received. She was surprised to find that James had set aside only 15 shillings (not even, she noted, rounding up to a full pound) out of his pay to maintain the family in England.[19] Other EIR wives she knew got over twice as much from their husbands, and, she reported, rumors were circulating that she must drink or James would have left more funds at her disposal.[20] The landlord, a Mr. Jackson, came around to collect rent Ann did not have and "told me you was serving me shameful" with such a small remittance to live on.[21] Exacerbating Ann's financial troubles, the EIR had been late disbursing payments out of their London offices, stretching what was supposed to be a monthly payment schedule to five weeks. Ann sent a friend to the company's offices to complain about the late payments on her behalf, and was told that she "must not be so particular." Two or three days, Ann noted, was nothing to the company, but "them and me are different."[22] Even amid her financial worries, Ann wanted to understand what James was experiencing so far from her. "Dear," Ann wrote, "when you write again send me more what you are going to do with all the money you save and tell me all particulars about the country."[23] Ann attempted to foster shared experiences with James, nudging him to set aside funds and help her imagine his present circumstances and the family's future fortune.

Though Ann Palmer likewise worried about money, her James' departure seems to have made her more financially secure, at least while he was alive to send needed funds. James signed a four-year contract, promising a significant increase in salary and years living apart from his wife and daughters. He was hired to work as an inspector of the permanent way, responsible for insuring that a segment of rail in Colgong (present-day

---

[17] Ibid.   [18] Ibid.
[19] Ibid. Presumably Ann received these 15 shillings on a weekly basis from the company.
[20] Ibid.   [21] Ibid.   [22] Ibid.   [23] Ibid.

Kahalgaon, Bihar) was in good repair. James was in charge of some twenty native workers. He made a significantly larger sum working in India than he could have made in England – £15 a month.[24] The average English railway worker, in contrast, could expect to make about £40 a year in 1851, with the average engineer's salary at £110 a year in the 1860s.[25] James' salary was high for a working-class man, suggesting that the four-year separation mandated by his contract would be well worth the trouble in financial terms. But the benefits were likely to be future ones for the Palmers. The family made no formal arrangement with the EIR to have part of James' salary paid at home.

In spite of these unstable financial arrangements, Ann was able to receive pay through the EIR offices at irregular intervals and used the money to improve the family's conditions. She moved to a new house with four rooms in Hitchin, only a few miles from her father's home in Wymondley and large enough for the family and lodgers to live comfortably. She spent money on new clothes for the children and considered moving young Ann, the more promising scholar of her daughters, to a better school where "they learn all sorts of learning ... for I think they cannot know to[o] much."[26] But Ann had difficulty managing this new influx of money, especially as it was unreliably dispersed. Months after her spending spree, she noted that children were once again without clothes – possibly because she had pawned some of her new acquisitions. Ann also spent money sending material reminders of the family to James. She put together a box containing likenesses of the children, James' watch, and a Bible. This box was not simply the gift of a wife missing her husband and sending a gentle reminder to remain virtuous, but a sign that the Palmers felt comfortable with their finances. James had left the watch behind in England to be pawned. Ann had only been able to redeem it some months before and send it out to India, signaling that she would no longer require it as collateral for future loans. In return, she asked for "a nice broad ring to wear around my finger ... if they are cheap," and young Ann asked for a pair of earrings, noting in what might

[24] James Palmer's contract with the EIR stipulated he pay his own rent, but, with passage provided, his pay remained remarkably generous. He *was* subject to a £100 fine if he chose to break his contract. Presumably George Cole was subject to the same fine, or one proportional to his income (his contract has not survived), making the decision to join the EIR all the more fraught and life altering.

[25] As an inspector, James' English salary would likely have been somewhere between these two numbers. The £40 figure is troublesome, because it is an average that includes everyone from the poorly paid navvies through the professional classes. Figures from Williamson, "Earnings Inequality in Nineteenth-Century Britain," 474, and Porter, *The Thames Embankment*, 176.

[26] Ann Palmer to James Palmer, December 11, 1861, IOR MSS Eur. F133/112.

have been her own unspoken editorial aside, "but I daresay you will think we want a great deal."[27]

Material items received from family and friends at home likewise played an essential economic and affective role. Erika Rappaport has argued that for elite families, "the money and goods that often travelled with correspondence ... were central to the smooth functioning of domestic and imperial economies."[28] For working-class families as well, these goods mediated experiences between India and home, strengthened bonds, and helped maintain relationships between family members. Among poorer families, like the Palmers who shipped James's watch back and forth, they could act as financial and social capital. Home goods were inextricably bound up with written correspondence. Material objects and letters most often arrived together in one parcel, a single package composed of different parts, each of which was required to make sense of the whole.[29]

Regardless of financial circumstance, most requests for material goods tended to be sentimental. Pollie Keen, missing the farm near her home in Woolwich, asked her mother to send butter. "Put it in a tin," she instructed in her letter, "and let dear Tom solder it down and please sent is as an experiment for the country butter is not nice and the tinned butter from other parts of the country is not nice. I think the parcel post is 6d per pound to India. I expect you will laugh at the idea."[30] Pollie, who was experiencing a period of temporary luxury in India, acknowledged the oddness of the request and was careful to note the cost of her experiment for her laundress mother. Gunner Barney Sheridan's sister-in-law sent him a letter with a lock of her hair enclosed, reminding him to behave himself with the women of the regiment, as if sending a sisterly chaperone in material form along with the verbal warning.[31] James Commack's sister promised "a bit of English reading" and asked him to tell her his preferred newspaper.[32] Even Lucy Cole sent her husband the home papers every week, although the hotels he stayed in carried the major British papers, and their copies were likely more up-to-date. Postal rates made this a relatively minor expenditure, but for a thrifty and time-

---

[27] Ann Palmer to James Palmer, February 9, 1862, IOR MSS Eur. F133/112.
[28] Rappaport, "'The Bombay Debt'," 235.
[29] Pollie Keen notes when she has received a package without a letter – suggesting such an experience was unusual enough to be remarked upon. "Till sent me a Mrs. Leach's book of fashions for children some of them are very pretty. She did not send any letter." Pollie Keen to Mary Holloway, September 28, 1890, IOR MSS Eur. F528/9.
[30] Pollie Keen to Mary Holloway, January 5, 1890, IOR MSS Eur. F528/8.
[31] John and Margaret Sheridan to Barney Sheridan, August 27, 1859, IOR MSS Eur. F133/142.
[32] Fanny Winter to James Commack, November 24, 1861, IOR MSS Eur. F133/43.

pressed wife, the weekly activity was a gesture of love. When the Wonnacotts first arrived in India, Emily's parents sent newspapers and picture books. Later, William Wonnacott would beg his mother-in-law for photographs of the children he had sent home to her; the pictures arrived some three years after his first request. Correspondents could take delayed requests as slights – Emily Wonnacott's relationship with her own parents suffered after they refused to send out her dead brother Tom's watch as a memento.

Marriage and Fidelity

Any parcel sent from home enclosed sentiment alongside the letters, material goods, and much-needed money. But for couples managing marriage across distance, correspondence served as a means of reminding one another of the importance of fidelity. This was an especially significant concern for wives at home, as infidelity in India carried with it the possibility of racial as well as sexual transgressions. Anxieties about marriage were threaded throughout the letters. None of the correspondents have much evidence of infidelity, but they use the notion to express their distress at being so far distant in space and experience. Ann Palmer, whose marriage to James appears to have been a happy one, still worried about the temptation of other women in his life. Through her daughter's pen, she addressed her husband: "Dear husband you say that there is two or three a lodging together you dont say wether you are all by yourself but I daresay you have got a black woman to wate upon you"[33] Ann imagined an unknown "black woman" taking over her own domestic duties and possibly posing a sexual threat. The presence of this supposed servant underscores the growing gap in experience between Ann and her daughters in England and James in India. Though she had no direct experience of Indian life and James had made no mention of it in his letters, Ann was aware of the racial hierarchies in the country and the benefits they afforded working-class men. Likely because of the communal nature of the letter, any questions Ann may have had about James living in the company of a "black woman" remained subtext. Using young Ann as a scribe may have prevented Ann from revealing some of her more intimate feelings. On the other hand, it could have allowed her to share more family gossip and news that she would not have wanted to reveal to a stranger. By filtering her letters through her daughter, Ann Palmer was able to keep more information within the

---

[33] Ann Palmer to James Palmer, January 19, 1862, MSS Eur. F133/112.

immediate family circle, something she would have been unable to do had she sought outside help in composing her missives.

Ann Commack wrote more freely to her James: "you said in your leter you were lodging with an Englishman and Woman i hope you wont be led away by her ... but i dont supose you will be true to me all the time you are away." Seemingly pragmatic and resigned to an unfaithful husband, she nonetheless assured James, "my Dear if it were for 20 years i will stick to you for ever i dont say but what i have my feellings sometimes but i dont let them overcome me."[34] She concluded this letter with a stream-of-consciousness expression of the worries that plagued working-class correspondents – death, distance, jealousy, money, and love. "Untill death us do part write as often as ever you can i hope my Dear husband you will send me the money as soon as you can and i hope you wont forget your affectionate wife and tender child and i hope you will ever be true to me."[35]

Both Ann Commack and Ann Palmer worried about their respective husbands falling under the influence of women in India. For Ann Palmer, the concern came from an overt discussion of blackness. Having a black servant, even one whose labor was shared between multiple men living in one dwelling, distanced Ann from James. The domestic space in which he lived transformed from one that was created and cared for by both members of the couple to one that included an outsider – made even more so by her race. In the case of Ann Commack, race appeared in the specification of the Englishwoman that her husband was living with. Though the reference appears at first to be joking, Ann Commack was realistic about her prospects of marital fidelity. Unlike the Coles, however, for neither Ann Commack nor Ann Palmer did fears of infidelity lead to marital breakdown.

The Coles lobbed accusations of infidelity at one another as they bickered across the distance. Though none but the last of George's letters have survived, it is clear from Lucy's responses that by the beginning of 1862 he had started accusing her of being unfaithful. It is hard to imagine that Lucy was surprised at these accusations, given the extent to which she bragged about her male lodgers. She defended herself nonetheless, even offering up her own wifely devotion as a model he should seek out in any ladies he might take up with. "I think my Dear husband you torment me enough about the Men but neaver mind I will not worry and fret ... I shood like to live with my husband but you wanted a change so of crs I can not have you My Dear George I hope if you form an atachment to

---

[34] Ann Commack to James Commack, October 31, 1861, IOR MSS Eur. F133/43.
[35] Ibid.

any one out there she will Prove as faithful to you as I have done."[36] The Cole correspondence is remarkable for the openness of the accusations of sexual infidelity and emotional cruelty. While correspondence was ostensibly private, letters were likely to pass through many hands, as Lucy's forwarding practices make clear. News from England was at a premium, and friends were willing (or eager) to wade through pages of marital infighting to hear about home. Lucy was offering up her marital discord to unknown readers continents away.

But if Lucy had no qualms about letting her personal affairs become public knowledge, she was just as willing to use public matters to intervene in her personal life. One of her more creative techniques for shaming George was her use of press cuttings to send intimate messages. While sending along news clippings and entire papers was common practice, Lucy preferred to send items of particular relevance to her marital problems. Tucked in among the letters in the Cole family file is an article entitled "A Domesticated Husband." The article described a trial for domestic assault and the familiar story of a husband, who, having abandoned his family, suspected his wife of having an affair with one of her male lodgers. The wife, Ann Watkins, claimed her husband "has left me two years, during which time I have supported myself and the children by taking in lodgers, all of whom are respectable."[37] Ann Watkins lived in Stratford New Town, the same railway suburb as the Coles, and the Coles knew the family. While Lucy could have meant the clipping to do nothing more than update George on the local scandal, it is unlikely that she failed to notice the similarities between her own family's situation and that of the Watkinses. The article continued to recount the trial, noting that Richard Watkin had threatened his wife repeatedly with violence since returning home. Ann Watkins testified, "My husband came home about three weeks ago, and the first night, he told me he would lay me under the turf.... He is causing all my lodgers to leave me through his dreadful conduct." Richard Watkins received a sentence of hard labor for attempting to beat the man he accused of being his wife's lover. Lucy's inclusion of this particular case would seem to be a warning of what might come if George continued to accuse her of infidelity. Once again drawing upon popular and local opinion, Lucy attempted to show how a wayward husband might not merely be subject to condemnation from his friends and neighbors, but to legal censure.

---

[36] Lucy Cole to George Cole, April 18, 1862, IOR MSS Eur. F133/42.
[37] "A Domesticated Husband" [no additional publication information survives], MSS Eur. F133/42.

Dreams and Worries

Though letter writers expressed love and care through material means, they also turned to the immaterial. Talk of dreams allowed correspondents to say things they might otherwise keep hidden or have difficulty finding a way of articulating. In George Cole's only surviving letter to his family, he defended himself against Lucy's accusations of neglect: "Dearest Lucy i feel as if i loved you quite more every day you cannot imagine my feelings when i am a writing to you i just fancy i am in Bed with you once again i Dream about you all."[38] Among letters replete with accusations of extramarital sex, this is one of the few with direct references to intimacy within a marriage. George turned away from the community focus that characterized the rest of the Cole correspondence and focused on the private space of fantasy, interiority, and dreams. Lucy likewise used dreams to forge imagined connections. She wrote to George "You are neaver out of my mind sleeping or waking I very often came to India and back of a night in my sleep."[39] Dreams, like letters, could compress the distance. George and Lucy used dreams rhetorically to express love amid the persistent conflict that marked their waking lives and letters.

Pollie Keen, whose weekly letters to her mother Mary were relentlessly upbeat, was an enthusiastic reteller of dreams. Though pampered, Pollie's life in India was far from perfect. Perhaps to shield Mary from worry, she employed a cheerful tone to recount tales of illness among friends and neighbors, a dangerous childbirth, and her husband's trouble with drinking. Homesickness, fear, and ambivalence only appear in Pollie's dreams, which break through the narratives of Army life as expressions of longing for home. As in Lucy's letter, dream travel between India and England was a common theme. A few months after the Keens arrived in Sialkot, she wrote to her mother, "I was so disappointed one morning last week, I dreamed that I was coming to see you and had got as far as old Atfields in the meadow and I was just thinking you would be just home when our cook woke me up to have a cup of tea so I soon got back to India but it was all so real."[40] Pollie's imagined stroll across English meadows was interrupted not by a crying child or the sounds of soldiers drilling, but by the cook. For a working-class woman like Pollie, such an experience was characteristically Indian.

---

[38] George Cole to Lucy Cole, September 8, 1862, MSS Eur. F133/42.
[39] Lucy Cole to George Cole, undated 1861, IOR MSS Eur. F133/42.
[40] Pollie Keen to Mary Holloway, April 14, 1890, IOR MSS Eur. F528/9.

That she recounted it on paper suggests the disjuncture between her imagined or remembered English life and her Indian present.

Conveying inner life on paper was a challenge for working-class writers. Though Pollie might have been taught letter-writing form at school, the templates provided offered nothing but stilted models of emotional expression. Pollie's dreams allowed her to represent home-sickness and feelings of dislocation with a depth the formal resources available to her would not allow. Pollie recounted dreaming of coming home on three months leave. "I can't remember anything of my Holiday only the night I was coming away ... I saw a lot of Lancers coming along marching through. I saw a girl run over and she had both legs broke, then there was a big fire somewhere, I saw lots of smoke."[41] This chaotic vision gives way to a scene at her Aunt Clara's house, in which Clara refused to speak to Pollie because she had not yet come to visit her. Finally, Pollie "shouted to a cabman but called him gharry wallar so he took no notice of me, then I remembered I must say cabman so got him at last."[42] Through her dream, Pollie was able to express worries that she was growing distant from family and losing parts of her English self. She ended her account saying, "I don't think I did so bad in one night do you."[43] Pollie lessened the nightmarish effect of her dream experiences by concluding with a quip and turning her worries ridiculous. Among the tasks letter writers performed was emotional management, assuring relations that they were well, that they would come home, and that their experiences had not made them unrecognizably foreign. Pollie's final statement aimed at diffusing the impact of her dream suggests that she understood the vision to be an expression of some disturbing inner thoughts and felt the need to moderate them for her audience – a caring but geographically distant mother.

Children and Parents

Parent–child relationships changed when families moved to India. For adults like Pollie or Emily and William Wonnacott, leaving parents behind spurred voluminous communication aimed at maintaining connections. For women like Ann Palmer, who moved closer to her father after her husband James left, parents could be a source of practical and emotional support. Indian service reorganized working-class families in a variety of ways, weakening marriages and making parental relationships

[41] Pollie Keen to Mary Holloway, July 2, 1893, IOR MSS Eur. F528/12.
[42] Ibid. Pollie likely meant *gharry-wallah*, a horse-drawn cab driver.   [43] Ibid.

more important for some, emphasizing the primacy of maternal bonds for others.

Though the Wonnacotts experienced India as a gradual descent down the social ladder, William did make one major decision that marked his more elite roots. William Wonnacott had the means, the connections, and the cultural competency to send his children home to England. The ability to send children back for schooling, as Elizabeth Buettner has argued, was one of the key ways for English families in India to protect their class and racial status.[44] And keeping children in India opened families up to meddling and discipline from the state and charitable organizations. William kept his son Willie with him for six months after Emily's death in September of 1871. By March, though, he had arranged passage for Willie on a troopship headed for England, and the boy's grandparents met him after a month's voyage.[45] It is not clear whether William had planned to keep his daughters Nellie and Emmie with him until his regiment was scheduled to return to England, but those plans were disrupted by Emmie's death.

William wrote the news directly to Willie after informing the rest of the family separately, in a letter that seemed calibrated more to relieve his own feelings than comfort his son. "I got your last very nice pencilled note yesterday. In it you desire to be remembered to your sisters; my dearest son you have not but one Sister my sweet little Nellie. Poor Emmie one month ago was looking so fat and was so lively and so full of frolic." After describing in detail Emmie's fever and death, he shifted to a description of the burial, sliding between personal pronouns and the impersonal "it" to protect his feelings. "It was buried the following morning in the graveyard here and little Nellie and Agnes Rea threw flowers upon her little coffin after it was lowered into the grave."[46] This expression of unfiltered emotion was unusual among William's correspondence with his children – under normal circumstances he reserved his worry for his parents alone.

William's middle-class upbringing and education were evident in the way he communicated with his children. He either wrote directly to Willie or Nellie or instructed his mother to communicate for him. In a letter to his mother, he wrote, "Tell Willie & Nellie I have now to amuse me in the bungalow when alone three pets ... a mastiff pup, a young deer, so tame, directly he sees me come home he runs into the house, and if

---

[44] Buettner, *Empire Families*, 2.
[45] William Wonnacott to parents, April 18, 1872, IOR MSS Eur. 376.4.
[46] William Wonnacott to Ernest (Willie) Wonnacott, September 3, 1872, IOR MSS Eur. 376.4.

I don't take a notice of him he butts me gently, and a mongoose."[47] This move allowed him to communicate with his children and effectively set aside the remainder of the letter as for his mother's eyes only. When not in the throes of grief, William reserved stories for his children that he perceived to be appropriate for their young ages. He likewise put value in the physical artifact of writing – encouraging Willie to become proficient at his letters so the father and son could write directly to one another. To his daughter Nellie, William acted as a tour guide to an England she was seeing for the first time without him. "Such a lot of houses, so big & close together. You remember how in India the houses are separate, with compounds around them, and seldom more than one storey high. What lots of people too, and all white & nicely dressed, instead of the black & nearly naked."[48] William attempted to comfort his daughter by teaching her to understand her new English surroundings as superior to the India she knew, emphasizing racial difference and putting a positive spin on what he worried might be the unwelcoming architecture of English cities.

William interpreted his own actions in sending his children to England as an act of paternal self-sacrifice, in the process of losing his last connections with Emily and weakening his relationship with Willie and Nellie. By breaking up his family, he tried to ensure that his children would regain the status that he and Emily had lost when his schoolmaster post took him to India. But while family separation allowed the Wonnacott children, if not William himself, to stabilize their class position, it could make for a much more volatile childhood for children from working-class families.

While the Wonnacott children, for the most part, had a grandparental buffer from their father's emotions, young Ann Palmer had a different experience. At the age of nine, young Ann became the recorder and disseminator of her family's strife and her mother's worry, rather than merely an observer. Ann was a member of a relatively privileged set of working-class children, in that she herself attended school and did not have to work, so it was not material deprivation that blurred the borders of her mother's life and her own. Nor did she perceive herself to have been abandoned by her father, as Lucy Cole's children seem to have done. The valentines Ann and Diana sent to India and her own interjections into the family correspondence suggest that James continued to play an important role in the Palmer daughters' childhood.[49] Julie-Marie

---

[47] William Wonnacott to mother, August 20, 1873, IOR MSS Eur. 376.4.
[48] William Wonnacott to Nellie Wonnacott, August 27, 1873, IOR MSS Eur. 376.4.
[49] No date, James Palmer Inspector EIR family letters 1861–63, IOR MSS Eur. F133/113.

Strange and Ginger Frost have demonstrated that even absent working class fathers played central roles in their families' lives and that absence and work could signify love and care rather than neglect.[50] Young Ann's role as a correspondent was shaped by the conjunction of such working-class practices at home and life in an imperial world.

In one of young Ann's earliest letters, her voice and her mother's are almost fully blended:

> Dear father we was glad to hear you was quite well Dear father we should very much like to see you mother ... mother said she will make herself as hapy as she can about you but she cannot be comtable here ... let me know more news about the country and how deer the living is no more from your loving daughter Ann Palmer[51]

Though young Ann was ostensibly the author of the entire letter, starting with a salutation to Father and ending by signing herself as daughter, her mother's voice is clearly dictating the letter. From reports on Ann Palmer's emotional state to inquiries about the cost of living in the country, the text reads as a communication from an anxious wife to a distant husband. Young Ann, in fact, shared no information about herself and only wrote that she hoped to be able to write him a longer letter soon. It was only later, as she became more comfortable writing, that young Ann started to include her own news.

Even without the medium of letters, a working-class child in the mid-nineteenth century would likely have more information about her parents' marital and money troubles than a middle-class child. The Victorian working-class family in Britain was thought to be a poor copy of the middle-class ideal, and children suffered the most from their parents' failure to provide a sheltered and innocent childhood.[52] There was little privacy in the homes of the poor, and their family problems infamously spilled out into the streets, much to the chagrin of middle-class reformers. The vast distance between Hitchin and Kahalgaon would presumably have created a bit more space for keeping family business private, but the same conditions that kept poor families involved in one another's affairs at home prevailed in an imperial context. Working-class communities functioned through reputation and neighborly interest; pawn shops loaned money based on character attested by

---

[50] Strange, *Fatherhood and the British Working Class*, 84; Ginger S. Frost, *Victorian Childhoods* (Westport, CT: Praeger, 2009), 14.

[51] Ann Palmer to James Palmer, undated, MSS Eur. F133/112.

[52] Ross, *Love and Toil*, Chapter 1.

neighbors, children were looked after by any mother available, and women kept an eye on the activities of one another's husbands. Many of these same mechanisms remained in place as members of the working class relocated from the tight-knit communities at home to imperial outposts. Community pressure and gossip had the potential to exert a powerful influence on a wayward father and husband, even if they had to be conveyed by envelope, rather than by a sharp word or sideways glance. It is perhaps because of the porous boundaries between private matters and community knowledge that Ann Palmer used her daughter as a medium to confide in her husband without any evident concern about the emotional repercussions of sharing family secrets.

Lucy Cole and Anne Commack's children were too young to write to their fathers, and so appear in the family letters only through the accounts of their mothers and relatives. Lucy used her daughters to shame George for leaving her, while Anne Commack offered up her infant daughter as a reason for James to support her, if he refused to on her own account. In contrast, the Keen daughters appear in Pollie's correspondence not as well-loved but worrisome burdens, but as children in their own right, with their own quirks and interests. Dorothy and Eva's experience of childhood in the empire was one of relative privilege. Dick's Army service did not accelerate Dorothy and Eva's adult responsibilities, as James Palmer's EIR job did for young Ann. Nor did it lead to a period of economic and emotional instability, as in the case of Lucy and Anne Commack's children. Rather, Indian service extended to the Keen girls a period of childhood indulgence. Time in India preserved the Keen daughters' childhood, in contrast to the disruption seen in the Cole, Commack, Palmer, and Wonnacott family letters. This was in large part the result of real improvements made in British education, children's welfare, sanitation, and living conditions for the Army in India. Dick could not only marry, but bring his wife and children along with him to India with the expectation that they would be fed, clothed, and receive a decent standard of education. Pollie could read, write, and communicate with her mother without having to resort to outside help. The Keens, in India at the end of the century, could expect to survive their time there without too great a risk of dying of disease. Indeed, the only child the Keens lost was sick with the whooping cough that eventually killed her in Malta before the family embarked from England.

The notion of a working-class family living an upwardly mobile life in Army housing in India ran contrary to a variety of elite imperial anxieties about the "demoralizing influence of barrack life," the destructive effects of climate, and the painful practice of separating families and returning children back to England.[53] Two letters from Dorothy demonstrate the difference between the lifestyle the Keens were living and how their military commanders understood the family's situation. Dorothy wrote about receiving gifts from the Major on Christmas day, an act interpreted as one of charity by the officer: "the major sent an order for us children to go to the office at twelve oclock he gave me a workbox and eva a box of pictures puzzle and in my workbox there was four packets of niddle and a pair of sissors but they cannot cut and a lookinglass in the lid."[54] The bigger girls also received two balls to blow up, and the baby got a doll. Pollie described these presents in a letter to her mother as "very sensible," combining cheap childhood fun for the younger children with a hint of Dorothy's growing domestic responsibilities. In other words, appropriate if dull charitable gifts. Writing about her birthday, Dorothy reported to her grandmother that both she and Eva had tea sets, though Eva broke hers.[55]

The Keen children's Indian childhood was enshrined in letters to their grandmother and in artifacts lovingly collected and sent between Mary's home in Greenwich and the Punjab. The surviving Keen children, Dorothy (called Dolly) and Eva, figure prominently in Pollie's letters and were encouraged to write to their grandmother from a very early age. Taking advantage of penny post rates for the military, Pollie sent anything and everything to her mother, including a "letter" from Eva (undated) that was nothing more than the sort of loopy scribbles small children make when they are attempting to imitate handwriting. Pollie added a note: "this is eva's letter to you/she can write man and can and small words but she said I will write 'm's to grandmother."[56] Pollie had an affinity for the act of writing and put value on the physical artifact handwriting left behind – an affinity her mother, who saved these letters, shared. These letters maintained family bonds by tying grandmother and granddaughter together through a material artifact of childhood. Ann and Diana Palmer did something similar when they sent their father valentines, though those two cards are the only evidence of playful mail James received. By contrast, the Keen girls wrote dozens of letters, scrawls, and fragments to their grandmother. Dorothy, who at eight was old enough to have progressed beyond scribbling, wrote more

---

[53] This phrase from the Lawrence Asylum's charter is repeated throughout documents on the dilatory effects of the India climate on European constitutions and morality. *Report of the Lawrence Military Asylum, for the Orphan and Other Children of European Soldiers, Serving of Having Served in India, for the Financial Year Ending 30th April, 1861* (Sanawar: Lawrence Asylum Press, 1859).

[54] Dorothy Keen to Mary Holloway, undated 1893, IOR MSS Eur. F528/12.   [55] Ibid.

[56] Pollie Keen to Mary Holloway, undated, IOR MSS Eur. F528/17.

substantively. Her writing style is not too different from young Ann's missives to her father, but the content speaks to a much securer childhood experience. Dorothy's breathless accounts of dances, picnics, and the social life of the troops described a childhood situated in a secure community and happy family. Dorothy never gave any hint of strife between her parents, and indeed any such letters would never have been sent, as the mail went through her own literate mother.

Conclusion

Regardless of their level of education, correspondence was a communal practice for working-class letter writers. Illiterate correspondents hired professional readers and writers of letters and sought help from friends and family. Those who could read and write for themselves sent letters, printed matter, and material objects from recipient to recipient. Marital strife and financial trouble became matters for wider consumption. Letters served as proof of both emotional and economic care for working-class correspondents. A neglected letter could mean not just emotional distress, but serious financial trouble as well. Correspondents shared their dreams – both sleeping and waking – in efforts to reach emotional worlds across distance. Each person who wrote, read, heard, and passed along these missives became part of a growing communication network that spread intimate information on an imperial scale. This communal form of correspondence did not create a lack of privacy; it reflected an already extant indifference toward the notion.[57] While letter writers did not expect their correspondence to be private, the need to communicate across long distances forced people to reveal aspects of their own personal lives to a wider range of audiences. The increase in correspondence made necessary by imperial separation transformed news that would have been spread by word-of-mouth into information that spanned continents and was preserved, however unknowingly, for posterity.

Letter-writing reshaped working-class correspondents' domestic worlds, drawing in company, state, friends, neighbors, and family alike. Those in financial straits corresponded with companies and state entities that might be able to forward money that was either owed or anticipated. They turned to extended family, who might provide material aid in the form of money, childcare, or housing. The common elements of working-class domestic life – feeding the family, paying the rent, keeping marriages as content as could be expected, and raising children – shifted

---

[57] See Cohen, *Family Secrets*, 7–8.

from a local to an imperial scale. Rather than being based in the street, the neighborhood, and the nearby factory, domestic life expanded to shipping routes, cantonments, and empire-spanning companies. Both Anne Commack and Lucy Cole were well acquainted with the salaries available to other men in their families' circles. Anne Commack used the differences in rate to try to convince her husband into increasing her living stipend, while Lucy Cole used her knowledge to berate George for having left her when good jobs were available closer to home. For adult correspondents, letters always married the practical and the emotional. Conveying essential information about practical matters, from organizing the shipment of butter to arranging for much-needed increases in incomes paid at home, was an act of caretaking aimed at holding families together.

But the act of writing could serve to emphasize differences as well. The changing nature of their domestic worlds was a major theme in the letters of working-class British correspondents in India. Letters conveyed new experiences and helped spread information about Indian life to people far beyond India. For some recipients, like Pollie Keen's mother Mary, these reports of Indian experiences created a shared bond through storytelling. For Ann Commack, a resigned acceptance of her husband's new life maintained her marriage, if not her own happiness. While for Lucy Cole, George's new experiences, mostly imagined, threatened the couple's marriage. Attempts to sustain relationships might further fray them as correspondents realized physical separation had mutated into emotional and experiential distance as well. Those families who best maintained their ties through correspondence learned how to bridge this distance by performing acts of emotional and economic care – whether a tin of British butter sent to India or an advance on the monthly pay arranged in England.

This chapter has argued that the need to maintain affective and economic relationships through correspondence shifted the boundaries of British working-class domestic life from a local to an imperial scale. The following considers what new forms domestic life took for working-class British in India. The men and women of the British Army in India created domestic lives within military spaces and institutions designed to avert just such domesticity in cantonments and hill stations across the Subcontinent. Domesticity specific to the imperial working class in India grew on the ground out of practices brought from British working-class communities and shaped in response to the exigencies of military life. These domestic worlds developed by single men and married families in the cantonments and hill stations across the Subcontinent challenged elite military, governmental, and reforming ideas of what working-class sexuality and sociality ought to look like.

3   Military Domesticity
Creating Working-Class Worlds in British India

William Wilkie, a private in the 79th Cameron Highlanders, joined the Army just in time to serve in the Crimean War and fight against the Indian Rebellion. By the time his regiment made its way to the cantonment at Rawalpindi, in the early 1860s, Wilkie had tired of fighting and was happy to find himself in an orderly, peacetime station. In his memoir of his time in the Army, Wilkie described Rawalpindi as "a beautiful station. The duty was pretty light and so was the drills, and that made us all the more comfortable. Such is life here the married women that was on the strength of the Regiment joined their respective husbands they got the nickname (the locust tribe)."[1] For Wilkie and his regiment, Rawalpindi was a place of respite and one in which domestic order could be reestablished. He wrote affectionately of the "locust tribe" of women, the regiment's teasing pet name for the wives who managed to organize "extra dainties" for the soldiers – extravagances like eggs, butter, and extra vegetables.[2]

Wilkie and the locust tribe can help us understand Indian cantonments as enlisted men, camp followers, and married families did. These permanent military encampments, intended by their British builders to hold within them the fighting power of the British Empire and imprint British authority on the Indian landscape and population were, to the British working-class men and women who populated them, both domestic and military in nature. To the military commanders, imperial officials, and social reformers who made the construction, regulation, and reform of cantonments their business throughout the nineteenth century, Britain's Indian cantonments were both a cause of and a potential solution to bad behavior. Anxieties about the type of domestic worlds British military non-elites created within them were evident in funding appeals from

---

[1] William Wilkie's Reminiscences during his sojourn in the Crimea and during the Indian Mutiny was written from memory while night watchman in the Angus Jute Works, Dundee, 1890–91, British Library, IOR MSS Eur. B221, 85.
[2] Ibid.

charity schools, reports aimed at improving conditions for soldiers, and exposés on military-regulated prostitution.[3] This interplay between domestic and military, reform and degeneration, shaped British military life in the Indian cantonments.

Most Britons of working-class origin made their way to India in the lower ranks of the British Army. They came as enlisted men, attempting to create and maintain emotional connections over the course of lengthy terms of service. And they came as families, traveling together, but separated from larger social networks and familiar surroundings. One-third of all troops enlisted in the British Army in the late Victorian period were stationed in India at some point during their military careers.[4] The academic literature on the nineteenth-century military and working-class experience has largely examined working-class army life to determine how it inspired, or failed to inspire, class consciousness. Working-class histories have frequently ignored military service, implicitly treating it as one of the moves that could declass, or at least depoliticize, a man. Women's experiences of military life have been all but ignored.[5] But historians who have looked at class and military service have found that the British Army, at home or in the empire, was hardly a sure force for maintaining the political status quo. Peter Stanley and Nick Mansfield have explored the nascent working-class consciousness that developed among the armies of the East India Company. The "white mutiny" uprising of EIC troops, who objected to being forced to join the British Army and not properly compensated for their labor, destabilized the British military forces in India mere months after the Indian Rebellion. And Carolyn Steedman has shown how military service could lead to working-class radicalization rather than conformity.[6]

This chapter focuses not on the implications of military life for class consciousness, but rather on the ways in which soldiers and their families

---

[3] See Levine, *Prostitution, Race, and Politics;* Wald, *Vice in the Barracks;* Ronald Hyam, *Empire and Sexuality* (Manchester: Manchester University Press, 1991).

[4] Heathcote, *The Military in British India*, 127.

[5] Notable exceptions include Myna Trustram, *Women of the Regiment: Marriage and the Victorian Army* (1984; reis., Cambridge: Cambridge University Press, 2008), and Lara Kriegel, *The Crimean War and Its Afterlife* (Cambridge: Cambridge University Press, 2022). For military wives in the South African context, see Eliza Riedi, "Assisting Mrs. Tommy Atkins: Gender, Class, Philanthropy, and the Domestic Impact of the South African War, 1899–1902," *Historical Journal* 60, no. 3 (2017): 745–69.

[6] Mansfield, *Soldiers as Workers*, 2016; Steedman, *The Radical Soldier's Tale John Pearman 1819–1908*, 1988; Peter Stanley, *White Mutiny: British Military Culture in India* (New York: New York University Press, 1998).

built homes and communities within India, at odds with the intentions of military command. As we shall see, soldiers worked to fashion interior lives and personal connections within military hierarchies, developing a practice of military domesticity. These seemingly apolitical ways of living could pose a problem for the imperial army. They threatened to undermine regulations that aimed to make soldiers obedient and the military in India an unimpeachable representation of British military and moral force.

This chapter takes Rawalpindi cantonment and its associated hill station, Murree, as a case study and Wilkie's memoir as a counternarrative to that of the dominant discourse around cantonments, enlisted men, and married families in the ranks. This approach allows us to look at Rawalpindi from multiple angles. From above, Rawalpindi appears as a planned military space superimposed onto multiple pre-existing communities, Indian and British alike. From below, seen through the experiences of Wilkie and other working-class residents like him, Rawalpindi appears as a temporary home, one that facilitated the building and sustaining of relationships. More difficult to root out are the experiences of South Asians who lived in and around the cantonment. Wilkie mentions them seldom in his account, and, as we have seen, they make infrequent appearances in correspondence. This erasure on the part of working-class correspondents and memoirists was integral to domesticating military spaces, making them not only homely but British (or in Wilkie's case specifically Scottish), and at least discursively white.

Through these opposing angles of view, we can see how British nonelites formed their own social worlds in response to and in spite of official attempts to control their private lives. Soldiers and their families domesticated military spaces over and over, remaking homely customs and relationships each time a new regiment cycled through. Camp, cantonment, bazaar, and hill station became domestic as well as military and commercial spaces, ones in which connections to home played a paramount role. The same military domesticity that troubled British officialdom for its potential to create a settler population worked to prop up British rule by creating networks of familiarity and care among enlisted men, making the experience of family separation and arrested adulthood easier to manage. The following pages explore how elite anxieties surrounding domesticity, sexuality, and marriage intersected with working-class realities in military spaces. I do so first, by establishing the lay of the land in the cantonment of Rawalpindi and the nearby hill station of Murree. I then turn to a close examination of William Wilkie's experiences to question how working-class Britons' understanding and experiences of domesticity changed in India.

Soldiering and the Limits to Private Life

In the years immediately following the Indian Rebellion, men enlisting with the British Army gave over a large portion of their lives to that service. Men enlisted for ten years and could then either leave or renew their enlistment for another eleven. Only men with twenty-one years of service were eligible to receive a pension, meaning that many men who enlisted were left with nothing at the end of their service.[7] Even men who had served this full twenty-one-year term lost their pension eligibility if they did not sign on to the reserve. In effect, the term of service was almost lifelong.[8] Enlisted men were required to sign their youths over to the British Army; as a result, all classes of British society looked down upon enlistment in the ranks of the Army as a last resort employment of the unemployable.

To add to the difficulties surrounding these long terms of service, most British enlisted men were forbidden from marrying while in the Army. Enlisted men could not officially marry without the permission of their commanding officer. If they did so, they could not be supported on "the strength of the regiment," which meant their wives and children would not be acknowledged, housed, and financially supported by the Army.[9] Life was precarious even for officially recognized military families. They were not eligible for pensions and depended instead on the kindness of the regiment, which would take up collections for the temporary support of the families of fallen comrades.

Reforms in the 1870s and 1880s to length of service requirements and support offered to families improved matters marginally, but more in theory than in practice. In 1870, the required length of service was drastically reduced to a mere six years, with an additional six years optional.[10] In practice, however, troops in India needed to be transported and redistributed around the empire and could wait long and potentially deadly years to return to Britain. A further set of reforms in the early 1880s increased the number of enlisted men who could marry "on the strength" from a maximum of 7 percent to a maximum of 12 percent.[11] The higher one's rank, the easier it was to marry on the strength; half of all men who had achieved the rank of sergeant could

---

[7] French, *Military Identities*, 11.   [8] Ibid., 13–14.
[9] Soldier's documents of Pte William Randall, 1st Battalion Wiltshire Regiment, 1889–1907, include pay book and discharge certificate, National Army Museum 9703–34.
[10] Ibid.   [11] French, *Military Identities*, 129.

rely on regimental support for their families.[12] But with these reforms, most enlisted men could not and did not marry.

The Victorian Army was not foolish enough to think that these men would remain celibate for their entire term of service. The British Parliament and the Government of India spent a great deal of effort trying to control and direct soldiers' lives, movements, and sexual practices, in order to preserve British prestige. As Philippa Levine has argued, providing for soldiers' sexual needs through state-regulated prostitution was a priority, thought essential to avoiding the homosexual relationships, venereal diseases, and sexual violence that would damage Britain's moral reputation.[13] These concerns shaped how British soldiers could live and where they could move. By constructing sexual violence and moral disorder as a lower-class threat, military leadership both rendered upper-class misconduct invisible and made an argument for disciplining enlisted men and native women. The association between enlisted men and immorality further confused their racial status – allying them with the native male population, which had already been solidified in the British imagination as a threat to British femininity in the Rebellion.[14] It was not until the First World War that the lower ranks of the Army shrugged off their reputation for immorality – when that reputation was recoded, among the British at least, as boyish exuberance.

Imperial policy required a large body of men to maintain British rule, but for the most part, these men had little to occupy them and few opportunities to fight. Between the Indian Rebellion and the First World War, the British Army led twenty-nine expeditions into Afghan areas on the northwest frontier and engaged in one large-scale war in the late 1870s, the Anglo-Afghan War. These forays west did not require many British soldiers – the Army overwhelmingly sent Indian troops to engage with the western tribes. As a result, soldiers spent much of their time looking for ways to fill the hours. As their fighting capacity fell away, sexual danger became a way of identifying the soldier as both masculine and classed. This image of the insatiable private obscures a reality that is

---

[12] Ibid. and *Army and Militia Pamphlets showing the Conditions of Service in the Army and Militia Respectively* (London: Eyre and Spottiswoode, 1898).

[13] Levine, *Prostitution, Race, and Politics*.

[14] Patrick Brantlinger, *Rule of Darkness: British Literature and Imperialism, 1830–1914* (Ithaca, NY: Cornell University Press, 1988); Christopher Herbert, *War of No Pity: The Indian Mutiny and Victorian Trauma* (Princeton, NJ: Princeton University Press, 2008).

far more complex. The concept of the unattached enlisted man was powerful in official discourse because he confirmed British ideas about the nation's role in India as rulers, not settlers. British soldiers were constructed as individuals always looking toward a future return home, rather than part of a growing local community. If the ruling members of the Raj did acknowledge such a community, such an acknowledgment would undermine claims that the British role in India was always temporary, never permanent.

Thus, when enlisted men and NCOs tried to enter into marriages, rather than informal or paid sexual arrangements, they suffered from official opprobrium. Marriage among the troops, whether to British or Indian women, was discouraged by policies that limited the number of wives who would be financially supported "on the strength of the regiment." Marrying and setting up a household, even if done respectably with the consent of a man's commanding officer, cost the Army money. If men contracted marriages and sexual relationships in a disreputable manner, without official approval, across racial lines, their partnerships could undermine British military authority. With or without official approval, setting up a household with a woman created conditions in which India became attractive as a site of family life and made the Subcontinent look like a plausible colony of settlement. Regardless, enlisted men brought along wives from Britain who were not supported on the strength of the regiment or married – to British or Indian women – in opposition to military regulations.

Elite concerns about the unsuitability of enlisted men for domestic life – and the unsuitability of the domestic life they might create – structured the geography of military camps and hill stations, as well as the possibilities for mobility between them. Men, women, and families developed and maintained essential social connections to one another and to family and friends in Britain in response to official structures created to discourage domesticity. But military domesticity did not offer a respectable alternative to non-elite immorality and sexual danger. Instead, it threatened to undermine the divisions between rule and settlement, ruler and native, respectable and unrespectable, on which British control was based. And it held the threat of future demands on the imperial coffers, from widows, orphans, and veterans who preferred to remain in India. Men who did marry, particularly those among the higher ranking NCOs, could solidify their respectability, but might also produce children and remain in India. Staying on after a term of service expired meant throwing one's lot in with the "domiciled Europeans" and effectively renouncing Britishness. Marriage could produce respectability, but only if done in the right way – which is to say as close to the middle-class ideal as possible.

Making Military Space: Rawalpindi

Over the course of the nineteenth century, the cantonment of Rawalpindi grew into the largest permanent military camp in India. Today, Rawalpindi is the home of the Pakistan Army, which has built its head-quarters on the bones of the British site. In its most basic form, the cantonment was an encampment for the British Army that functioned as a military town. These camps were usually built near already existing Indian towns, though, as was the case with Rawalpindi, the scale of the Army installation sometimes outgrew the original settlement, which swelled with native workers and merchants supplying the camp with goods and labor.[15] The cantonment was at the center of an intercon-nected constellation of British spaces, which included the town as well as the nearby hill station of Murree. Murree was developed first into a sanitarium and retreat for troops, and later into a summer hill station, housing an invalid hospital, cottages for civil and military families, hotels, a brewery, and a Lawrence Memorial Asylum for the education of poor and orphaned European children.[16]

Rawalpindi cantonment and town symbolized the strength of British military power to a subject population and to the military working class who occupied it. The British Army began to build up a military canton-ment alongside the existing town of Rawalpindi in 1840s and 1850s in response to the Anglo-Sikh Wars and the threat of future frontier skir-mishes. Rawalpindi's size allows us to see what happened when ideas about social hierarchies and racial boundaries came into contact with the lived experience of the inhabitants of the cantonment. For military people, cantonments made the social stratifications of Indian society visible, revealing both the liberties and limitations associated with Indian service.

Rawalpindi cantonment was one of the last major military outposts the British possessed in the west, leaving only the buffer of the questionably loyal North West Frontier Princely States between the Punjab and

---

[15] Touring Pakistan in the 1980s, the writer Geoffrey Moorhouse noted what he called the "imperial encrustations" of the cantonments starting to bleed into the older native towns, making the divisions between each indistinguishable. Geoffrey Moorhouse, *To the Frontier* (London: Hodder and Stoughton Ltd., 1984).

[16] The Murree Brewery is one of the few still in existence in Pakistan today.

Afghanistan. As a gateway to the frontier, the cantonment at Rawalpindi created the appearance of imperial permanence amid the instability and ever-shifting population of a borderland. But the cantonment itself was unstable. Regiments cycled through the encampment; a year or two of service in the Punjab was a fairly common part of a posting in India.[17] Because military leadership considered local knowledge of little benefit to their enlisted men, there was no incentive to maintain troops in any given location. While the cantonment was far enough away from any border disputes that there was little fear of immediate danger to the residents, there was always the potential of the troops being called to engage in or support frontier skirmishes. Men stationed at Rawalpindi after 1858 had a higher likelihood of seeing some sort of combat during their time in the district than those at the capital of Calcutta or the more stable outlying areas.[18] Even John Brand, who spent the majority of his time in India sick in bed, had his "swords sharpened" and his uniform camouflaged in anticipation of being deployed to fight in the Khyber Pass.[19] Brand understood, better than most, Rawalpindi as a staging place for military incursions into the northwest. From his convalescent bed, he saw the men of his regiment sent out to fight and the women shuffled from cantonment to hill station to keep them safe from feared enemy incursions.

Rawalpindi district's population swelled in size and shifted in composition in response to frontier conflicts, British acquisition of territory, and epidemics and famines. The famine of 1876–1878 that killed millions in the south and was exacerbated by British inaction and hoarding also took a toll on some parts of the north and sent refugees out of Kashmir toward Rawalpindi. The Second Anglo-Afghan War (1878–1880) displaced people from Afghanistan. The town and cantonment of Rawalpindi held 73,795 people by 1885 and had grown rapidly, increasing its population by nearly 20,000 since the beginning of the decade.[20] Europeans made

---

[17] Robertson, FA. *Final Report of the Revised Settlement of the Rawalpindi District in the Punjab* (Lahore: The "Civil and Military Gazette" Press, 1893), 172. The 1893 Settlement Report noted that there were large numbers of Indian and British forces garrisoned at the cantonment: "there is always a large garrison at Rawalpindi during the winter months comprising usually one battery of Horse Artillery, one regiment of British and one regiment of Bengal Cavalry several batteries of field or Mountain Artillery with a Garrison Battery in the fort; two or three regiments of British Infantry, and two regiments of Bengal Infantry."

[18] Roy Kaushik, *The Army in British India: From Colonial Warfare to Total War 1857–1947* (London: Bloomsbury Academic, 2013), 44–45.

[19] John Brand to Peter Gardiner, October 30, 1878, Papers of John Brand, NLS Acc. 6386.

[20] Digital South Asia University of Chicago Spreadsheet No. 23. As a point of comparison, Halifax, another peripheral British colonial outpost, had a roughly similar population size in 1881.

up a small proportion of that population, though they represented far greater numbers in urban than rural areas.[21] In 1881, 3,661 people claiming whole or part British ancestry lived in the district, 837 of whom had been born in India.[22] These numbers increased as a result of migration from other parts of India, eastern Europeans trickling over the borders from the west, British in the military, and Eurasians on the railways.

The vast majority of these migrants would have lived in and around cantonments, towns, and railway communities, making these urban sites ripe for British regulation of a potentially disruptive population. In addition to the British troops in the cantonment and the civil servants staffing the town of Rawalpindi, native workers flooded into the district and its major cities as the North-Western Railway expanded west in the 1860s and 1870s. By the 1890s, railway workers came from many of the tribal and ethnic groups spread across the Punjab, Afghanistan, and northern India.[23] They joined Eurasian and European workers who supervised the construction of the railways. As was the case with the Army, divisions of race and class segregated the railway works around Rawalpindi, with Europeans and Eurasians playing the most substantial role in management and native workers used as hard labor. South Asian men and women flooded into Murree from across the Punjab to obtain temporary employment in the summer months.[24] Even the practice of prostitution in Rawalpindi was more international than in many other stations. In their surveys of Britain's Indian cantonments, investigators researching the persistence of state-sponsored prostitution with the Ladies National Association found that there were "women of many nationalities" residing in the brothels of Rawalpindi's Suddar Bazaar.[25] Some of the women who found employment in the bazaar were likely migrants from Kashmir and Afghanistan, fleeing war and famine.[26] By 1914, there were records of Austrian and American women in the bazaar as well.[27] Rawalpindi town, then, replicated all the troubling hybridity

---

[21] People of British ancestry made up less than 0.4 percent of the total district population, but likely represented nearly 5 percent of the population of the urban areas.

[22] Robertson, *Settlement Report*, 39.

[23] The settlement report lists among incoming migrants to Rawalpindi Kashmiris, Hazaras, Pathans, western Punjab Muhammadans, Jats from the Rechna Doab, and Hindustanis from Oudh and the North-West Provinces. Robertson, 39.

[24] Robertson, *Settlement Report*, 1893, 181.

[25] British Committee of the Continental and General Federation for the Abolition of State Regulation of Vice, Women's Library, 3BGF/C/4/4 Index to Indian File p 209–467.

[26] Notes from Rawul Pindee, *Times of India*, September 10, 1878, 2.

[27] Minutes of Special Sub-Committee Appointed July 17, 1914, to arrange a Private Conference on India & the Regulation of Vice in Cantonments, Women's Library

that made the metropole such a problematic space in Victorian thought. The same moral contagion infected the working-class spaces of the adjoining cantonment by proximity.

The most distressing manifestation of military domesticity for British officialdom could be seen in the streets of the cantonment. The reports of anti-Contagious Diseases Act investigators offer insight into the conditions for soldiers and their families in British and India. Kate Bushnell and Elizabeth Andrew, investigators with the Ladies National Association – part of an organization dedicated to fighting against government-regulated prostitution – explored the cantonment and bazars of Rawalpindi in the 1890s. They were appalled to find soldiers' families living in ramshackle buildings in the bazaar that also housed prostitutes.[28] Men whose wives and children were not supported by the strength of the regiment, either because allotted marriage slots had already been filled or because they had married Eurasian or Indian women, housed their families where they could. Both military leadership and moral reformers viewed these families as inconvenient adjuncts to a disordered military lower class. The men who imported their wives from Britain or married in India were attempting to create a home life while serving out up to twelve years of their lives in India. Though these families were well aware of the opprobrium attached to living near houses of prostitution, their options were otherwise limited, and they valued family continuity over adherence to elite moral norms.

The enlisted soldier was assumed to be unmarried and sexually frustrated, to assuage his frustrations through alcohol and prostitution, and, as a result, to make what was called barrack life untenable for the few families who were living on the strength of the regiment. By a circular logic, these Army families, who should have been a bulwark against martial immorality, had failed to create a familial atmosphere in the barracks sufficient to domesticate the vast body of unmarried troops and were therefore themselves morally unfit. Charity schools (discussed in greater detail in Chapter 4) used variations on this argument to justify family separation and their own existence. Thus military policy forced many to live outside the Victorian ideal of marriage and tautologically

3AMS/A/03/04. Informants seemed to think that European prostitutes were not regulated by the government, but traded in the less-regulated Suddar Bazaar, where they also took on Indian clients. There is little more information on the European and American women, but it is likely that data were collected on them in response to the white slavery moral panic.

[28] Katharine Bushnell and Elizabeth Andrew, Summary of Evidence Records of the Association for Moral and Social Hygiene. Women's Library. London Metropolitan University, 3BGF.

established their lack of respectability on the basis of their unmarried state.

The figure (and reality) of the unrestrained working-class British soldier proved rhetorically potent to elite British officials and elite Indians alike. Both British and vernacular press printed accounts of the misbehavior of British soldiers, ranging from skipping out on a rail fare to far more serious violations like assault and rape. These newspapers, reporting on assaults directed at native men and women, took up British officialdom's anxieties about the uncontrolled nature of the British working-class population to argue for self-rule.[29] This focus on potential and committed crime by enlisted British soldiers, and attempts to regulate these actions, had real consequences for working-class Britons in India, both in and outside the military.

We can see in an 1874 report from the *Times of India*'s Rawalpindi correspondent how concerns about crime and misbehavior bleed across the borders of cantonment, town, and district.[30] The brief column is full of transgressions, from a European officer under threat of a court martial for borrowing money from a native officer and refusing to pay it back to a violent robbery. A group of bandits broke into a house near the town dispensary and within sight of the police *chowkey*, stole the jewels from the neck of a woman identified as a prostitute, slew the man sleeping outside her house, and remained at large.[31] A small group of European soldiers had been arrested for assaulting the residents of a nearby village, handed over to the civil courts, and received the lenient sentence of a small fine rather than a court martial. And an out-of-work European had been making the most of the summer crowds in the neighboring hill station of Murree by selling liquor to European soldiers stationed there. He was arrested and brought down to the jail in Rawalpindi, where he served a fifteen-day sentence, to be followed by a much more serious punishment – he would be deported to England under the Vagrancy Act.

Rawalpindi seemed to be in the grip of everything British India feared. Dacoity and murder made their way from the countryside and into the confines of the town, impinging on what should have been a

---

[29] Jeremy Neill, "'This Is a Most Disgusting Case': Imperial Policy, Class and Gender in the 'Rangoon Outrage' of 1899," *Journal of Colonialism and Colonial History* 12, no. 1 (2011), https://doi.org/10.1353/cch.2011.0003.

Selections from the Vernacular Newspapers Published in the Punjab Received up to August 29, 1896, Punjab Native Newspaper Reports, 1896. Nehru Memorial Library, Acc. No. 94.

[30] "From Our Own Correspondent Rawul Pindee," *The Times of India*, August 18, 1874.
[31] Ibid.

well-regulated British space. The Civil Dispensary, adjacent to the site of the robbery and murder, was located in the heart of the town, with the Civil Hospital close by.[32] Police chowkeys, staffed by night watchmen, poorly paid though they may have been, dotted the city and cantonment. These sites of European power failed in their function if murder and robbery could take place right alongside them. That one of the victims was a prostitute, and the men in the house likely involved in the sex trade in some way, added an additional layer of unseemliness to the incident. A European officer borrowing money from a native officer – and refusing to pay it back – transgressed codes of gentlemanliness and racial suprem- acy, though the act itself was far from unusual. Men at all levels of service complained about their pay and how difficult it was to stretch a military salary to cover the higher cost of living in India.[33] If this officer's antics had spread around the cantonment enough to merit inclusion in major newspapers, it would have turned local gossip into a matter of public record. The European selling alcohol to troops activated all the fears about the bad behavior among non-elite British men. There is a good chance that the European, who was described only as "unemployed," had himself been a soldier. The men buying liquor from him were trading outside the regulated sales of alcohol that the military used to ensure a measure of control over the behavior of their men. And the man's likely deportation under the Vagrancy Act was further evidence that the Government of India had no interest in tolerating a disruptive population of lower-class British who could no longer uphold imperial power by performing imperial respectability.

Articles like these served to depict Rawalpindi (and other civil-military urban areas like it) as a site of transgressions against British power. This reflected everyday realities – neither police *chowkeys*, alcohol laws, nor the ideals of elite Victorian masculinity could be relied upon to smoothly govern a diverse population with often competing interests. But it also played upon the anxieties felt more acutely by those in power in the Raj: Army officers who could not control their own men or their own finances; civil servants who worried about the increasing and uncount- able population of poor Europeans making money where they could with little concern for their reputation or the reputation of the empire that had left them in an impecunious state; and Europeans of all classes who feared the sometimes real, but more often illusory figure of the native

---

[32] *Gazetteer of the Rawalpindi District* (Lahore: Civil and Military Gazette Press, 1895), 219.
[33] Erika Rappaport discusses the emotional toll taken by unanticipated expenses on middle- and upper-class military families in "'The Bombay Debt'": 223–60.

dacoit whose reputed innate criminality had been created and codified by the British and remained uncontrolled.[34]

As we have seen, both popular and official thought about Rawalpindi figured the town was an urban space, shifting and migratory, and apt to replicate in India the evils of Victorian city life. The cantonment would ideally quell both the disorderly aspects of town life and the dangers of an uncontrolled working-class British population. Orderliness could be created by confining races and classes to their own separate areas. The British relied on natural barriers to maintain their racial divisions.[35] The river Leh ran through the town, separating the European community from the larger Indian town.[36] Spatial signifiers, like the attractive pine trees reminiscent of a European landscape that surrounded the elite Civil Lines at Rawalpindi, kept up class distinctions.[37] These signs of Europeanness divided the respectable and white from the disreputable and Indian, and they created an even starker contrast in the hill station of Murree.

Class, Britishness, and Mobility: Murree

The hill station of Murree was situated some forty miles northeast of Rawalpindi. While Rawalpindi represented British military force, Murree was intended to provide an idealized version of European life, free of the complications of imperial rule. Murree had started life as a cantonment, placed far enough up the hills to provide soldiers with respite from the summer heat. A sanitarium and hospital attracted troops recovering from a range of ailments. This military lineage stuck to Murree, which lost many of its civilian visitors when the British government of the Punjab shifted its summer quarters to Simla.[38] A reporter traveling into

---

[34] Heather Streets-Salter, *Martial Races: The Military, Race, and Masculinity in British Imperial Culture, 1857–1914* (Manchester: Manchester University Press, 2004), Aidan Forth, *Barbed-Wire Imperialism: Britain's Empire of Camps, 1876–1903* (Berkeley: University of California Press, 2017).

[35] William Glover, *Making Lahore Modern: Constructing and Imagining a Colonial City* (Minneapolis: University of Minnesota Press, 2007), 34–5.

[36] "Colonel Timler's Diary in India," *The Times of India*, November 20, 1888. The Times excerpted The Pioneer's original translation.

[37] Robertson observed that the Civil Lines, an area of the cantonment reserved for the highest-ranking officers, "are the best wooded portions and here many specimens of the pinus longifolie [a variety of pine tree] are to be seen which give an almost European aspect to this large North Indian Station. Robertson," Final Report, 175–6.

[38] The Government of India moved summer residences in 1876, leading to what was described as a dull summer season for elites at Murree. "The Viceroy's Tour From Murree to Domal," *The Times of India*, November 13, 1891, ProQuest Historical Newspapers, British Library, Kennedy, *Magic Mountains*, 113.

Kashmir at the turn of the century described the population as "almost exclusively military, which means geniality, good-fellowship."[39] Flora Annie Steel and Grace Gardner recommended Murree for its convenience and well-stocked shops and called it "with the exception of Ooty ... perhaps the most English place in India ... good society; you can be as gay or as quiet as you like."[40]

While these depictions of Murree aligned with popular descriptions of the officer class as simple, hearty, friendly, and English, they paid little mind to the working-class population of soldiers and families who also traveled to the hills. In addition to these itinerant populations, hill stations like Murree often housed charity schools for the children of poor British and mixed-race families – Murree had its own branch of the Lawrence Asylum. These children, soldiers, and families complicated the vision of the hill station as a pleasantly white, middle-class, and English environment free from the military trappings of cantonment life. The military and class hierarchies established in Rawalpindi bled over into the summer retreats of the hills and were likewise made manifest in the landscape.

NCOs and their families spent summers, when they could, at Cliffden, located some four miles below Murree. Those four miles brought the residents that much closer to the heat of the plains. Cliffden reminded upwardly mobile NCOs that they could not achieve either the social or physical heights of their betters. Housing for enlisted men was separate from the general population of Murree or Cliffden, situated on neighboring plateaus. The barracks and small huts for regiments were designed in plain Army style, without the decorative flourishes that distinguished elite residences. "There are some 1,500 troops scattered amongst the various gulleys," the *Times of India* reported in a glowing 1875 account of the station. "The benefit derived by the troops from the bracing climate is simply incalculable, and saves the State a mint of money in reducing the number requiring to be invalided."[41] NCOs, enlisted men, and their families attended their own social functions, separate from the higher ranks. The Murree Brewery spent a small fortune on two nights of balls to promote its product – one for the officers and one for NCOs.[42] Working-class military men and families could

[39] "Along the Kashmir Road A Northern Sanitarium," *The Times of India*, September 25, 1902, 4.
[40] Flora Annie Steel and Grace Gardner, *The Complete Indian Housekeeper & Cook: Giving the Duties of Mistress and Servants the General Management of the House and Practical Recipes for Cooking in All Its Branches*, 7th ed. (London: William Heinemann, 1909), 44.
[41] Our Own Correspondent, "A Visit to Murree," *The Times of India*, October 30, 1875, 2.
[42] Ibid., Rs. 20,000, according to the *The Times of India*.

enjoy the European landscape and holiday atmosphere, but they had to accept British class divisions along with it.

Murree simulated European landscapes – visitors praised flourishing European gardens, pine forests, and Alpine architecture. They also noted the winding road that ran up the hill to Murree, in contrast to the precise grid lines that marked off the soldiers', officers', and South Asians' quarters in the cantonment. As Dane Kennedy has argued, hill stations adopted at once an organic and European look, with their builders working with the lay of the land and interpreting Himalayan landscapes through a European architectural language.[43] Pollie Keen, summering in Murree, described the hills from her vantage point in the NCO's married housing. "Dear Mother it is wonderful country [the hills] are covered with trees, fir, silver birch and holly and ivy, the first I have seen in India and lots of wild fruit trees, pears and plums."[44] Europeanization of the Indian landscape was an elite project, but working-class men and women likewise spent summers embedded in these spaces. Some like Pollie, who had grown up near the countryside, appreciated reminders of home. Others, especially those from cities, might have encountered these Anglicized rural idylls for the first time in India. The Alpine embellishments created a hyperreal environment, relocating an imagined Europe to Indian space.

Signs of Britain were everywhere in Murree and can be seen in the descriptive publications designed to lure travelers to the remote location. Houses in Murree harkened back to Britain, with names like Dulwich, Norwood, Willow Bank, and farther afield with the literary Uncle Tom's Cabin.[45] By the end of the century, elite Indians began to purchase these properties as well. They maintained the naming tradition – Mount Pleasant was jointly owned by Mr. Mamoojee and Mr. Dhunjibhoy. The presence of elite Indians, however begrudgingly accepted by British inhabitants, where enlisted men and NCOs could not go, reinforced the complexity of India's race/class system. E. B. Peacock's 1883 travelers' guide to Murree was eager to reassure its readers they would easily find European food and services in the station. A pensioner named Mr. Dean baked high-quality brown and white bread, and the orphaned girls of the Lawrence Asylum sold cakes and biscuits.

[43] Kennedy, *Magic Mountains*, 2–3 and Queeny Pradhan, *Empire in the Hills: Simla, Darjeeling, Ootacamund, and Mount Abu, 1820–1920* (Oxford: Oxford University Press, 2017).
[44] Pollie Keen to Mary Holloway, May 1, 1892, British Library IOR MSS Eur. F528/11.
[45] E. B. Peacock, *A Guide to Murree and Its Neighbourhood* (Lahore: W. Ball, Printer, 1883), appendix.

Europeans and Parsees, noted for their assimilation of British customs, ran many of the shops and hotels.[46] The orderly streets and shops described by Peacock contrast sharply with the chaotic atmosphere correspondents ascribed to the bazaar attached to cantonments in the plains. European customers preferred to patronize European merchants in the hills in hopes of maintaining the illusion of home, and European shops hired a largely European population to serve them.

These British merchants added yet another layer of complexity to the class stratifications of British India. They were potent representatives of home and Englishness, responsible for supplying the material products of Britain in empire. Among the chemists, photographers, tailors, milliners, watchmakers, opticians, stationery sellers, and fishing outfitters were various strata of the British commercial classes. Some of these establishments were profitable enough to support families and homes in both Britain and India. Lawrence Christie, a wine merchant who had shops in both Rawalpindi and Murree, made enough to keep a house in Edinburgh as well as Rawalpindi and to support his institutionalized brother.[47] The commercial population in Murree and Rawalpindi was divided between those who styled themselves merchants, traded between Britain and India, and maintained homes in Britain, and those shopkeepers whose only residence was in India. In keeping with the whitewashing of the Eurasian population in publications aimed at travelers, these shopkeepers were described as European, with no hint of Indian antecedents. The orphaned girls of the Lawrence Asylum were similarly described as soldiers' and potentially civilians' children – never Eurasians.

A Disgraceful Scandal

The effects of these divisions between merchants, soldiers, and officers among Indian, European, and Eurasian populations can be seen at work in a rape case that shocked Murree in the summer of 1876. The Rawalpindi correspondent for the *Times of India* reported on the assault:

When we consider that those who mostly resort to the hills are European ladies and gentlemen of fair education, and, in the majority of cases, undoubtedly good breeding, it is perplexing to find that the moral barometer ranges so tremendously low ... Murree is an Indian hill station, and as such not without its complement of

---

[46] Ibid., 6.

[47] Lawrence Christie Will, ScotlandsPeople NAS. Christie left £500 to support his brother's care, with the remainder of his estate going to his wife. These amounts suggest Christie was quite affluent and would have been more likely to mix socially with the upper levels of the Civil Service and military.

scandals; the first this season has been a disgraceful one. A young officer of H.M. 17th regiment, celebrated for his sportsmanship, was recently charged with rape, said to have been committed by him on a European lady assistant serving in a millinery establishment.[48]

Rape became a gauge of the character of British India. It was not the assault itself that qualified this incident as a scandal, but the status of the person who committed it and the race of the victim. Violating claims to "fair education" and "good breeding," the officer's actions threw elite British moral (and thus racial and class) superiority into doubt. That the officer in question was once celebrated as a "sportsman" further destabilized British notions of elite physical prowess in the service of upright morality. The way in which this incident was reported also suggested a dual vision of the social life of the British hill station. Ladies and gentlemen "resort to the hills," while the shop assistant who was attacked lived in them. In a dynamic common to tourist towns, it was the ability to move back and forth between the work of military and civil life on the plains and the respite of the hills that created the distinction in status.

The unnamed European lady shop assistant was part of the commercial class of Murree. She may have been a domiciled European, possibly a former student of the nearby Lawrence Asylum. Less likely, she had traveled out to India in search of employment or with a husband and stayed on to work in the shop after his death. Little of the woman's life apart from her Europeanness survives in the archives – and that fact alone was likely responsible for the assault being prosecuted or reported on at all. The case did not make its way from the *Times of India* into any of the British papers, though it was common for snippets of Indian news to end up in the metropolitan press. English-language papers did not report on rape cases when the woman was native unless they became a *cause célèbre*. This was what happened in the case of the 1899 "Rangoon outrage," in which a Burmese woman was assaulted by a number of soldiers of the West Kent Regiment.[49] The case made its way into the English-language newspapers in India and into the British press as well. That case followed a pattern that aligned better with elite notions of working-class disrespectability – involving as it did a native Burmese woman and British enlisted men. The subject positions of the people involved likely help to explain both why the British government attempted to cover up the case and why it became so notorious in the press when news of the incident became public.

---

[48] "Notes from Rawul Pindee," *Times of India*, June 10, 1876, 2.
[49] Neill, "'This Is a Most Disgusting Case'."

The Murree rape case further blurred the boundaries of the supposedly open, unregulated retreat of the hill station and the necessarily ordered cantonment. Officers removed to the hills as a matter of course; they could be trusted in the wider world. NCOs went almost exclusively with families in tow.[50] Enlisted men were confined to hill barracks that provided only climatic respite from the oppressive atmosphere of the plains. The relative degrees of freedom and quality of accommodation for each group depended upon their perceived ability to self-regulate sex, drink, and violence. The assault on the shop assistant suggested deviant sexuality could not be contained in either one space or one social group. British official ideas of class and morality were built into the organization and operation of Rawalpindi and Murree. The Murree rape case broke these ideas down in a spectacular way, while the everyday domestic practices of enlisted men and families did the same in subtler ways over time.

The Enlisted Man and the Locust Tribe

The work of men and their families to construct a military domesticity can be seen in the memoir of William Wilkie. Wilkie recorded his memories of Army life in a small notebook, jotting down stories of the Crimean War, the Indian Rebellion, and his conversion to evangelical Christianity, while working as a night watchman in a Dundee jute mill some thirty years after he left India.[51] The memoir was both a show of Wilkie's faith and a means of passing down some part of his military service to his daughter Martha. Wilkie left his medals and ribbons to his son, but reserved his tale of moral development for his daughter.[52] Perhaps because his account was intended for a female readership, Wilkie took greater pains to record incidents of domestic life alongside the marches and battles that more typically feature in military memoirs.

Wilkie joined the Army at nineteen on a whim and spent the next eleven years of his life in service, most of them far from his native Scotland. His life trajectory took him from the heights of British working-class masculinity in the mid-nineteenth century – starting life

---

[50] Pollie Keen wrote to her mother that of the nine NCOs she knew, only the four with families would be going to the hills. Pollie Keen to Mary Holloway, May 1, 1892, IOR MSS Eur. F528/11, British Library.

[51] William Wilkie's Reminiscences during his sojourn in the Crimea and during the Indian Mutiny was written from memory while night watchman in the Angus Jute Works, Dundee, 1890–91, British Library, IOR MSS Eur. B221.

[52] Wilkie, William (Wills and testaments Reference SC45/34/4, Dundee Sheriff Court Wills) Image 293 Scotlands People, 1902. Accessed June 7, 2023.

as a disaffected weaver, joining the Army just in time to serve in the Crimean War and the Indian Rebellion – to the complementary shallows of post-Army life. The Dundee jute mills, where Wilkie punctuated his nightly rounds with spates of memoir-writing, represented the last gasp of a once-prominent Scottish industry. By the second half of the nineteenth century, jute production had been taken over by cheaper Indian factories and growers, enriching British investors and impoverishing workers. Wilkie spent his middle age guarding an industry increasingly irrelevant to a working-class man like him and his youth protecting the British industrial interests that made it obsolete. These economics likely explain the profession listed in his 1902 death record – "pedlar."[53]

In his memoir, Wilkie acts as a rambling guide through some of Britain's mid-century imperial adventures. Though he converted to evangelical Christianity while in the Army, and it was through that conversion that he learned to write, his narrative is not one of salvation. Rather, joining the church and signing the pledge to renounce alcohol were merely two of many events in a long life. In common with many working-class autobiographers, his writing style is blunt and matter-of-fact, following no coherent narrative besides that dictated by recording incidents of interest.[54] Alongside the battles, raids, and skirmishes in which his regiment engaged, Wilkie was interested in the connections between the people he encountered as the Highlanders moved throughout India. In Wilkie's telling, Army life in India was a series of marches and resettlements made sense of by an overlaying web of acquaintance, the filaments of which reached from the Crimea to the Punjab to his native Kirriemuir in Forfarshire. He experienced the cantonments and hill stations he moved through in India in terms of their effects on his friends and comrades. A station was good or not depending on how many died there, how easy or onerous the work was, and whether social relations remained harmonious. Ying S. Lee has argued that this is typical of working-class autobiography style – writers understood themselves not by delving into the depths of their psyches, but "through family and community bonds."[55] Wilkie seldom wrote of himself in the first

---

[53] Ibid.

[54] Carolyn Steedman, John Burnett, and David Vincent note this tendency in working-class autobiographies. Jonathan Rose argues that evangelical impulses were one among many reasons working-class writers created memoirs. Rose, *The Intellectual Life of the British Working Classes*, 2010. See Steedman, *The Radical Soldier's Tale John Pearman 1819–1908*, and John Burnett, David Vincent, and David Mayal, *Autobiography of the Working Class: An Annotated Critical Bibliography* (Brighton, Sussex: Harvester Press, 1984).

[55] Ying S. Lee, *Masculinity and the English Working Class: Studies in Victorian Autobiography and Fiction* (New York: Routledge, 2007).

person, referring instead to "we," "us," and "our," capacious terms that encompassed the regiment and its associated crew of married women, children, and camp followers.

The "we" of Wilkie's regiment included men and women equally. Camp followers had long worked as laundresses for the regiment, even in India where male dhobi wallahs would generally have taken on the task. Some of the married women who joined their husbands in the Army traveled from Scotland to do so. These reunions could be a source of joy or anxiety for the regiment. Wilkie fondly recalled encountering a woman who had been close friends with his own mother and joked with her about how far they were now from home. "One day she was trying to light her fire & she was sore put about for it would not burn I said to her send ... for my mother's bellows she looked and laughed no doubt thinking over the distance ... for it was reckoned we were 20000 miles from home."[56] Scotland was far away in Wilkie's account, but made closer by the proximity of those who shared acquaintances, experiences, and knowledge.[57] Being stationed in the cantonment for a length of time allowed the men and women of the regiment to restore a gendered order. Married men were no longer responsible for cooking for themselves, and family units were not separated as they had been on the march. Even for unmarried men like William Wilkie, the presence of the women of the regiment and the reestablishment of family life in the cantonment domesticated military life in India.

Friendships, sexual relationships, and marriages all formed a regular part of working-class military life, in spite of the Army's attempts to keep its soldiers unattached. Even single soldiers created a domestic culture within the military. Holly Furneaux has argued, in relation to soldiers' quilt-making practices, that British soldiers brought the domestic and military together by maintaining connections to home and taking on domestic tasks in army camps.[58] Soldiers understood themselves as caretakers and took pride in the domestic arts, from cooking to quilting. The activities required of military men in their daily lives likewise encompassed what in other contexts would be considered domestic work. On the march, men were responsible for cooking, maintaining their clothing and equipment, and making camp, literally a kind of homemaking. In a

---

[56] William Wilkie's Reminiscences, IOR MSS Eur. B221, 87.

[57] See John M. MacKenzie and Tom Devine, eds., *Scotland and the British Empire* (Oxford: Oxford University Press, 2011) on developing Scottish identity in empire.

[58] Holly Furneaux, *Military Men of Feeling: Emotion, Touch, and Masculinity in the Crimean War* (Oxford: Oxford University Press, 2016) and Holly Furneaux and Sue Prichard, "Contested Objects: Curating Soldier Art," *Museum and Society* 13, no. 4 (2015): 447–61 https://doi.org/10.29311/mas.v13i4.346

similar dynamic, Clare Anderson has shown how sailors and soldiers replicated the intimacy of shipboard life by creating domestic spaces on land while stationed in the Andaman penal colonies.[59] In cantonments, hill stations, and sanitaria, soldiers did the work of sustaining connections between themselves and their comrades in India and family and friends in other parts of the empire.

Domestic practices like these were not actively discouraged by the military command. For camps, cantonments, and regiments to run smoothly, men had to take on some labor that in Britain would have been gendered as female. Furneaux points to sewing classes promoted by temperance activists and tolerated by officers as an example of elite acceptance of enlisted men's domestic work. Work like mending and practical sewing needed to be done and provided the added benefit of keeping men out of trouble. And because enlisted men could often rely on a bearer to perform heavier labor, they were freed up to do the necessary but less physically taxing handiwork. Single, enlisted men could strengthen their bonds to the military and improve the conditions of their service by creating home-like spaces for themselves, whether by making quilts, darning socks, or caring for pets.

Pets added to the domestic feeling of the cantonment for enlisted men and families. Working-class families in Britain kept pets, but they would have had neither the space nor the money to devote to large menageries. Some animals did make their way back to Britain with their owners. In her study of Victorian pet ownership, Sarah Amato has found advertisements for a wide assortment of animals native to India for sale or trade to buyers of varying means in British papers.[60] William Wilkie recalled that most of the men in his regiment had pet animals – rabbits and hens were particularly popular. Wilkie devoted a significant section of his memoir to the pet sheep he bought for one rupee when his regiment was stationed at a convalescent camp outside of Simla.

It was a perfect treat for it followed one like a dog. I fed it on pear & Indian corn and bread from the mess table, it did not cost me much for its keep. If I jumped over a charpoy (or bed) it would do the same, If I crawled in below the table it would follow me or even under the beds too.... I used to go out for a walk to harden my feet for the march it ran after me in fact almost every place I went before leaving I sold it for what I paid for it it was very much made off by all who knew it it was so tame.[61]

[59] Clare Anderson, *Subaltern Lives: Biographies of Colonialism in the Indian Ocean World, 1790–1920* (Cambridge: Cambridge University Press, 2012), 183–4.
[60] Sarah Amato, *Beastly Possessions: Animals in Victorian Consumer Culture* (Toronto: University of Toronto Press, 2015), 36.
[61] Wilkie, 81.

Wilkie's pet sheep was at once a companion, an unofficial regimental mascot, and an object of caretaking. Wilkie was clearly attached to the animal, creating a home for his pet and admiring its loyalty. But he left it behind nonetheless as his regiment moved on. Wilkie's treatment of his pet sheep, purchased, cared for, loved, and then left, was typical of the types of domestic arrangements enlisted men made in the cantonments or hill stations they passed through. Each place was turned, however briefly, into as much of a home as possible and then left behind for another regiment to repeat the same process.

Temperance and Domesticity

Drinking culture and the debates surrounding it provide a useful lens into the ways in which official regulation, elite standards, and non-elite practices intersected in India. Working-class men and women would have been familiar with the British temperance movement and its top-down approach to regulating working-class behavior.[62] These same currents existed in India, but there they were joined by officials' concern over how non-elites' actions reflected on British rule and ideas of British superiority. Drinking, like sex, was a point at which elite concerns over Britain's public image in India and non-elite morality came together to make drinking a major social problem with racial undertones.

Regulations on the consumption of spirits among enlisted men were established in India as early as the 1800s, and by the 1850s, the sale of liquor and beer had been moved into the cantonment.[63] Because the Army itself was the only authorized purveyor of alcoholic beverages to the troops, intemperance reflected poorly on the command as well as the soldiers. Elite concerns over alcoholism were practical as well as cultural – sick soldiers could not work or fight; they required additional care, often in expensive hill station sanatoria, and were frequently invalided home. Temperance was one of the few movements in which working-class organizing and elite interests aligned. But the decision to drink or not had little bearing on how class was perceived. A working-class man who signed "the Pledge" – a promise to abstain from alcohol – may have been rendered more respectable, but the fact that he needed outside inducements to keep him that way reified his class position instead of challenging it.

---

[62] Brian Harrison, *Drink and the Victorians: The Temperance Question in England 1815–1872*, 2nd edn. (1971, London: Faber; ACLS Humanities E-Book, 2012).
[63] Wald, *Vice in the Barracks*, 131.

But drinking also played an important role in military sociability and military rations. Pollie despaired of her husband's drinking, writing to her mother after almost four years in India that Dick was "killing himself not by inches but I should say by yards through the drink."[64] It was a liver complaint (a diagnosis encompassing any number of alcohol- and climate-related ailments) that eventually invalided Dick and his family's home. Tensions between the restriction and tolerance of alcohol played prominent roles in working-class culture in Britain, and they were translated to India. Emily Wonnacott, the regimental schoolteacher's wife, received copies of the temperance newspaper *The British Workman* from her parents.[65]

Signing the pledge, as Wilkie did, allowed soldiers to assert themselves in response to military authority.[66] Wilkie was convinced to join the temperance cause by an itinerant preacher. He put his new-found sobriety to the test at one of the regiment's public displays of Scottish identity – a Highland games. Wilkie interpreted his experiences through the lens of temperance. Recovering from a scorpion bite, Wilkie was not in the mood for caber tossing. He spent the Highland games keeping sober and reading the Bible with a traveling chaplain, but begrudgingly admitting that he "did not see any real harm … in such amusements."[67] He later recalled a rainy march through the Himalayas when "the grog was to be served out but we had to pay for it … a crpl came to me & said (Willie) I wonder at you not taking your grog on such a day as this, I will pay for it if you'll drink it i replied if I wanted it I could pay for it (thanks)."[68] Refusing alcohol became a way for Wilkie, both in life and in the memoir, to differentiate himself from the mass of soldiers and to make choices within the limited range of possibilities open to him in the military. As Sam Goodman points out, the British in India used drinking and the choices around the act as a way to form colonial identities.[69] Wilkie was careful to make it clear to the corporal and to his reader that his abstinence was a matter of choice, not a necessity born out of poverty. Notably, neither his officers nor fellow soldiers seem to have been put off by Wilkie's temperance. Wilkie's temperance placed him somewhat outside the norm of army relations, which might have been part of the appeal. By removing himself from one of the main forms of socialization that

[64] Pollie Keen to Mary Holloway, July 24, 1893, British Library, IOR MSS Eur. F528/12.
[65] Emily Wonnacott to parents, March 9, 1867, British Library IOR MSS Eur. C376/1.
[66] William Wilkie's Reminiscences, IOR MSS Eur. B221, 74–79.
[67] William Wilkie's Reminiscences, IOR MSS Eur. B221, 79.   [68] Ibid., 79.
[69] Sam Goodman, "Spaces of Intemperance & the British Raj 1860–1920," *The Journal of Imperial and Commonwealth History* 48, no. 4 (July 3, 2020): 591–618, https://doi.org/10 .1080/03086534.2020.1741840.

enlisted men enjoyed, he carved out space to create his own social circles, with varying degrees of success.

The pledge could just as easily be used to attempt to control behavior. Thirty years after Wilkie's experiences in India, Dick Keen signed the pledge at the urging of his wife and his commanding officer. "Dick has signed the Pledge at last," Pollie writes to her mother, "and as the Major knows of it may have a little hold on him. I hope please God it will."[70] Pollie, acknowledging the limits of her own influence on her husband, turned to the combined power of working-class temperance organizing and military hierarchies to attempt to stop her husband from drinking. This effort worked for a time, though Dick drank on and off throughout his service.

Marriage, Morality, and Infidelity

The small number of British women allowed on the strength meant that single women were in high demand. As a result, the enlisted men and families of the regiments developed a morality around marriage and fidelity that was responsive to their surroundings. Like the letter writers we encountered in Chapter 2, Wilkie and his regiment took a harsh view of extramarital affairs, but they looked with equanimity at speedy remarriages and economically motivated relationships. When Wilkie's regiment moved on from Rawalpindi to Sialkot, single men and women in a position to marry did so. "The women that was bereaved of their Husbands got other ones to fill their places the sergeant who lost his wife so suddenly in Rawlpindee got another."[71] Wilkie responded to these marriages gladly, but pragmatically. The sergeant's wife was the same Kirriemuir woman he had been so happy to reminisce with about home. She had died of a hemorrhage, which Wilkie attributed to having resumed her duties as a washerwoman too soon after giving birth.[72] The communal life of the regiment was based on relationships that were created out of both necessity and affection. Husbands and wives filled practical roles as well as emotional ones.[73] The moral worldview that developed out of these circumstances adhered to certain elements of elite

---

[70] Pollie Keen to Mary Holloway, October 19, 1891, British Library IOR MSS Eur. F528/10.

[71] William Wilkie's Reminiscences, IOR MSS Eur. B221, 98.

[72] William Wilkie's Reminiscences, IOR MSS Eur. B221, 87.

[73] Burnett et al. also remark on this tendency among working-class autobiographers: "autobiographers are uncomfortable with the language of love, preferring to speak more of solid calculation than emotional obsession." *Autobiography of the Working Class*, xxviii.

normative morality and rejected others. Marital fidelity was paramount, but the "decent" periods of mourning required by elite Victorians were not a requirement of respectability for those in the military working class in India. Neither speedy remarriage nor unions born more out of practicality than affection were unique to India, but the practices intensified there. Women and men alike lacked the support of nearby family and could not rely on long-established community bonds.

The distance from home presented other dangers. Wilkie made note of marital infidelities or gossip in the regiment, much as he would among his community at home, but would not record more illicit activities. When a sergeant was caught in a sandstorm coming home from a regimental bazaar (notorious as the location of brothels for the troops) and narrowly saved himself from suffocation, Wilkie makes no explicit mention of his likely activities.[74] Wilkie discussed morality in terms of the women of the regiment, not the men. He told the story of a friend and his wife as "a warning to all (that sin is sure to find us out)."[75] The wife "had misconducted herself with an old comrade of his in Glasgow, came out with child in her arms, she was the cause of the poor fellow's death." Distraught, the husband began to act strangely and was disciplined for being drunk on parade. But the man had not been drinking; he had developed a case of brain fever.[76] Victorians understood brain fever to be a disease brought on by a great emotional shock.[77] The diagnosis suggests not only the unfaithful wife's culpability, but general knowledge of the affair in the regiment, extending to the medical staff. The cuckolded husband died a few days later in a hospital.

The moral of this story is obscure at first glance (it is after all the wronged husband and not the wife carrying another man's child in her arms who dies). But in the context of military marriages and the realities of widowhood, the account can be read as a warning for women. Coming out to India with an infant, the unfaithful wife was left without the support of her husband, who died, as Wilkie understood and represented it, as a result of the shock produced by the discovery of his wife's infidelity. The death of a husband left women in dire financial distress; widows received no Army pensions until the 1880s.[78] Military communities banded together to take up collections for the support of women

[74] See Elizabeth Andrew and Katharine Caroline Bushnell, *The Queen's Daughters in India* (London: Morgan and Scott, 1899) for a contemporary account of the regimental bazaar system, and Levine, *Prostitution, Race, and Politics*, for historiographical perspective.

[75] William Wilkie's Reminiscences, IOR MSS Eur. B221, 87–88.   [76] Ibid.

[77] Audrey C. Peterson, "Brain Fever in Nineteenth-Century Literature: Fact and Fiction," *Victorian Studies* 19, no. 4 (1976): 448.

[78] Trustram, *Women of the Regiment*, 93.

left behind, but an unfaithful wife would have been unlikely to enjoy that level of generosity. Violating the moral precepts of the community she was joining, the wife was cut off from its support and left friendless and destitute. A hasty second marriage, a popular option among many widows desperate for support, would have been difficult to arrange among a betrayed husband's loyal comrades.

Instances of sexual immorality among women had wide-ranging effects. An 1871 letter to the *Pioneer* questioned the wisdom of removing a European woman from barracks and sending her to live in the bazaar as a punishment for, in the same language Wilkie used to describe sexual misbehavior, "misconducting herself."[79] The correspondent referred to a similar case as precedent, in which the commanding officer of the regiment "was ordered to let her return, as a European woman should never be allowed to live in a bazar to find a subsistence in the only way possible for a woman in such circumstances. Surely she should be 'deported' and not allowed to remain a standing disgrace to our community."[80] The correspondent assumed, and expected his audience to understand, that women regardless of race could only live alone in the bazaar as prostitutes. His solution – to deport the woman rather than provide for her or allow her to return to living in barracks – suggests less concern with the woman's fate or even her morality than with her potential to remain "a standing disgrace to our community." An impoverished woman was just as likely to take up prostitution upon being deported back to England as she was in India. The community in question was clearly British and likely military, but it was just as clearly not one that had room for disgraced non-elites or sexually promiscuous European women. However bad the conditions in barracks were, leaving the protection of the Army meant losing the sexual respectability the Army afforded.

Maintaining the image of a respectable soldiering life meant leaving certain subjects unmentioned. Native women made no appearance in Wilkie's account. This was not unusual among men writing about their experiences in letters or memoirs. Letters home were likely to be shared around, and those containing salacious content were less likely to be preserved. William Wonnacott wrote to his brother Thomas in 1874 that he had all but stopped going out in the evening: "Matters have proved to me that the class of people about me are not the sort I ought to associate with. One can't handle pitch without being contaminated, so I've thought it wisest to have none rather than bad associates."[81]

---

[79] "Summary," *The Pioneer*, July 3, 1871, 4.   [80] Ibid.
[81] William Wonnacott to Tom Wonnacott, August 3, 1874, IOR MSS Eur. C376/4.

The activities those "bad associates" engaged in remained unmentioned. In unpublished memoirs like Wilkie's, written for family, friends, or local historical associations, there are similarly scant references to sexuality or interracial relationships.

The excision of Indian women from these written accounts meant that readers or correspondents in Britain had limited access to knowledge about this part of British-Indian life. Enlisted men were officially forbidden to marry Indian women, and wives or children of such marriages could make no claims on support from the Army, but such families did exist. Working-class men were loath to write back to Britain about short encounters with Indian women or longer-term relationships with mistresses and wives. This near silence on sexuality in their correspondence suggests that many non-elites adhered closely to middle-class notions of respectability.

At the same time, the existence of mixed-race families indicates that not all non-elites perceived interracial sexual encounters as incommensurate with their ideas of sexual and marital respectability. Francis Phillip Woodruff, in a memoir remarkable for its frankness on sexual matters, wrote plainly of soldiers' Eurasian families.[82] The presence of mixed-race families further brought into question the respectability of soldiers' families as a group. Often clustered on the margins of cantonments or in the native bazaars just outside the cantonment proper, mixed-race families were to the ruling class living evidence of the failure of Britain's moral mission. The limited opportunities for marriage and sexual relationships with European women afforded to non-elite British men meant that for many, relationships with Indian women could not hold the stigma they did among elite Europeans.[83] Many of those who did create sustainable relationships with Indian women and started families chose to remain in India, rather than returning home. The existence of interracial families living together as family groups suggests a more open response to mixed-race marriages than existed among elites in this period. These marriages could fit into a framework of working-class respectability while in India,

---

[82] Frank Richards [Francis Phillip Woodruff], *Old-Soldier Sahib* (London: Faber & Faber Ltd., 1936), 234.

[83] This is not to suggest that elites did not engage in interracial sexual relationships. While scholars like Ronald Hyam have argued that Indian civil servants did indeed maintain sexual distance between themselves and native women, others, like E. M. Collingham, have suggested that outside of the major cities of the Presidencies, relationships between elite men and native women were fairly common. Hyam, *Empire and Sexuality*, 157–160; E. M. Collingham, *Imperial Bodies: The Physical Experience of the Raj, c.1800–1947* (Malden, MA: Polity, 2001), 183–184.

but enlisted men hesitated to bring either Indian families or Indian notions of respectability back to Britain with them.

Conclusion

In the late 1880s, the *Civil and Military Gazette*, one of the favorite papers of the elite Anglo-Indian readership, published a series of short sketches of Indian life. One of these "turn-overs" dubbed the married quarters at Rawalpindi "a curious colony ... a republic within an autocracy."[84] The *Gazette* marveled at how "helpful to themselves and to one another, and how careless of outside opinion! Their children grow up as do no others in India. They are in no degree exposed to the influence of native servants, and treat the sun with perfect indifference, and even contempt."[85] Though the tone was affectionate, the *Gazette* identified a number of factors that suggest that the social life of the married quarters existed somewhere outside the rules of British respectability. In their own quarters, the married families seemed unaffected by the military hierarchies they otherwise operated within. Raising their children themselves and taking (to the writer, at least) little care to preserve their place in the racial hierarchy, the *Gazette* treated the married families with the same sort of anthropological curiosity that characterized discussions of native Indian cultures.

Working-class families, in developing their own "curious colony," undermined the social boundaries built up by British military and civil elites. Their "republican" idyll, run on a spirit of communal cooperation, was to the *Gazette* a charming, and ultimately harmless, display of working-class solidarity. It is also evidence of the persistence of the kind of domesticated working-class military culture that Wilkie had identified in his memoir – one with its own standards of how to have a good family life and how to be British in India. Men and their families worked to build homes and communities and create connections across these spaces. Though intended to contain, regulate, sort, and organize diverse populations, the cantonment could not perfectly regulate the contingencies of empire. While reformers might have seen cantonments as sites where working-class British masculinity ran rampant, military life as it existed in the cantonment and its satellite sites was far more complex. In some cases, like those of the soldiers and their needlework, the cantonment created military domesticity that broke down gendered practices.

---

[84] Centurion, "The Married Quarters," in *Turnovers from the Civil and Military Gazette* (Lahore: Civil and Military Gazette Press, 1888), 94–95.
[85] Ibid.

In others, as in the example of the locust tribe gathering up extra food for the men of the regiment, it reinforced them. In the case of working-class men who created families with Indian women, or British families staying on in India after military service ended, such choices threw into question British claims about their role in India as moral exemplars and temporary rulers always looking to a desired return home. To people like Wilkie, and the families of the curious colony, Rawalpindi was a place that could contain multitudes: military work, domestic practice, living space, Scottish culture, and Indian landscapes.

This chapter has considered the ways in which non-elite military men and women domesticated military space, but the story has been told largely from a male perspective. The next chapter picks up on these themes of domesticity and gender to look more closely at the experience of women of working-class origin and their India-born daughters. Whereas single men might take on a larger burden of domestic work in India, married British women transferred some of that domestic burden to servants. The British wives of NCOs, many of whom had been raised in working-class families and worked as servants themselves before coming to India, found themselves in charge of household staff. The differing ways in which these women understood servants, their responsibilities as housekeepers, and their own altered subjectivities as employers have much to tell us about how non-elite women managed their social mobility in India for themselves and their families.

4   Servants in Empire
Wives, Daughters, and Domestic Service

When George Lee's commanding officers learned that his wife had lost their baby, they summoned him to the orderly room. Mrs. Tucker, the district commissioner's wife, was planning to spend the summer in the foothills of Nanga Parbat and needed a new lady's maid. Would Lee's wife like to go along? Ada Lee wanted to get away from the plains and spend the summer out of the heat, but men of her husband's rank were only offered time in the hills every other year. She decided to join the Tuckers and their staff for the summer.[1] For Mrs. Lee, this was part vacation, part job. She occupied a special position in the family – one determined by strict demarcations of race and malleable borders of class. Mrs. Tucker liked to employ European lady's maids. The woman Mrs. Lee replaced had returned for the summer to her native France. As likely the only white servant in the Tuckers' household, Mrs. Lee was responsible for providing companionship to her employer as much as a stylish coiffure and well-looked-after wardrobe. She would also serve as an object of conspicuous consumption; European help was hard to find in India.[2] A European lady's maid provided not simply the usual benefits of personal care and grooming, but added ones – companionship, familiarity, and the luxury of a white servant in a country where even poor whites could afford help.

Mrs. Lee told the story of her summer in the hills to Charles Allen in the 1970s for his *Plain Tales from the Raj* BBC radio series. In her discussion of "servants" and "service," we can see Mrs. Lee attempting

---

[1] Charles Allen's Plain Tales from the Raj recordings and transcripts list the family's names only as A Lee. A search through the census records brought up husband and wife Ada and George Frederic Handel Lee (!) whose locations, ages, occupations, and children fit with the history Mrs. Lee relates. I use George and Ada when introducing the couple, but returned to Mrs. Lee, as she seems to have preferred, for the remainder of the chapter. Mrs. A Lee, Plain Tales of the Raj oral interview transcripts, IOR MSS Eur. T40.

[2] In one of the scarce household management guides aimed at men, the author explicitly refers to European servants in Indian as "most expensive luxuries." L.J. Shadwell, *Notes on the Internal Economy of Chummery, Home, Mess and Club* (Bombay: Thacker & Co. Ld., 1904).

to maintain and explicate racial boundaries as she recounted her experience over half a century on. She recalled a "real lovely summer, enjoying
the help of Goanese servants [who were marvelous] and a wonderful
cook."[3] In this telling, Mrs. Lee maintained the distinction between
herself, the Goanese servants, and the local servants in the Kashmiri hill
station. Though she was in service, she was also being served. But she
was not just summering; she was also an employee and as such subject to
the personality and moods of her employer. She described Mrs. Tucker
as "a bit of a snob, but she was alright really that was just the way she'd
been brought up to talk to servants."[4] When considering her position in
relation to Mrs. Tucker, Mrs. Lee understood herself to be a servant as
well. This duality was typical of the position working-class women found
themselves in as they accompanied their husbands to India – at once in
service and served, working and leisured.

It was in caring for homes or homely spaces, buying and preparing
food, and looking after children that the differences in everyday life
between India and Britain became most stark for women. The gender,
race, and status of people who did domestic labor were different in India,
as was the meaning of that labor for those who performed it and those
who benefited from it. Native men worked as cooks and did housekeeping work. British men in camps took on the cooking and did mending.
British men and women alike employed servants or had servants provided for them by their regiments. For women born into working-class
families or who managed working-class households of their own in
Britain, running an Indian household with servants presented a range
of possibilities. For some, it was a chance, possibly the first since young
childhood, for leisure. For others, the change in responsibilities led to a
sense of aimlessness or loss of control. Determining who was in service,
who had servants, and under what circumstances these categories shifted
can show us when class was made mutable by race in India, and when it
was not. Pregnancy, miscarriage, childbirth, illness, death of a spouse,
entering or leaving school, arriving in India, or returning to Britain could
shift families from lives in service to being served and back again. This
chapter is divided into three sections that follow working-class women's
experiences of India through a life cycle – marriage and motherhood,
through Mrs. Lee's oral histories; childhood, through the lives of the
Keen daughters; and schooling, through the experiences of the female
pupils of the Lawrence schools. This inverse order, which centers on
marriage and motherhood, followed by the raising and schooling of

---

[3] Mrs. A Lee, Plain Tales of the Raj oral interview transcripts, IOR MSS Eur. T40.
[4] Mrs. A Lee, Plain Tales of the Raj oral interview transcripts, IOR MSS Eur. T40.

children, echoes the ways in which most British working-class women encountered and experienced India. These moments of change in women's and girls' lives expose the tension between material circumstances, practical needs, and the desire to preserve or maintain social position.

Historians of empire have long identified the relationship between native servants and European employers as a particularly fraught one and as a useful site for understanding the intersecting relationships between race, class, gender, labor and care. Bringing a servant into a domestic space, as Ann Laura Stoler and others have argued, meant violating the sanctity of that space and opening it up to commerce, as well as racial and moral impurity.[5] This action was further complicated among working-class British households in India as their members transformed from servants to served, while still occupying a lowly social position in relation to both the British and Indian upper classes. In the British context as well, Alison Light notes that "being taken care of by another person who is seen as subordinate … is never without its anxieties and fears."[6] Much like the stories of soldiers, or of empire itself, servants' histories have played little role in studies aimed at understanding class formation or working-class politics. It is only with the revival in working-class history and the import accorded to histories of service by historians of empire that histories of domestic service in the metropole have started to gain traction.

The history of both white servants and white lower class employers in empire has been less studied, as they were far fewer in number than their Indian counterparts and have left few obvious traces of their experiences. Fae Dussart has argued that the habit of maintaining multiple servants in poor white households in India was "necessary" to preserve racial and social status.[7] Even those who could barely afford to do so would continue to pay servants as their incomes fell. The position having servants afforded them was valuable enough to justify the expense. As Stoler put it, "no one needed to tell those 'wavering classes' on the borderlines of

---

[5] See Light, *Mrs. Woolf and the Servants*, 4; Stoler, *Carnal Knowledge and Imperial Power*, 2010, xii. See also Ann Laura Stoler, *Race and the Education of Desire: Foucault's History of Sexuality and the Colonial Order of Things* (Durham, NC: Duke University Press, 1995) on race, caregiving, and domestic service, and Carolyn Steedman, *Labours Lost: Domestic Service and the Making of Modern England* (Cambridge: Cambridge University Press, 2009) on domestic service and intimacy in the eighteenth-century context.

[6] Light, *Mrs. Woolf and the Servants*, 4.

[7] Fae Ceridwen Dussart, "'That Unit of Civilisation' and 'the Talent Peculiar to Women': British Employers and Their Servants in the Nineteenth-Century Indian Empire," *Identities* 22, no. 6 (November 2, 2015): 710–11, https://doi.org/10.1080/1070289X.2014.950971.

colonial categories that management of home, sex, and sentiment was at the forefront of governance."[8] But those wavering classes did not understand service and its meanings in the same ways. European women in empire have been described as clinging to their status as mistresses of households in an effort to ward off accusations of racial degeneracy. But this analysis flattens European women into a monolithic group, aiming only to achieve or maintain middle-class status and thereby to insure their claims to whiteness.

In the letters and recollections of working-class women and families, we see instead the relationship to service change depending on class of origin, generation, and geography. The experiences of Mrs. Lee and other women like her complicate this narrative. What is notable about the experiences of the working-class women considered here, then, is that they felt comfortable enough in their racial and social position to write of and recall the shift between servant and served with little anxiety. This sense of security suggests that the relationship between class, race, and service in British India was more complicated than a desperate attempt to maintain class and racial standing by virtue of employing, rather than being employed. Service was not just a bulwark against slippage in categories. For non-elite military wives, in spite of many years spent in India and embedded in a globe-trotting British military culture, hiring servants remained a novelty, not a source of identity. Domiciled Europeans, in contrast, had a much more fraught relationship with the instability of class and race that characterized Indian life than those women who, though they might spend much of their lives in India, remained temporary sojourners. Similarly, female children raised in India with the help of servants adjusted to the return to Britain with relatively little trouble (or at least trouble that went unrecorded). This embrace of temporary status – one which the British administration was eager to maintain among its military families – helps to explain why there was little talk of *wives* being ruined by the aid of Indian servants, while *daughters* were very much at risk of growing up with incorrect expectations and a weakened sense of their position in the world.

Domestic Service in Britain and India

In Britain, domestic service was a normal part of life for women and girls of the working and lower classes. There was almost no part of the population that did not have some relationship to service, whether as

---

[8] Stoler, *Carnal Knowledge and Imperial Power*, 2010, xii.

employer, servant, or relation to one. Alison Light puts the number of servants in Britain in 1860 at just over one million and the proportion of women in service under the age of twenty at 40 percent.[9] But girls raised in India would not have seen their aunts or sisters go into service. Instead, they would have seen Indian servants looking after enlisted men, serving noncommissioned officers, and working by the dozens at the picnics and fetes officers occasionally put on for subordinates and their families.

It was a commonplace among both metropolitan observers and Anglo-Indians themselves that the British in India had too many servants. From the view of the metropole, the size of Indian households of all classes provoked wonder, while those living in India bemoaned the difficulties of managing their bloated household staffs and blamed caste and local prejudice for their existence. Anxieties about the effects of excess household help in India cut across class lines in the form of figures like spoiled middle-class wives, colonels returned from India with an outsized sense of self-importance, and charity school girls and India-raised soldiers' wives who could not or would not cook or clean for themselves. For the women who had been accustomed to keeping a middle-class house in Britain, the change in scale and style of responsibility could be overwhelming.

Advice books for brides setting up households in the country for the first time warned their readers that much of their time would be devoted to managing household staff. *The English Bride in India*, aiming its advice at middle-class women working with limited budgets, recommended managing with a minimum of eight Indian servants – an "ayah, two boys [performing the roles of butler and valet], cook, cook's mati [assistant], sweeper, bhisti or waterman, dhoby [washerman], and the syces [grooms] (one to every horse you keep)."[10] The author also recommended readers rely on their husbands' orderlies if available, thrusting these men into positions of domestic as well as military service. In contrast, Mrs. Beeton's tome of middle-class household management recommended that British households add one additional servant per £200 pounds income – so that a family living on £1000 a year would employ a cook, upper and under housemaid, nursemaid, and man servant.[11] *The Complete Indian Housekeeper and Cook* promised to help its

[9] Light, *Mrs. Woolf and the Servants*, 13.
[10] Chota Mem, *The English Bride in India: Hints on Indian Housekeeping*, 2nd ed. (Madras: Higginbotham & Co., 1909), 54.
[11] Mrs. Beeton (Isabella Mary), *The Book of Household Management* (Farrar, Straus, and Giroux, 1861), 8.

readers prevent "the best years of her life" from being wasted in the "scolding and petty supervision" required to run a massive household staff.[12] In her published account of her years in Punjab, Lady Annie Campbell Wilson wrote that when she first arrived in the country, she had "visions of attaining professional skills as head-housemaid, dairy-maid, and shepherd!" after receiving warnings that Indian servants were so hard to manage that it would be easier to do the work herself.[13] Guides for middle-class readers likewise depicted marketing as an encounter with the Indian other, an onerous and potentially dangerous endeavor, in which shoppers grappled with cheating servants, overcharging merchants, and adulterated food.[14]

Women who had grown up in working-class communities in Britain had little advice of this nature to draw on when they arrived in India. Middle-class wives and daughters had libraries of published advice to turn to, but if working-class women appeared in these texts at all, it was as servants themselves. British men, in fact, had better access to domestic advice literature written for their needs. The *Indian Manual of Military Cooking*, for example, offered guidance to military cooks on managing rations and purchasing ingredients, as well as advice on training British and Indian soldiers in cookery, and recommendations for the best equipment for feeding large groups of men.[15] Soldiers' wives, then, had to rely on one another and on the knowledge their own servants possessed to figure out how to live in a new environment. The sole volume dedicated to providing information on Indian life for working-class women that I have been able to locate is *Cookery for the million*, one of the cheaply printed For the Million guides for working-class readers. *Cookery* offered advice on the price of curry powder, how to stretch greens and lentils for a hungry crowd, and recipes for eel stew with Indian spices.[16] It provided no guidance on how to set up a household in India, how to manage a staff, or how to navigate unfamiliar markets or foodways.

[12] Flora Annie Steel and Grace Gardner, *The Complete Indian Housekeeper & Cook: Giving the Duties of Mistress and Servants the General Management of the House and Practical Recipes for Cooking in All Its Branches*, 7th ed. (London: William Heinemann, 1909), 1.
[13] Anne Campbell Wilson, *Letters from India* (Edinburgh: Blackwood, 1911), 10.
[14] Chota Mem, *The English Bride in India*, 35; Wyvern (A.R. Kenney-Herbert), *Culinary Jottings for Madras: A Treatise in Thirty Chapters on Reformed Cookery for Anglo-Indian Exiles, Based upon Modern English & Continental Principles* (Madras: Higginbotham and Co, 1878), 87.
[15] *Indian Manual of Military Cooking* (Calcutta: Office of the Superintendent Government Printing, 1906).
[16] Harriet Lawrance and JS Stirling, *Cookery for the Million Being 202 Practical, Economical, Recipes in Indian Cookery*, 2nd ed. (Bangalore: Daily Post and Examine Press, 1886).

If cookbook and advice publishers had trouble conceiving of a non-elite woman in a managerial role, the women in question seemed to have little desire for more detailed guidance on keeping house as mistresses rather than servants. In contrast to their middle- and upper-class counterparts, who bemoaned the labor involved in organizing meals and managing a household staff, working-class British women did not conceive of this type of organizational work as labor. None of the working-class women whose letters and memoirs inform this book mention managing servants or purchasing food as a source of stress or discomfort. Having performed the physical labor of cooking, cleaning, and caregiving, women of working-class backgrounds found managing to be a reprieve, rather than a burden. If conflicts with their staff became too intractable, they simply fired them. Instead, these women focused on the leisure servants afforded them.

Mrs. Lee Said She Would Do the Cooking Herself

Ada Lee, whose story started this chapter, was one such working-class woman. Mrs. Lee was born into a military family and married into one as well. Her father served with the Third Dragoon Guard in Egypt and in the South African War. When asked in her interview to recall her thoughts about India before traveling to the country, she responded with the seeming nonsequitur: "but you see my father was a soldier, we'd come from a soldier's family."[17] Being part of a soldier's family did not imply any special knowledge about India, but instead a readiness to pick up and go to unfamiliar lands. George Lee, Ada's husband, started army life as a "boy soldier," a coronet player, at the age of 9 and had risen through the ranks to corporal by the time the couple headed for India in 1909. For Mrs. Lee, being "in service" had multiple and sometimes simultaneous meanings. The experience of military service entailed a disruption to family life – both geographically and socially. But service also meant domestic service. Removed from her extended family and networks or friends, Mrs. Lee had to remake connections in India – relying on other women of the regiment to fill care-giving positions and in some cases hiring help to fill in gaps.

While living in India, Mrs. Lee hired a succession of bearers and occasionally cooks as household help. Basic housekeeping, she recalled, was covered by bearers. Cooks were not available to everyone – and were considered something of a luxury, not necessary for running a good

---

[17] Mrs. A Lee, Plain Tales of the Raj oral interview transcripts, IOR MSS Eur. T40.

household but certainly useful if you could afford one. Finally, ayahs might be hired for temporary childcare, though never as a lady's maid. Mrs. Lee recalled "You can get as many servants as you like if you like to pay for them. Everyone had a bearer … you called them all boys but I daresay he'd be about 25 or so."[18] The comedian Spike Milligan, when interviewed by Charles Allen for *Plain Tales*, likewise remembered the ease with which working-class families could hire household help. Recounting his own Indian childhood, Milligan recalled that "every standard [of living] went up. It automatically went up because you had access to this work force."[19] This higher standard held across classes; the two or three servants Mrs. Lee employed, though far more than she would have had in England, pale in comparison with the eight- to ten-person household recommended for more elite families.

In addition to a bit of leisure for their employers, servants created distance between British women and South Asians unconnected to the household or regiment. When Mrs. Lee hired bearers to do the shopping for her, she avoided, intentionally or not, glancing acquaintance with vendors and shopkeepers, or learning the few words and phrases necessary for navigating the bazaar. Even within the household, Mrs. Lee kept her distance. She did not know much about the bearer in her employ. She never knew his religion or caste, remembering simply that he did not go home for holidays – because, she believed, he had no family to go to. This was not the case in all employer–servant relations Pollie Keen chatted with her household staff and asked about their home lives. Despite this perhaps unusual level of interest, her relationship with them never went beyond the surface, and she learned little of substance about their religious practices or lives. And even Pollie wrote about these servants only half a dozen times in many years of nearly weekly correspondence. Such distancing came from servants and employers alike. On the part of Indian servants, keeping information private helped to maintain a portion of their selfhood separate from British colonizers and employers. British women used distancing to manage racial and class boundaries. Anxiety about middle-class women and their imagined or real sexual relations with Indian servants hovered constantly.[20] This threat persisted across classes, with women attempting to manage their own respectability in households staffed with male servants.

---

[18] Ibid.
[19] Spike Milligan, Plain Tales of the Raj oral interview transcripts, IOR MSS Eur. T47.
[20] It came to a head most notably, at least historiographically speaking, in the Hume Case used to drum up opposition to the Ilbert Bill. Mrinalini Sinha, *Colonial Masculinity: The "Manly Englishman" and the "Effeminate Bengali" in the Late Nineteenth Century* (Manchester: Manchester University Press, 1995), 52–54.

For working-class women, the threat was not only sexual but also racial. Wives of NCOs, like Pollie Keen, or band members, like Mrs. Lee, had weak claims to respectability. Their status was dependent upon their husband's good behavior, and their own. Become too friendly with the servants, and you ran the risk of being lumped together with them. Creating close connections with Indian servants would demonstrate too close a commonality between the white and Indian working and serving classes.

Even as they provided labor and much-needed respite, Indian servants could represent a loss for working-class women of the opportunity to use their domestic skills and be useful to their households. What had been necessary tasks in Britain – like feeding a family – became optional outlets for creativity and identity in India. Pollie Keen hired and fired her cooks because she preferred the autonomy of cooking for herself. Mrs. Lee, whose husband was a Band Sergeant, described herself as "a bit fussy" with her cooking and preferred to do it herself. Doing the cooking herself involved wrangling a grill and a camp stove while in the hills or staking out a place in the cookhouse in the barracks. Both options were labor intensive and required more effort than similar activities would have in Britain. Both Pollie Keen and Mrs. Lee were in the financial position to hire help but chose not to, turning this element of housework into a hobby. Maintaining control over the cooking was one way for these women to retain some sense of themselves in India. And taking control of your own cooking meant cooking with familiar recipes and ingredients. Neither Pollie nor Mrs. Lee complained about Indian food or flavors explicitly, but being "a bit fussy" could cover a wide range of tastes, dislikes, and demands.

Given the option to spend money on childcare or cooking, working-class British women seem to have considered cooking optional, while the work of mothering was not. Hiring an ayah was a way for military wives to fill in the missing pieces in their social networks. This practice was not that different from what working-class women would have done in Britain. Ellen Ross has written about mothers in the poorer districts of London hiring temporary nurses immediately after giving birth, either at home or in the hospital.[21] Women in British Army regiments had access to military hospitals during childbirth and often spent many days there. Dick Keen hired an ayah to look after his daughters when Pollie was hospitalized for two weeks with complications after her daughter Marjorie's birth. The woman, whose name neither Dick nor Pollie

---

[21] Ross, *Love and Toil*, 111–14.

recorded, looked after Marjorie's older sisters, Dolly and Eva, and likely her father as well, as Dick spent much of those two weeks getting drunk.

British women of all classes hired ayahs, but they understood their roles differently. Elite women hired ayahs as a matter of course. They might work caring for children or as lady's maids. The term itself could mean both nursemaid and lady's maid, depending on context.[22] *Hobson-Jobson* identifies it as deriving from the Portuguese for nurse or governess, which helps to explain the slipperiness in the meaning of a role that could encompass childcare as well as care of adult women's bodies and dress.[23] While Anglo-Indian households were notorious for maintaining what metropolitan observers considered to be an excess of servants, an ayah could fill – or refer to – two roles in one. Elite women used the term ayah interchangeably to refer to servants who performed childcare and the tasks of a lady's maid. This is a meaningful conflation, suggesting that women understood childcare and personal care to be interrelated. For working-class women, there was a distinct line between those who could temporarily hire help with their children and those who hired help dressing and grooming themselves. The distinction did not hold for men – working-class men reported being shaved and having their clothes and shoes looked after by servants. This proximity was not the case for working-class women – or if it was, it went unrecorded. Working-class families typically hired ayahs to look after their children temporarily when they went into hospital to have babies. In these circumstances, ayahs only did childcare, only worked on a temporary basis, and only were hired in extremis.

Mrs. Lee, happy to hire servants as needed in other capacities, never had an ayah, not even when she went successively into the regimental hospital to deliver her three children. She gave birth to her first baby in a hill station while living in tents, and this experience perhaps left her unimpressed by hospital births. In the hospital, "all you had was the midwife," Mrs. Lee recalled, "and more often than not the midwife was Eurasian, but as I say there isn't a lot of difference."[24] Mrs. Lee was happy with her experiences with the midwives until her final pregnancy, during which she was "neglected by midwife [and] suffered all my life for

---

[22] Elizabeth Garrett, *Morning Hours in India: Practical Hints on Household Management, the Care and Training of Children, &c.* (London: Trübner & Co., 1887).

[23] Henry Yule and A.C. Burnell, and Kate Teltscher (eds.), *Hobson-Jobson: The Definitive Glossary of British India*, Oxford World's Classics (New York, NY: Oxford University Press, 2015), 57, 71–72. "Amah" referred to nursemaid and "ayah" to nurse or lady's maid, but the correspondents and memoirists considered here use "ayah" exclusively.

[24] Mrs. A Lee, Plain Tales of the Raj oral interview transcripts, IOR MSS Eur. T40.

that."[25] Mrs. Lee recalled her initial reactions to Eurasians upon arrival in India as a sort of gruesome fascination, but though in retrospect she recalled that some Eurasian girls she met socially were "very nice."[26] It is not clear whether Mrs. Lee attributed her birth injury to the care of the midwife in particular, or an understaffed hospital more generally. She never took advantage of the nursing staff at the hospital when her own children were admitted for various childhood injuries or illnesses, as "matron was always overworked."[27] She did note that there were native doctors treating the children, which might have led to her taking the children's care upon herself. Paying for childcare and companionship was one of the points where class difference remained stark in India. There is little evidence that the families of NCOs or enlisted men were cared for by ayahs long term. Even in the case of the death of a mother, babies would more likely be given over to another woman in the regiment for feeding and care. Mothers who needed childcare instead pieced together arrangements for their children. Pollie left her girls at home in the evenings while going out dancing with Dick, popping back into the house to check on them and leaving her eldest daughter in charge.[28] For officers' and civil service wives, ayahs numbered among the score of servants necessary to run a household *and* had an obvious British corollary in the nurse.

Elite British women employed Indian servants to help with childcare, but considered working-class British women a suitable substitute. Quality European servants, advice manuals warned, were both notoriously difficult to come by and well worth the trouble, as they could better understand and sympathize with the needs of Englishwomen. White servants were a status symbol and social support in a country where Indian labor was cheap and available, but familiar faces and close relationships were harder to come by. Advice for women headed to India frequently suggested trying to hire a European nurse or lady's maid, as they would provide superior service and would not require the kinds of training Indian women supposedly needed. *The Englishwoman in India* reassured its readers that if they did not want to spend the "trifle" required to employ an ayah to look after their children on board ship, "there are generally one of two decent soldiers' wives who would gratefully accept a small sum and any old clothes in return for their services to a lady or children."[29] This practice echoed the treatment of servants in

[25] Ibid.   [26] Ibid.   [27] Ibid.
[28] Dorothy Keen to Mary Holloway, undated, IOR MSS Eur. F528/17.
[29] *The Englishwoman in India: Containing Information for the Use of Ladies Proceeding To, or Residing In, the East Indies, on the Subjects of Their Outfit, Furniture, Housekeeping, the*

British households – who could expect to receive their mistresses' cast-off clothing as an unwritten part of their compensation.[30] This sharing of clothes and a nominal sum suggested a relationship of favor, rather than formal employment. Indian ayahs, in contrast, could expect little sense of connection between themselves and their employers – and those that traveled to Britain with their employers often found themselves abandoned, left to find their own passage back or to languish in the Ayah's Home, waiting for a means to return.[31]

Amy Macnabb's letters to her mother-in-law give us a good view of how elite women – the wives of officers and civil servants – understood the relationship between white servants and employers. Amy's husband, James Macnabb, was a British officer, and the couple spent the 1860s moving from station to station in Punjab. As generations of both Amy and James' family had served in India, both James and Amy would have been familiar with the particularities of Indian life.[32] Soon after her marriage and arrival in India, Amy gave birth and hired an English nursemaid, Mrs. Robertson, to care for her and the baby. Amy had a fraught relationship with her English servants. Though she had nothing but praise for Mrs. Robertson, she feared her departure and despaired of finding another English servant who could fulfill her exacting requirements. Mrs. Robertson's husband served in a regiment that was fighting on the frontier, and Amy had offered her leave to go nurse him in the event that he was injured. But the possibility of losing her servant drew some unguarded comments from Amy while writing to her mother-in-law. "Should it chance that her husband were killed she might remain altogether of which I should be very glad." Quickly revising her statement (though not so embarrassed as to strike it out), Amy continued, "I mean I should be glad if she would stop with me not that I should be glad if her husband were killed poor woman!"[33] Fearing that Mrs. Robertson's departure would leave her without a European servant or a connection

Rearing of Children, Duties and Wages of Servants, Management of the Stables, and Arrangements for Travelling to Which Are Added Receipts for Indian Cookery By A Lady Resident (London: Smith, Elder and Co., 1865), 11.

[30] Lucy Lethbridge, *Servants: A Downstairs View of Twentieth-Century Britain* (London: Bloomsbury, 2013), 78; Lucy Delap, *Knowing Their Place: Domestic Service in Twentieth-Century Britain* (OUP Oxford, 2011), 56.

[31] Arunima Datta, "Becoming Visible: Travel Documents and Travelling Ayahs in the British Empire," *South Asian Studies* 38, no. 2 (July 3, 2022): 141–160, https://doi.org/10.1080/02666030.2022.2111087.

[32] Amy's father Sir James Weir Hogg had been a member of the East India Company Board of Directors. www.oxforddnb.com/view/article/13473?docPos=5.

[33] Amy Hogg Macnabb to Jean Mary Macnabb, November 1, 1863, British Library, IOR MSS Eur. F206/132.

to home, Amy asked her mother-in-law to look out for a "respectable experienced woman" who would be willing to organize her own passage to India and to sign a three-year contract. Amy's list of requirements was substantial; she wanted a nurse who could "understand" children and oversee their preschool education, while also fulfilling some of the functions of a lady's maid.

Amy understood English nurses in India to fill a special position in the lives of the families they lived with. "I lay a particular stress upon her being kind to the weens and good tempered as in India you see so much of an English Servant that if they are ill-tempered it is simple misery." And yet, she complained that "They will take airs and expect to be waited on.... In this country it is almost impossible to find a woman who does not drink or steal or such like."[34] Though complaints about good help were by no means limited to India, Amy's issues with her servants indicate the multiple roles she expected these English women to play. They should foremost be English and provide a connection to home, an understanding of English customs, and a familiar method of child-rearing. But the range of English women available to Amy left something to be desired – they did not understand or correctly occupy their class positions. They were either too loose with their morals, drinking and stealing, and thus insufficiently English, or they were too Indian – expecting to be waited upon. In either case, class and national identity became jumbled in a way that troubled Amy Macnabb.

While experienced Anglo-Indian housekeepers encouraged women to form friendly relationships with their white servants, the same was not true for native servants. Native servants appeared in advice literature only as potential problems to be managed. This attitude toward native servants trickled down to working-class mistresses – as we have seen, of all the correspondents and memoirists considered in this book, it is only Pollie Keen who provides any detail at all about her servants apart from the mere fact of their existence.

For those working-class women in India who did not intend to stay, service functioned not as a boost in social status, but rather as evidence of the fundamental instability of women's lives in the empire. Reliant on husbands and the support of the regiment, separated from their family and friends, these women were aware that their time as ladies of leisure was limited. Even those families that remained healthy and intact would have to renegotiate their social status once their terms of service expired. Those who returned to Britain would return to working-class

---

[34] Amy Hogg Macnabb to Jean Mary Macnabb, February 16, 1864, British Library, IOR MSS Eur. F206/132.

communities and lives. The transition back to Britain – described by Elizabeth Buettner as so destabilizing for those middle- and upper-class Britons who returned from imperial service to a far less lavish lifestyle at home – was easier for women of the working class.[35] Their experience of empire had always been marked by status instability.

Cossetted Childhoods

Women raised in Britain who came to India later in life experienced wild vacillations in status. But their children, whether brought along at a young age or born in India, knew little else. We can see this play out in the childhood of Pollie Keen's daughter, Marjorie. Marjorie was the third Keen daughter and the only one born in India. She spent her days accompanying her mother on social calls around the cantonment. Dolly and Eva, aged six and three, were considered old enough to look after themselves for a few hours, especially in a house attended by a bearer and surrounded by familiar neighbors. Pollie makes no mention of the older Keen girls doing any household labor apart from some light babysitting. Though this may be an oversight in her letters (not bothering to say the obvious), the volume and detail of Pollie's correspondence suggest that if she were training her girls in housework, she would have mentioned it. Marjorie accompanied her mother on walks around the cantonment, drives to the bazaar in a borrowed carriage, and chats with the wives of other high-ranking NCOs. The regiment was experiencing something of a baby boom in Marjorie's early years, so there were plenty of children to visit. Dressed in hand-me-downs from her sisters and a bonnet Pollie had knitted with lightweight wool, Marjorie was the model of a well-loved, well-cared-for child.[36]

The military officers surrounding the Keens understood the family to be of lower status, and thus grateful for charitable impulses. Pollie recalled one such incident: "One day the Captain saw them having their bit of bread and butter while they were out to play and he asked them if their mother never gave them jam so young Dolly said 'No Sir' so he told them to go to the coffee shop and tell the corporal in charge to give them a pot and he would pay for it."[37] Every morning after that, the children went to the coffee shop where their pot of jam was waiting for them. A pot of preserves, among the homelier pantry items, was in fact something of a luxury in India, though one that would have been within

[35] Buettner, *Empire Families*, Chapter 5.
[36] Pollie Keen to Mary Holloway, July 20, 1890, MSS Eur. F528/9.
[37] Pollie Keen to Mary Holloway, June 29, 1891, IOR MSS Eur. F528/10.

Pollie's grasp if she chose to purchase it. The Captain, though, saw two little girls going without. He reserved the gift for the children alone, requiring them to come every day to the coffee shop for their treat. This passing encounter replicated many of the power relationships that characterized elite responses to working-class child-rearing in India. The Captain observed children he thought deserved a treat and offered to provide something they seemed to lack. Bypassing their parents, he spent a little of his own money to sponsor the children through an institution run by the Army.

The Keen children spent much of their Indian childhood in a mixed state of luxury, surveillance, and charity. Dick and Pollie appreciated being driven around in carriages, going to parties, and having servants at their disposal, and Dolly, Eva, and Marjorie were too young to know anything different. The Keen girls, like so many other working-class children born or growing up in India, did not fit into the categories the army, civil service, and government of India had developed to manage its population. They were not the deprived children of the lowest ranking soldiers; they were not being raised in "the barracks," nor in cramped and unkempt rooms in the bazaar. Though the Army had worked to improve conditions for soldiers, and in particular for soldiers' families, since the mid-century flurry of concern around the issue, popular opinion had not kept up with conditions on the ground.[38] From an elite perspective, the Keen children could be understood to be growing up in substandard conditions, exposed to all elements of regimental life, bad climate, and wanting small luxuries and reminders of home. Contrary to popular opinion, children like the Keens grew up in a relatively privileged and secure manner, though the family lacked that key marker of elite status – the ability or desire to send their children home for schooling. Instead, they relied on the regimental schools – of the sort that Emily Wonnacott would have taught in. What protected the Keens (and the Lees) from the bad conditions that working-class families were supposedly subject to is that they remained largely intact. The death of a parent frequently meant family disintegration. And when that happened, India's charitable schools were there to step in.

Children who were old enough could go to the schools for orphans of full or partial European descent scattered throughout the major cities and hill stations of India. While regimental schools often closed with the hot weather and only met for a few hours a day, hill schools boarded their pupils and offered reliable, if indifferent, care all year round. The

---

[38] French, *Military Identities*, 248.

Government of India relied heavily on charity schools like the Lawrence Asylums, the Bishop Cotton Schools, and La Martinière, or schools set up in railway colonies, to educate the children of working-class British and mixed-race families.[39] As a result, these schools' policies played a major role in shaping the futures of non-elite children. It is in these schools that class instability and state intervention intersected in the form of an ever-changing curriculum that neither helped to create a pliable British-identifying population nor responded to the realities of these children's situations.

These institutions developed out of a mix of care and concern over the futures of children of partial or full European descent born in India. India was the birthplace of a number of charitable educational initiatives aimed at providing – first for soldiers in the East India Company and British Army, and later for railway workers – what their employers would not, a safety net for their families. These projects, though, required that parents give up the care and raising of their own children. Some parents sent their children to these institutions willingly – for others, separation came as the result of intervention from the military, state, or community.[40] The same impulse that led the Captain to buy the Keen children jam, but required them to receive it from the Army coffee shop, led concerned officers and philanthropists to set up educational and orphan funds aimed at protecting children by removing them from familial care.

"The Wives of Working Men"

By the mid-1860s, the governors of the Lawrence Military Asylum in Sanawar started noting a worrying tendency among the school's female pupils. The girls, the daughters of soldiers, many fully or partially orphaned, some of mixed heritage, and all being educated for lives of domestic work (whether in service of employers or husbands), refused to take positions as domestic servants. The school's 1864 Report noted with surprise that "out of all the grown up girls only *one* volunteered to go into Service, and she had lived in England."[41] This refusal among working-class girls who had been raised in India to enter into domestic service – a

---

[39] On the development of these schools and their role in family separation, see Satadru Sen, "The Orphaned Colony: Orphanage, Child and Authority in British India," *Indian Economic and Social History Review* 44 (2007): 463–488; Ghosh, *Sex and the Family in Colonial India*, 2006; Buettner, *Empire Families*, 2004; Bear, *Lines of the Nation*, 2007.
[40] Sen, *Colonial Childhoods*, 33–34.
[41] *Report of the Lawrence Military Asylum, for the Orphan and Other Children of European Soldiers, Serving of Having Served in India, for the Financial Year Ending 30th April, 1864* (Sanawar: Lawrence Asylum Press, 1864), 4.

first step into adulthood and earning a living for many girls of their station in Britain – raised a number of concerns for the school's governors. Sanawar aimed to educate children to be useful and tractable imperial subjects, who identified and behaved as did their contemporaries raised in Britain. That meant understanding and accepting what was expected of people of their class. But Sanawar students, almost all of whom had been born in and lived their whole lives in India, had little experience of the British class system outside of either the Indian or military context. Raised largely in military cantonments, the children who ended up in charitable hill schools like Sanawar had spent their early years waited on by servants. Taking up such jobs themselves would mean transgressing the racial boundaries they had been raised with and relinquishing what little remained of the social status they had enjoyed as the children of white soldiers in a British colony.

Indian boarding schools were part of a much wider movement across the British Empire to "save" children by removing them from environments deemed unhealthy or uncivilized. "Saving" children in this context meant placing them in environments designed to make them as white, Christian, respectable, and British as possible. Extending beyond the geographic and temporal bounds of the British Empire, boarding schools in India, orphan trains in the USA and Canada, the Stolen Generations in Australia, and supported childhood emigration schemes all formed part of this trend.[42] Starting in the eighteenth century, subscriptions from officers and men of the East India Company armies to the Bengal Military Orphan Society supported the care and education of the mixed-race children of British officers and soldiers. Durba Ghosh has argued that these schools were already working to subvert family relationships in the eighteenth century by forcibly removing children from their Indian mothers.[43] Family separation was not only for the imperial poor; as Elizabeth Buettner has shown even elite British Indian childhoods were built on a foundation of family separation, with the children of officers and civil servants sent home to England at young ages to preserve class, race, and health.[44]

The Lawrence Asylum Schools, the most prominent among these institutions, stated their purpose as providing their students with "the benefits of a bracing climate, a healthy moral atmosphere, and a plain, useful, and above all religious education, adapted to fit them for

---

[42] For British examples, see Ellen Boucher, *"Empire's Children: Child Emigration, Welfare, and the Decline of the British World" 1869–1967* (Cambridge: Cambridge University Press, 2014); Mizutani, *The Meaning of White*; McCabe, *Race, Tea and Colonial Resettlement*.
[43] Ghosh, *Sex and the Family in Colonial India*.   [44] Buettner, *Empire Families*.

employment suited to their position in life."[45] The problem was no one could agree on what exactly that position in life should be. The Lawrence schools in particular played a formative role in working out ideas about childhood, race, and moral inheritance in the second half of the nineteenth century. They were the first charity schools in India founded under the influence of Victorian, rather than eighteenth-century, ideas about race, religion, class, and childhood. The first and largest among them, the Lawrence Asylum at Sanawar, became famous for educating the displaced children of soldiers and featured in *Kim* as an appropriate – if despised – home for that novel's protagonist.[46] They spread across the Subcontinent in four different hill stations and, despite their name, eventually drew children from military and civilian populations. Faults in the girls of Sanawar suggested, by extension, faults in the entire population of non-elite British girls in India.

An 1863 Report on gaps in the girls' training noted that "it is really a reproach to a young woman of this class to be totally unable to cook" and fretted over the school's reputation as a training ground for future wives: "Instances have been brought to the knowledge of the Guardians, of soldiers complaining that 'Lawrence Asylum wives were more helpless than black girls'."[47] To encourage domestic labor, the Report pointed to examples in other institutions. The women of Mount Holyoke Female Seminary (now College) in the United States did not bring servants to school with them, though they were drawn from the "higher and middle class" and lower-class students in German schools tended to their own needs.[48] This directive extended to students of all genders, encouraging "the sons and daughters of hard working men and women" to learn a litany of tasks that in India were performed by servants, from bed-making and boot-cleaning to gardening and washing clothes. The children, the Report noted, "would all have had to" take on these tasks in their "English homes" and "may be called upon to take [them] up in this country as Soldiers and Settlers, or Settlers' and Soldiers' wives."[49] Slipping between these two tenses, Sanawar addressed a past that the children never experienced and planned for a future the conditions of which were unknown.

---

[45] *Brief Account of Past Ten Years of the Institution Established in the Himalayas by Sir H.M. Lawrence for the Orphan and Other Children of European Soldiers Serving, Or Having Served in India* (Lawrence Military Asylum Press, 1858), 81.

[46] Hubel, "In Search of the British Indian in British India."

[47] *Report of the Lawrence Military Asylum, for the Orphan and Other Children of European Soldiers, Serving of Having Served in India, for the Financial Year Ending 30th April, 1863* (Sanawar: Lawrence Asylum Press, 1863), 23.

[48] *Report of the Lawrence Military Asylum, 1863*, 25.   [49] Ibid., 22.

This list of skills proceeded from two assumptions about British Indian life, neither of which were universal. First, that the children in question would, as adults, live in the same way they would have "in their own English homes." This ignored the reality that most of these children had either never stepped foot on English soil or had left the country so young that they would have few memories of English life. Though many children of working-class parents who were born in or spent their childhoods in India did ultimately return to Britain, they tended to be children of intact families. Those who attended boarding schools, in contrast, were either full or half orphans or came from families that had been marked as at risk of moral and racial degradation. The second assumption guiding this curriculum was that the skills these children acquired should be at least to the standard of those they would have acquired had they never left Britain. Both these assumptions were born of a belief among the Lawrence school guardians that they could successfully replicate English life in a foreign land. Neither the experience of the girls nor the teaching style of their instructors bore out this belief.

The 1865 Report shows the Sanawar board grappling with their desire to train up, as they put it, "really English" girls while making some concessions to the realities of Indian life. The school wanted to "import a Matron from England with English notions" and a "really English cook."[50] The Matron should "know how to put her own hand to household work; and how to teach others to do the same" while the cook, having been raised in England, would "be accustomed to do everything for herself, and free from wants and prejudices."[51] Sanawar undertook this expensive project after the existing Matron refused to teach the female students housekeeping. The school claimed the girls had wanted to learn, but the Matron appeared to have considered it beneath her dignity to instruct them in domestic tasks that were left to servants in India. From the Matron's perspective, she would have been demeaning herself by engaging in work that was appropriate to people for a lower class and racial status and she would have been preparing the girls in her care to demean themselves as well. A "really English" cook would avoid these problems. She would be both culturally and racially English, knowledgeable about English foodways, eager to take on the work appropriate to her class, and infected with none of the laziness associated with Indian ancestry.

But at the same time, the Board considered expanding the girls' language education in response to the realities of Indian life. They sought

---

[50] Ibid., 36–37.   [51] Ibid.

a Hindustani teacher, arguing that "a soldier's wife should be able to market in the Bazar."[52] By 1871, Sanawar recommended all its female pupils be taught to speak enough Urdu to direct native servants. Here again, we can see the influence of various and sometimes contradictory ideas about race and class at play. In spite of their efforts to make their female students domestically self-sufficient, by 1871 Sanawar was ready to acknowledge that its students might indeed be in a position to direct native servants. But the students who came to the school already speaking fluently, likely because they came from mixed-race families or communities, were not encouraged to maintain their skills.[53] Language instruction of this sort would never have been on the curriculum for girls of a comparable status in Britain. Their middle-class counterparts might learn French to establish themselves as accomplished ladies, but the language had little practical purpose beyond marking its speakers as members of a particular class. For the Lawrence students, learning vernacular languages in India was seen as a survival skill at best and a sign of racial mixing at worst, not as a means of intellectual improvement or social advancement.

These discussions surrounding language indicate a shift in the way the Lawrence schools conceptualized their students. In spite of their, and the British government's, best efforts, most of the schools' students did not return to Britain. The 1868 Report noted that "only a few have accompanied regiments to England. As in former years, the majority have therefore left then to settle in India."[54] Between 1858 and 1868, a total of 654 students left the school, of whom 279 were girls. Only 62 of the girls married NCOs; the others married "other persons holding equally respectable places in society, and it is believed that they are with one or two exceptions, doing well."[55] The girls who married "other persons" may have married into railway families, known as one of the few refuges for the largely unemployable Eurasian community. This imprecise accounting leaves the fates of the majority of the Lawrence alumnae in question. The other girls may have married lower ranking soldiers – with or without permission. *"Eight children* of former pupils," an emphatic 1868 Report notes, "or eight of the *second* generation of soldiers' children

---

[52] Ibid. Hindustani was the lingua franca of much of North India at the time and would allow the girls to engage in basic transactions with South Asians of various first languages. The girls would likely already have had at least a little knowledge of the language.

[53] *Report of the Lawrence Military Asylum, for the Orphan and Other Children of European Soldiers, Serving of Having Served in India, for the Financial Year Ending 30th April, 1868* (Sanawar: Lawrence Asylum Press, 1870), 22.

[54] Ibid., 2.   [55] Ibid., 3.

are in the asylum, and they belong to three families."[56] These suggestive italics are left unelaborated in the report. They may have been meant to express pride at a developing school tradition or dismay at the repeated need for charitable schooling across generations.

Female education always carried with it the additional burden of shielding girls from sexual danger. In an appeal for private donations to support the female students of the Lawrence School at Ootacamund, the committee wrote, "there are many orphans of British Soldiers growing up in a very neglected state in the parcherries [married soldiers' quarters], and even in the bazaars, of the great Military stations, in an atmosphere of moral and physical impurity."[57] The only way the schools had of securing respectable futures for their female students was by making sure they had the moral and practical tools to make good marriages; the schools had little control over their female students' choices. In 1872, the Government of India appointed a commission, headed by Major General Huyshe of the Royal Army, Inspector General of Artillery, for India to investigate the management and curriculum of the Lawrence schools. Huyshe was skeptical of the schools' dedication to ensuring or arranging good marriage for its female pupils. "The Principal has doubtless satisfied himself," Huyshe wrote, "as far as possible, that the marriages effected have been of a suitable character, so far as his influence may extend in this matter."[58] The schools kept indifferent records of their students' marriages and postleaving occupations, and what records they did keep were not specific – an Army rank rather than the name of the man who held it.

Whatever the fates of the married girls and their children, they were of less concern to the school than their unmarried counterparts. Huyshe found there were few provisions made for girls who "are, as is often the case, friendless, – or if, through colour, or temper or any other defect ... [not] very promising candidates for matrimony."[59] The category of "color" was of concern to both British men seeking wives and Eurasians.[60] The paler a prospective bride, the easier it would be to pass as fully British for purposes of both employment and

---

[56] Ibid.
[57] Appeal on Behalf of the Female Branch of the Ootacamund Lawrence Asylum, *The First Annual Report of the Ootacamund Lawrence Asylum, for the Year Ending 1859* (Madras: Adelphi Press, 1859), Appendix F, xi.
[58] *Report of the Commission Appointed to Enquire into the Constitution and Working of the Lawrence Military Asylums in India; with Reports by a Deputation Directed to Visit the Several Asylums* (Simla: Government Central Press, 1872), 42.
[59] Ibid., 4.
[60] Though color could also be deceptive – Francis Phillip Woodruff, writing as Frank Richards, told a tale of a soldier who married a Eurasian woman and had a child who

respectability.[61] Huyshe and his commission came up with a number of recommendations, most of which were, as the original Lawrence curriculum had been, based on the assumption that the girls in question would easily find employment suitable for the British working class in India. This was seldom the case. Having spent their early years with servants and their school days repeatedly being told they had been saved from moral ruin in the cantonment, the girls had little interest in taking positions as Army schoolmistresses and even less in going into service.[62] As Jane McCabe has shown, the mixed-race children of tea planters were hired out as servants after they left the Doctor Graham schools, but only after having been transported to New Zealand and left with few other choices.[63]

Neither were middle-class British wives interested in hiring Indian-raised girls. Amy Macnabb, who had enjoyed having a comfortable and familiar relationship with her English nursemaid, complained to her mother that "you seldom can get an English servant in this country to be like a servant. They will take airs and expect to be waited upon."[64] The difficulties in negotiating a relationship shaped by seemingly complementary viewpoints – that a servant who might fill the role of a friend would also expect to be treated as one – underline the instability in relationships formed by women in unfamiliar settings and shaped by changing hierarchies of class, gender, and race. *The Indian Cook and Housekeeper*, offering faint praise to the Sanawar girls, warned that "though some young girls from the Sanawar and Mayo schools have proved quite satisfactory, the general run of girls brought up in India have a strong cheechee accent, and are lazy, careless, and independent."[65] A servant who reminded her mistress not of a longed-for homeland, but of the volatility of race and class in India, could offer only the anxiety, and none of the comfort, of recognition.

Conclusion

British women's understanding of what service meant in India depended on geography and generation. British-born women who had an expectation of returning to Britain saw their time in India as a temporary sojourn, and as such one in which they could play around with status safely. Taking on the airs of the mistress of a household or performing the role of a servant to another British woman did not necessarily engender

was too dark to pass for white – meaning the family would not consider returning to England. Richards, *Old-Soldier Sahib*, 234.

[61] Hawes, *Poor Relations*, 78; Caplan, "Iconographies of Anglo-Indian Women," 877.
[62] *Report of the Commission* (1872), 42.   [63] McCabe, *Race, Tea and Colonial Resettlement*.
[64] Amy Macnabb to Jean Mary Macnabb, February 16, 1864, IOR MSS Eur. F206/132.
[65] Steel and Gardner, *The Complete Indian Housekeeper & Cook*, 166.

expectations of either upward or downward mobility. Those who remained in India, on the other hand, came to see their respectability as defined by their roles as employers, rather than employed. The second generation – the daughters of these women who spent most of their childhoods in India – were particularly protective of their position. These girls, whether remaining in the cantonment, educated at a hill school, orphaned, or with living parents, grew up with a different type of knowledge of Indian and Anglo-Indian social hierarchies. For these daughters, the role of servant was racialized first and classed second, if at all. While the worried Lawrence Asylum board saw working-class girls refusing the education suited to their class, the girls in question were attempting to secure futures, as they understood them, suited to their race. The issue became all the more vexing for the school's leadership as there were mixed-race girls among their pupils.

Underlying most of these practical concerns was the question of whether or not poor white and mixed-race children born or raised in India could ever be fully British. Appearing white was not enough. Britishness required the correct performance of class accompanied with a patina of moral respectability. Children who unthinkingly accepted Indian luxuries, like servants, represented a moral hazard. But while middle-class luxuries were thought to be morally degrading, deracing, and declassing, middle-class respectability was expected of those who sought to be characterized as unproblematically British. As we have seen, educators and charitable institutions feared the possible moral contagion of a childhood spent in cantonments. Those who enjoyed the material benefits of India without adhering to the moral standards of the British middle class ran the risk of being classed with native Indians and made a social problem. Schooling was a last chance to strip out the cultural and environmental Indianness and create good British subjects. But even schooling could not convince British girls born in India to accept a life of service.

The only way to really get girls to accept service as a viable option was to remove them from India altogether. No matter how much time and energy the Lawrence schools spent instilling an appreciation for the domestic arts in their pupils, only moving to an environment in which no other options were available made service an acceptable choice. By the time Dorothy Keen was seventeen and the family settled back in England, she too was working as a servant. Service seemed more reasonable in other settler colonies as well. The Lawrence board came to understand that service in India would never be either an attractive or practical course for their female students. Native Indian servants could be employed at a much cheaper rate, and treated much worse, than servants of visibly British descent.

5   Class and Colonial Knowledge
Miseducation for Empire

Like most soldiers in the British Army, Private Frederick Lambert knew little about the culture or language of India when he arrived in the country in 1889. Lambert was raised on a farm and attended a village school in Essex before joining the Army in his teens.[1] Unlike most of his fellow soldiers, Lambert spent his time in British India, which at the time included Burma, immersing himself in the study of Asian languages while attempting to make sense of the cultures he encountered with limited educational resources. In spite of his repeated attempts to prove his mettle as a multilingual autodidact, Lambert never managed to advance beyond the rank of private. He left South Asia disillusioned with the place and the people he encountered. Lambert's experience was at once the result of his own failures to navigate the military culture of British India, and a refusal on the part of the British military to embrace anything beyond the most basic level of education among its working-class soldiery.

The British Army offered some of the few opportunities for social mobility for working-class men in the Victorian world, but these were rewards for maintaining the status quo, not upending it through education. Though the British Army did require enlisted men to pass exams proving minimal levels of learning (including basic arithmetic, writing, and reading comprehension) to qualify for promotion, education beyond these basic proficiency levels was not rewarded. Obedience, respectability, and good relations with one's superior officers were far more likely to lead to promotion than hours spent studying Hindi. Knowledge of vernacular languages, especially among enlisted men and NCOs, suggested too friendly a relationship with the native Indian population. Autodidacticism and formal education were little valued in the military hierarchy because they did little to bolster British rule, while at the same time threatening to upset the British class system in the empire and at

---

[1] Diaries of Pte F Lambert, 1st Battalion Devonshire Regiment, India and Burma, 1889–1893, and South Africa, 1899–1901, 9506-75, National Army Museum, London.

home. Indian Civil Service officers, as the educated elite of the Raj, needed to acquire knowledge of local languages, but they were required to prove their classical proficiency first, as if to protect their class and racial status from too much Oriental learning. Working-class men curious about their Indian surroundings could not rely on this undergirding of respectable knowledge to bolster their own claims of Britishness.

Official lack of interest in imperial education and colonial knowledge for enlisted men and NCOs had far-reaching implications than individual failures to advance in rank. Working-class men and women approached India from a position of relative ignorance. Being part of a family with experience of empire or India did not necessarily mean one had special access to colonial knowledge. As we have seen, letters and material objects carried information about how working-class Britons valued family, status, and continuity with the past more effectively than they did specific information about India. When those letters did convey information about India, it was for the most part not colonial knowledge, but instead information about imperial culture. I use the term imperial culture to refer to the practices, communication methods, shared knowledge, and material world – the praxis of daily life – that developed among Britons in India. Colonial knowledge, in contrast, refers to usable information about native life, language, culture, and history.[2] A working-class British man could join the Army, travel to India, and live within and master imperial culture without gaining any significant colonial knowledge. Lambert became well versed in certain aspects of colonial knowledge as he spent more time in India and Burma, but never completely mastered imperial culture. If he had, he would have understood that his attempts at self-improvement were not the way to get ahead in his military career.

Lambert's case illustrates the class dimensions of colonial knowledge and the limits of social mobility for non-elites in British India. The

---

[2] Edward Said and Bernard Cohn shaped the first generation of scholars grappling with questions of empire, knowledge, and information, understanding colonial knowledge as a powerful tool used to define native Indian society and to enforce imperial rule. Edward W. Said, *Orientalism*, 1st ed. (New York: Vintage Books, 1979); Michel Foucault, Bernard S. Cohn, *Colonialism and Its Forms of Knowledge: The British in India* (Princeton: Princeton University Press, 1996); Nicholas Dirks, *Castes of Mind: Colonialism and the Making of Modern India* (Princeton: Princeton University Press, 2001). C.A. Bayly, *Empire and Information: Intelligence Gathering and Social Communication in India, 1780–1870* (Cambridge: Cambridge University Press, 1996); Matthew Edney, *Mapping an Empire: The Geographical Construction of British India, 1765–1843* (Chicago: University of Chicago Press, 1997); and Arnold, *Colonizing the Body*, consider the collaboration between British and Indian producers of what became colonial knowledge.

British Army was concerned with maintaining rule, corralling its troops, and managing its reputation. Enlisted men who could speak vernacular tongues aided in none of those pursuits. Access to colonial knowledge, though more difficult for a man of working-class origin like Lambert, was not the primary problem. Lambert's trouble came in figuring how to put that knowledge to use – not only as a means of communicating with others but also as a method of social advancement. Lambert could read and learn all he was able to – what he lacked was access to the institutional structures through which colonial knowledge could be put to use. His basic misunderstanding then was not that colonial knowledge was useful, but that it was useful for someone of his status, at least as a means of social advancement.

This notion of the utility of knowledge is essential to understanding why working-class Britons like Lambert failed to transform learning into social advancement. The production of colonial knowledge has been considered an elite pursuit, even as historians have moved away from understanding it as a top-down imposition of British control and increasingly as an act of shared creation.[3] Those elites who produced colonial knowledge used it not only as a method of managing a native population but also to distinguish those who conceived of empire from those who built it. If the quest for colonial knowledge was prompted by the desire to, as Nicholas Dirks puts it, "know India well enough to rule it and profit by it," then British non-elites like Lambert had no need to know because they could expect to neither rule nor profit.[4]

This chapter considers the relationship between colonial knowledge and the imperial culture in which it existed. Is colonial knowledge, as historians of imperialism have defined it over the past three decades, relevant to the lived experience of British non-elites? How much colonial knowledge were Britons of any class expected to have before embarking to India? How did preparations for empire differ between middle- and working-class Britons, and what happened when class positions destabilized in India? What did people learn once they got to India, and how did that new information change their interactions with the country and its people, their position within British Indian society, and their friends and relatives in Britain? What can we conclude about social mobility and

---

[3] As I. Sengupta and D. Ali put it, colonial knowledge is a "process rather than a finished product." See I. Sengupta and D. Ali, *Knowledge Production, Pedagogy, and Institutions in Colonial India* (London: Springer, 2011) and R. Roque and Kim Wagner, *Engaging Colonial Knowledge: Reading European Archives in World History* (London: Springer, 2011), which represent this newer form of engagement with colonial knowledge as a process, uneven and fractured like empire itself.

[4] Dirks, *Castes of Mind*, 6.

British conceptions of their own role in India from classed ideas about knowledge?

Education for Empire?

Imperial service, rather than being a subject of the British Empire, determined whether a British man of any class would be educated for India. For women across classes, opportunities for learning about India in particular or empire in general were far more difficult to come by. Girls' education covered the British Empire as part of history and geography lessons, with little practical information provided about the individual colonies. This was the case even for girls whose families had established themselves through generations of imperial service. Education for elite boys was different, depending on the career path chosen for them. Boys whose families decided on the Indian Civil Service after 1858 pursued a punishing course of study, first at elite schools, then at university, and finally in a "crammer," where they spent a year preparing for the exams that would insure their entry into the service. Candidates learned very little about India in any of these institutions – the ICS exam tested both a classical and liberal education, and so-called civilians were notoriously well prepared in classics and literature, but with varying levels of practical knowledge.[5] Elite schools shaped their curriculum and exams accordingly. Charterhouse asked its fourth and fifth form geography students to draw a map of "Hindostan," identify the presidencies and some key cities, and discuss the significance of Seringapatam.[6] Rugby awarded a prize of £10 to the best essay on an Indian theme.[7] Students were required to learn the specifics of Indian language and literature only once they had entered the service. This failure to train ICS candidates in practical local knowledge was in part a result of Thomas Babington Macaulay's formative influence on the ICS exam.

   Macaulay's best-known educational intervention is his "Minute on Indian Education," circulated in 1835. Macaulay argued that Indian (defined by Macaulay as classical Sanskrit and Arabic, not the vernacular) languages and knowledge were inferior to English and that the British government should only offer financial support to educational

---

[5] Christopher Hagerman, *Britain's Imperial Muse: The Classics, Imperialism, and the Indian Empire, 1784–1914*, Britain and the World (Basingstoke, Hampshire: Palgrave Macmillan, 2013).

[6] *Charterhouse Examination of the Upper School* (London, 1861), National Archives UK HO/73/59/35.

[7] "A List of Rugby School Midsummer 1861," National Archives UK HO/73/59/35.

institutions that taught English and Western languages and knowledge. Though Macaulay's policy recommendations were never fully implemented, his Minute came to represent the predominant view in the debate over Indian education that had raged since British rule was established.[8] But Macaulay also headed the committee that would decide to establish the ICS exam in 1854 and put an end to the India-specific training and system of patronage promotion that had led to imperial careers up to that point.

Following the ideology of the "Minute on Indian Education," the 1854 commission recommended that the ICS exam test exclusively knowledge that could be acquired from a good liberal arts education. Macaulay's reasoning was that the vast majority of men sitting the exam would not pass, and it would be foolish to force them to learn information they would never use outside of the Indian Civil Service. "We think it most desirable," the Macaulay-led committee reported, "that the examination should be of such a nature that no candidate who may fail shall, to whatever calling he may betake himself, have any reason to regret the time and labour which he spent in preparing to be examined ... the effect is merely to open, to invigorate, and to enrich the mind."[9] This classic defense of a liberal education helped to codify Indian knowledge, for members of the ICS, as local and practical, while preserving the status of Western knowledge as essential to the functioning of a first-rate mind. As a result, colonial knowledge was valued as professional knowledge acquired for advancement, not as knowledge for its own sake. And colonial knowledge was only valued if it supplemented a firm grounding in gentlemanly educational attainments. Without the protective underpinnings of an ICS score, colonial knowledge signaled dilettantism or "going native."

Though their labor was essential to the imperial project, imperial and educational policies did not include provisions to prepare British people of working-class origin for imperial service until very late in the nineteenth century. Whatever education on imperial matters working-class children in Britain received before the 1870s–1880s was entirely up to the whims of their instructors. Instead, metropolitan imperial culture did the work of education for empire. Music hall performances, penny novels, popular magazines, and cheap plays offered a random array of rumor, fact, and myth to their audiences. Jonathan Rose has searched for

---

[8] Martin Moir and Lynn Zastoupil, *The Great Indian Education Debate: Documents Relating to the Orientalist-Anglicist Controversy, 1781–1843* (Routledge, 2013).
[9] Great Britain Civil Service Commission, *Report of Her Majesty's Civil Service Commissioners* (H.M. Stationery Office, 1884), xxv.

evidence of imperial content in the reading and instructional materials most used by working-class British children in the nineteenth and early twentieth centuries.[10] Until the late entry of Empire Day in the years after the South African War, there was little mention of imperial possessions in the subpar geographic and historical education pupils received at state-funded schools.[11] Popular fiction featured imperial settings, but Rose argues this did little to create a real picture of imperial life in students' minds. And there is a difference between possessing an awareness of empire and acquiring practical information about native Indian life and customs.

Metropolitan school boards did little work to promote colonial knowledge among working-class children in Britain. The London School Board's (LSB) records for the last decades of the nineteenth century reveal intermittent attempts to provide materials on empire generally, though not India specifically, to students and teachers. Only three of the 104 books submitted to the LSB library in 1889 were on explicitly imperial subjects.[12] In 1894, the LSB received a series of general works for their reference library on the colonies as well as government publications. The publishers Cassell & Co. offered *The Queen's Empire* series of illustrated books, depicting life across Britain's imperial possessions. Spurred by the gold rush and tensions in the Transvaal, the LSB planned to purchase a map of southern Africa for their trainee teachers institute, so the student teachers could follow along with developments in the region.[13] The library volumes were intended for broad circulation among schoolchildren (and children did indeed bring these books home), while the reference works were accessible only to teachers. These volumes were donated by individuals and organizations or proposed for purchase by the board. The vast majority of books acquired by the LSB for school use were novels, with nonfiction offerings sparse and books on empire even farther between. The curriculum similarly ignored imperial subjects. Teachers could seek out colonial knowledge for their students depending on their interest, but had scant resources to bring this information to their classrooms.

There were some attempts to create explicit educational links between metropole and empire. In 1903, the LSB instituted a pen pal program for

---

[10] Jonathan Rose joins Bernard Porter in arguing that British workers had limited access to or interest in the particularities of empire. Rose, *The Intellectual Life of the British Working Classes* and Porter, *The Absent-Minded Imperialists.*

[11] Rose, *The Intellectual Life of the British Working Classes,* 335, 347.

[12] London School Board Library Report, London Metropolitan Archive 0750, 1889.

[13] "Reference Library Subcommittee Reference Book," 1894, London Metropolitan Archive, SBL/0124.

London school children. "A certain number of letters written by scholars in their schools shall be forwarded each year to scholars attending schools in such of the British Colonies and Dependencies.... It is hoped that some scholars who are learning English in Indian schools might be willing to enter into correspondence with English children."[14] The program was designed not as an exchange between equals, but as a way for English children to help their colonial counterparts. Any knowledge exchange that occurred in the process would be an accidental benefit.

Students may have had access to little imperial content in their British schools, but military schools had the potential to offer an alternate opportunity for imperial learning. Military education, however, was designed to make up for deficits in elementary education in Britain, not to create colonial experts. In 1861, 19 percent of recruits could neither read nor write, 20 percent could read only, and only 7.5 percent had anything beyond an elementary education.[15] This compares with a literacy rate of around 60 percent in the general population.[16] As a result, regimental schools were more concerned with basic competency in reading and writing English, as well as some mathematics. The Army touted this form of basic education as one of the benefits of military service. The 1865 Report of the Council on Military Education claimed that a good education was one of the main draws of military service, alongside such essentials as "good food, clothing, and good treatment."[17] Passing literacy and numeracy exams led to promotion for only some men – for the majority, Army education was designed to keep them out of trouble and provide them with the intellectual resources sufficient to enjoy a book rather than a game of cards or a night of drinking. Soldiers could only benefit from reading rooms if they could in fact read and could only avoid the temptations of sex and drink, it was believed, if they had the kind of moral training education provided.[18] The base level of educational attainment among working-class men entering the Army in the second half of the nineteenth century expanded greatly after the Elementary Education Act passed in 1870. By 1900, general literacy had risen to around 90 percent.[19]

Alongside the movement to improve education across classes in Britain, the Army began to incorporate exams into its requirements for

---

[14] School Board for London; scheme for correspondence between children in England and in India IOR/L/PJ/6/634, File 863, April 28, 1903.

[15] "Education in the Army," *The Pioneer*, May 26, 1865, 6.

[16] Vincent, *Literacy and Popular Culture*, 24–25.

[17] Blue Book Second Report of the Council of Military education on Army schools, libraries, and recreation rooms, following up on first 1861 Report, Quoted in "Education in the Army," *The Pioneer*, May 26, 1865, 6.

[18] "Education in the Army," *The Pioneer*, May 26, 1865, 6.   [19] Ibid.

promotion. By 1861, enlisted men were required to pass the 3rd-class education certificate to be eligible for promotion to corporal. This required the candidate to read aloud, write from dictation, perform arithmetic functions, and possess a basic understanding of currency. A 2nd-class certificate required men to write from more advanced dictation, accounting, fractions, and averages and allowed for promotion to sergeant. In 1871, a new 4th-class certificate was introduced to certify that the men had achieved an education on par with that of an eight-year-old schoolboy in England. Those who could not pass were required to attend school for five hours a week, although in practice attendance varied. As late as 1882, 36 percent of enlisted men still could not pass the 4th-class certificate.[20] The education certificates and the regimental schools served to make up for educational deficits within the ranks regardless of location. Soldiers serving in Punjab received the same training as those in barracks in Woolwich. Only after achieving the 1st-class certificate could an enlisted man hope to be promoted to commissioned status.[21] Most men who rose from the status of private to a low-ranking NCO position were first offered promotion and then attended the classes required to achieve the 2nd-class certificate, suggesting that the educational requirements were more symbolic than practical.

Military exams had little relation to the skills soldiers needed in their everyday lives. A soldier named Macpherson of the King's Own Scottish Borderers described his Indian military education to the Reverend William Marwick while they were stationed together in Meerut. Macpherson was born in Aberdeen and had worked as a lithographer before joining the Borderers. Though he met Marwick in 1912, his account of joining the military was similar to those of William Wilkie, who joined in the mid-1850s, and of Frederick Lambert in the 1890s: "he had joined the Army on a sudden impulse and was 'listed before he had time to change his mind'."[22] His profession, along with the late date of his enlistment and his Scottish upbringing, suggests that he would have had a firm grasp of basic reading and writing before enlisting.[23] By the time he met Marwick in Meerut, Macpherson had already served in the south of India as well as in Uttar Pradesh. Macpherson told Marwick "the different things he had learned in the Army, nursing, cooking,

---

[20] T.H. Hawkins and L.J.F. Brimble, *Adult Education: The Record of the British Army* (London: Macmillan & Co. Ltd, 1947), 36.

[21] Ibid.

[22] "Papers of William Marwick," December 9, 1912, ACC. 48801.1 National Library Scotland.

[23] Scotland had a different educational system than England and produced a more literate populace earlier, especially in urban areas. Rose, *The Intellectual Life of the British Working Classes*, 16.

Morse code, etc, & of his intention to settle in S Africa & for quarrying [t]here as one can earn pound a day."[24] None of the Army's education certificates tested these skills, though cooking was an important skill for Army life, and Morse code and practical nursing certainly had applications outside of the military. Macpherson came to the Army with a skilled trade for which the military had little use and acquired additional expertise useful within a military context. He did not, however, plan to return to Scotland and put his skills to use, but rather to South Africa, joining the working-class mining populace hoping to improve their status through a financial windfall, not educational attainment.

Though working-class Britons in India lived and worked among South Asians, their own knowledge of Indian culture and customs was limited. Historians have assumed that non-elite Britons had less substantive interaction with South Asians than did elites, who might work with educated Indians in the civil service or command troops in the Indian Army.[25] This argument ignores the informal interactions – in the bazaar, between employer and servant, in the mixed districts that sprang up in cantonments, in forced and consensual sexual relationships – that would have occurred outside the confines of occupational relationships. Relating colonial knowledge acquisition among non-elites to such informal relationships gave it a tinge of sexual disreputability.

If informal means of education became unspeakable among elites because of their association with interracial sexuality, formal education offered little hope of improvement. *The British Army and Navy Review*, surveying the results of half a decade of educational reform as early as 1866, concluded that military education had largely failed in its first few years, as military men were unreachable intellectually because they lacked moral fortitude.

The very composition of our Army should have taught those having control over its education, the futility of making attempts to extend its benefits of learning, while leaving it optional with the class of men who, for the most part, fill its ranks, to indulge in the idleness or intemperance which were the main causes of their enlistment, or voluntarily to undergo the slightest degree of mental exertion; the more irksome because never before enforced upon or practised by them.[26]

---

[24] "Papers of William Marwick," December 9, 1912 ACC. 48801.1 National Library Scotland.

[25] Thomas Metcalf, *Ideologies of the Raj*; Clive Dewey, *Anglo-Indian Attitudes: The Mind of the Indian Civil Service* (London: Bloomsbury Academic, 2003); Margaret MacMillan, *Women of the Raj: The Mothers, Wives, and Daughters of the British Empire in India* (New York: Random House Trade Paperbacks, 2007).

[26] R. Bentley, "The Council of Military Education on Army Schools, &c., &c.," *The British Army and Navy Review* IV (R. Bentley, 1866), 154–55.

Thus the lazy British soldier was unworthy of the educational opportunities generously extended to him by the British crown, and that unworthiness explained why he had become a soldier in the first place. This uneven rhetoric recurs in reference to military men in the discourse surrounding housing, families, and children – the soldier was at once a sinner to be saved and the instrument of his own destruction.

Echoing the concerns that prevented elites from acquiring practical knowledge until it was necessary for promotion, learning about Indian languages and cultures could only serve to bring the British soldier closer to his Indian counterparts – a result the British government was eager to avoid. In terms of promotion and social mobility, the Army's educational initiatives were designed to reward obedience to authority and adoption of middle-class morality rather than intellectual brilliance. As with many aspects of non-elite masculine life in India, elites thought about education in terms of sexuality. William Moore wrote in defense of prostitution, "We have not yet by the force of education reached that problematical social millennium in which moral force shall overcome animal instincts."[27] In Moore's usage, education signified moral education alone. As a result, improving an individual soldier's literacy and numeracy functioned as much to keep him in line as to develop him intellectually. Intellectual pursuits that fell outside of the parameters of Army education could not be tested, did not demonstrate an aptitude for working within military culture, and did not assure moral rectitude.

Learning Imperial Culture

If neither elementary education in Britain nor military education in India taught colonial knowledge, how and what, if anything, did British non-elites learn about the Subcontinent once they got there? The basic education soldiers received included little on India specifically. Instead, soldiers turned to other kinds of knowledge making.[28] British non-elites in the military circulated imperial culture through gossip and social interactions, and through poetry and songs. In the search for colonial knowledge, non-elites who did leave records relating to India and Indian

---

[27] William H. Moore, "The Contagious Diseases Acts: Worthlessness of These Measures Both in England and India Demonstrated by an Important Memorandum of the Army Sanitary Commission: Together with a Reprint of Professor Stuart's Reply to Sir William Moore, and of the Speech of the Secretary of State for War on the Army Estimates." January 1, 1895, www.jstor.org/stable/60240702.

[28] Kate Imy has written about British soldiers taking up indigenous practices and beliefs in "Queering the Martial Races: Masculinity, Sex and Circumcision in the Twentieth-Century British Indian Army," *Gender & History* 27, no. 2 (August 2015): 374–96.

cultures tended to rely on written sources combined with observation. They trusted European interpretations to guide their own observations. Those with a greater ability to record and create their own colonial knowledge developed written accounts, glossaries, and travel narratives to preserve and pass on this information. And, like their counterparts at home, non-elites in India turned to literature to get a glimpse of the country they were occupying.

Perhaps the most effective sites of military education and imperial knowledge dissemination were the reading rooms and libraries that military reformers and officials were so eager to establish in cantonments. Officials put a great deal of trust in the power of the library to quell the sexual appetites and alcoholic proclivities of the British soldier.[29] The Outram Institute in Dum-Dum, for example, boasted of its collection of "5000 volumes, ... *Army and Navy Gazette, All the Year Round, Cassell's Illustrated Family Paper, Chamber's Journal, Daily Telegraph, Freeman's Journals, Illustrated London News, Illustrated News of the World, Jackson's Woolwich Journal, London Journal, Lloyd's Weekly Newspaper, Oriental Budget, Overland Mail, Punch, The Field, The Scotsman, Delhi Gazette,* the *Englishman, Friend of India, Hurkaru.*"[30] These titles represented the best of the popular British press and some of the British Indian, though British publications dominated. The *Civil and Military Gazette* doubted the efficacy of reading alone and argued that allowing a small amount of card playing and similar activities in the soldiers' recreation rooms would not "do harm under proper regulations; and as a soldier can no more be expected to spend all his spare time in reading than any other man, the recreation may be fairly welcomed as a relief from the monotony of military life."[31] Reading rooms were eventually ordered to be "supplied with newspapers, periodicals, bagatelle, backgammon, and draught boards, &c., &c."[32] Thus reading rooms were intended for distraction first and edification second, if at all. But in spite of their original purpose, men did use them to develop both imperial culture and colonial knowledge. Dissuaded from any encounters with South Asians but sexual ones, or as employers, many soldiers turned to the contents of reading rooms to supplement their experiential knowledge of India.

These men had first-hand access to India, but turned to written forms of information, like literature, and Kipling in particular, for stories of

---

[29] Sharon Murphy, *The British Soldier and His Libraries, c. 1822–1901* (London: Palgrave Macmillan, 2016), 103–04.
[30] *Report of the Outram Institute to Which Is Added a Report on the Women's Sewing Class* (Dum-Dum: Outram Institute Press, 1861), 2.
[31] No title, *The Civil and Military Gazette*, January 23, 1878, British Library, 1.
[32] "General Orders. Supplements," *The Pioneer*, 1871, 1870.

Indian life. Francis Philip Woodruff, who recounted his Army service in India in a published memoir, recalled that he and his fellow soldiers did not think much of the accuracy of Kipling's accounts of barrack-room life, but wrote, "what interested us the most in them was his detailed accounts of native life."[33] Woodruff certainly had the opportunity to contact, if not necessarily communication, with South Asians. As a private soldier in the British Army in India, he was tended to by Indian servants and patronized Indian establishments. Woodruff's level of access to Indian culture was in many ways up to him – he could choose to ask questions, converse with South Asians, or educate himself in the collections of the regimental library. In other episodes of his memoir, he confesses visits to native Indian prostitutes and his own abuse of native servants, but he still got his stories of "native life" from the same source as any armchair traveler who had never left England. Woodruff's insistence on distinguishing between Kipling's stories of native life and his own encounters with Indians – which are never described in detail – is telling. The figures in Kipling's stories were set at a distance, viewed through a fictional lens and the haze of history.[34] The actual Indians Woodruff encountered were neither so picturesque nor so unthreateningly historicized.

Similarly, Kipling's soldiers were far more sanitized than the men Woodruff wrote about. Woodruff gained a small measure of fame after the First World War, with the publication of his memoir of life as a private in the trenches, which was edited and promoted by Robert Graves. His Indian memoirs were a prequel to that book, and the success of the workingman's perspective in *Old Soldiers Never Die* may have encouraged Woodruff to emphasize the earthier aspects of Indian military life. He proudly recounts his efforts to pass on local knowledge to new recruits.

I always remembered the old time-expired man's advice at Deolalie and never forgot to pass it on to young soldiers who were fresh to the country ... native girls, who being in the last stages of the dreaded disease and rotten inside and out, only appeared after dark ... it was a horrible form of suicide to go with them.[35]

Woodruff situated himself as a node in a network of knowledge transmission. He performed a similar role in the rest of his memoir, which functioned at once as a cautionary tale and a fond remembrance of the

---

[33] Richards, *Old-Soldier Sahib*, 138.

[34] This is not to say that Kipling himself had no information about the sexual aspect of military life, rather, that he offered a more sanitized version to his readers.

[35] Richards, *Old-Soldier Sahib*, 199.

hardships and liberties associated with British Indian life for non-elite men.

In a particularly colorful passage, Lambert describes the tattooing practices among the men of his regiment.

When I enlisted I had no distinguishing marks or scars on me but I was now tattooed with designs of animals, snakes and celebrities on my arms and chest ... some men I knew must have regretted it more than me. Some of them had tattooed on their backs a pack of hounds in full cry after a fox, with the fox seeking cover in the hole of the backside. I drew the line at designs of this sort...[36]

As in the much more famous case of British naval tattoos, these army tattoos united the men in a military experience embodied in the skin.[37] In military and imperial spaces, such tattoos suggested a sense of play. Woodruff's memoir demonstrates, however, that these jokes could be lost in translation once back in Britain, with the comic power turned back on the wearer. Woodruff mentions that the men would have become figures of fun in the communal baths in his mining town as women gawked. Their "distinguishing marks" were no longer a shared joke in a homosocial environment but a mark of military service and the incommensurability of Indian experience with British home life.

Woodruff's concluding remarks reiterate his role as a nostalgic interpreter. Once back in Britain, Woodruff returned home to Wales and relayed his tales of Indian life to his fellow miners. Outside of India, he shaped his textual narrative differently than he did the tales he spun in India that transmitted imperial culture. In recollection, his ambivalence fades, India is held up as an ideal, and Woodruff reasserts himself as a conveyor of imperial cultural knowledge. "'India', I would say, 'is a land flowing with milk and honey. And what I was thinking of when I left it to come back home here and work again deep in the bowels of the earth, I'm damned if I know'. The boys would fix their eyes on mine and drink it all in."[38] Like his tattooed compatriots, Woodruff believed that he came back from India different and that this difference was legible on his body.

Little of Woodruff's imperial knowledge nodded to Indian culture. He tended to confine his discussions of Army life to the British military community. Somewhere between this British insularity and working-class autodidacticism lies the acquisition of useful language and cultural knowledge. George West, stationed in Burma in the middle of the

---

[36] Ibid., 335.
[37] James Bradley, "Body Commodification? Class and Tattoos in Victorian Britain," in Jane Caplan, ed., *Written on the Body: The Tattoo in European and American History* (Princeton: Princeton University Press, 2000), 142.
[38] Richards, *Old-Soldier Sahib*, 339.

century, recorded a number of useful phrases in his notebook when he served with the 2nd Madras European Light Infantry.[39] These basic words and phrases reveal a lot about how West interacted with the native Burmese population. His vocabulary allowed him to buy food, clothing, and tobacco in the bazaar, to refer to weapons, uniform components, and common animals. He also noted the phrases for "stop quiet," "Robber," "Pox," "I want one woman," "kiss my arse," and "Do not flog."[40] In common with other soldiers, West used his notebook to copy down both translations and the lyrics of popular songs. This practice suggests that these notes were not merely for reference while in India, but made for either a future readership or as a memento of South Asian Army life. West's act of recording colonial knowledge with the intention of transmitting it either to other soldiers or back to Britain was one of the many beginnings of an informal archive of imperial culture.

Army schoolmaster William Wonnacott kept his own much more extensive glossary of Indian phrases. As we have seen, being a schoolmaster placed Wonnacott in an uncomfortable social position. By education, he was a member of the middle class, but by rank he was an enlisted man, and he and his family rankled at the limitations placed on them by their descent down the social ladder. Wonnacott's Indian glossary shows him struggling to understand and record elements of Indian culture and geography, along with his own perceptions of the country. Native Indian religious practices, places, monuments, and incidents in Wonnacott's own travels blend together. Hand-painted illustrations accompany some of the entries. The Indian glossary echoes some of the information that could be found in imperial gazetteers, settlement reports, and travel guides. Wonnacott is unlikely to have encountered detailed statistical accounts of native populations, agriculture, and geography contained in settlement reports. He might have stumbled upon the more readable imperial gazetteers, which provided information on local customs, population, and people to colonial officials on the move or the travel guides aimed at families relocating to the Subcontinent. Wonnacott cites no sources, but the level of detail in his entries suggests that he must have relied on a range of printed sources, either in his own library or the collections at Army reading rooms.

Wonnacott's notes were based on a mixture of experience and unattributed information and were organized according to his own life history, rather than any system legible to an outsider. A description of a palanquin – "unpleasant sensation lie at full length in cushioned box &

---

[39] Papers of George West. IOR MSSs Eur. F133/173.   [40] Ibid.

impose whole weight on shoulders of 4 men conveyance of despotism" –
flows into definitions of bazaars, the differences between caste signs, a
discussion of the merits of the ayahs in Bombay, and then the island of
Colaba, Bombay Harbor, Parsees, idols, the phallic stone Sinjam, and
the tamarind tree.[41] His account traces his entrance by ship into Bombay
Harbor, the sights he observed onboard, and his later jaunts around the
city. As he rewrote his notes into the glossary, he jettisoned this autobio-
graphical organization and increasingly interjected information gleaned
from outside sources. The glossary represents a formalization of knowledge, reorganized to leach out some of the personal experiences in
favor of a more official language and style. Wonnacott may have
intended the glossary to be used as a means of recording his experiences
and knowledge for future readers within his own family and considered
the glossary format more suitable for conveying knowledge than the life
history. In any case, he removed himself from the contents of
the glossary.

Wonnacott used his own knowledge to interpret Indian culture. He
discussed Indian ceremonies in terms of other polytheistic religions. He
indulged in a multipage tangent on the "pedigree of Sooryavansi Rana of
royal race" in Rajasthan and descriptions of the gods and history of the
tribe. He compared the "sacred Bardai (Bards) of Rajpool" to their
Saxon counterparts and notes that "the fallen in battle are borne to
'Mansion of the Sun' as Scandinavian children of Odin to feast in
Valhalla."[42] These comparisons to earlier European practices provide
an easy way of translating religion in Rajasthan. They also, as in the case
of so much Orientalist work, discursively tie contemporary Indians to
ideas Europeans had long-rejected as ignorant superstition.

When Wonnacott died at sea near Aden on his way back to England,
his colonel wrote a letter of condolence to his brother Tom. "His education & talents," wrote Colonel Woods, "made him a gentleman among
gentlemen and as such we all mourn his loss."[43] This turn of phrase was
more than a platitude – considered within the context of British military
hierarchies, Woods' praise elevated William Wonnacott's status in death
as he could not elevate his rank in life. Wonnacott did have a more
genteel education and family connections than many of the men who
took on the schoolmaster role. As such, Woods praised his learning and
his well-rewarded painting talents and framed his loss as the loss of a
gentleman, made all the more tragic for that reason.

---

[41] William Wonnacott, Glossary, IOR MSS Eur. C376/6.   [42] Ibid.
[43] Col. Woods to T. R. Wonnacott, November 9, 1878, IOR MSS Eur. C376/6.

Autodidact Orientalists

Frederick Lambert, in contrast, came to the Army with no gentlemanly credentials. Lambert enlisted with the Devonshire Regiment in 1889, the month before he turned nineteen. His Army papers list his trade as blacksmith, but he had far greater ambitions. His journals are full of scribbled alphabets and phrases in Persian, German, Hindustani (Urdu), Arabic, Russian, Punjabi, Turkish, Hindi, and Burmese.[44] Though Lambert enlisted as a private and remained a private until the end of his ten years of service, he undertook a massive self-improvement campaign during his time in the Army. He took and passed the proficiency exams required for promotion out of the ranks and went on to attempt to prove himself through exams in a range of Asian languages.[45] Lambert was never able to parlay his learning into advancement while enlisted, though he did manage to secure a clerkship after he returned to England in 1899, and later a position with the Post Office. The culmination of his learning came in his unpublished manuscript memoir, entitled "The Golden Penny." This was written in two segments: the first describing his early years in the British Army in India and his time in Burma, and the second his service in the South African War as an Army reservist. "The Golden Penny" reads oddly; it is neither a traditional memoir nor a journal. Some sections are written in the present tense, while others are written as if from memory sometime after the events occurred. Lambert seems to have created the document with the expectation that it would be published, or at least read, at some point in the future. He also wrote a number of journals that are much more clearly intended to be private documents, which likely provided the notes for "The Golden Penny."[46]

Lambert is highly observant of the landscape and people he encounters and is intellectually curious in a way that is uncommon even among elite correspondents and writers. In an early sketch of South Asians, he is

---

[44] Diaries of Pte F Lambert, 1st Battalion Devonshire Regiment, India and Burma, 1889–1893, and South Africa, 1899–1901, 9506-75, National Army Museum, London.

[45] Lambert reports sitting for the second-class certificate in 1891. This required only a basic level of proficiency in taking down dictation and performing basic mathematic functions. He is at the same time learning Burmese, suggesting that his educational ambitions far outpaced the scope for advancement available to him. "The Golden Penny and My Life in the Army: The Diary of a Soldier," 1889, 9506-75-61, National Army Museum, London.

[46] Only one of Lambert's diaries survives. The remainder were lost when the Lamberts' Ilford home was looted in the wake of a landmine explosion in 1941. Note from Alma White, who donated her grandfather's paper to the National Army Museum, February 1, 1991. "The Golden Penny and My Life in the Army: The Diary of a Soldier," 1889, 9506-75-24, National Army Museum, London.

careful to note diversity amongst the population. Lambert's knowledge was likely obtained secondhand; he makes no mention of interacting with Indians in this part of his account. What results is a mixed attempt to understand native life through rumor and misinformation. "Then there is their caste," Lambert writes, "which a European would call religion and they live on rice and jepatties. If the shadow of a white man passed over their food there would be an uproar. They would throw it all away. Everything, post, chatties could be seen flying in all direction and the white men would be the same if they did not quickly shift away from them The different casts generally are in groups and dont mix one with another."[47] Lambert's discussion of caste is typical of working-class writers in India. "Caste" as a concept in reference to India had entered British usage by the seventeenth century, and by the late nineteenth century, the term was being used widely in reference to any exclusionary social system.

Caste was one of the few concepts relating to Indian social structures that British of any class had familiarity with before arriving in the country.[48] Loss of caste is a common theme among both elite and non-elite writings – guidebooks for British traveling to India discuss prohibitions regarding food and overseas travel, as well as the dire consequences that will befall those who transgress them. Lambert understands caste here to refer to religion, but later uses the term in a more general sense, in reference to groups of natives defined by occupation.[49] Combining a general notion of caste with his observations, Lambert develops a schema of Indian life in which all aspects of society are ruled and defined by caste, a notion educated elites would not dispute, but one they would apply in different ways.[50]

"The Golden Penny" is replete with knowledge derived from incomplete information. "Their dress varies in different parts of India," Lambert writes. "The men wear what is called a Soarie leaving their legs

---

[47] Frederick Lambert, "The Golden Penny and My Life in the Army: The Diary of a Soldier," 1889, National Army Museum, London, 9506-75-24, 31–32.

[48] Dirks, *Castes of Mind*, 5.

[49] Frederick Lambert, "The Golden Penny and My Life in the Army: The Diary of a Soldier," 1889, National Army Museum, London, 9506-75-24, 32. Lambert refers to a group he calls "loose wallahs," who steal weapons and sell them to Afghan tribes, as a caste. "loose-wallah" was a general term for a thief and did not denote any particular caste. Julie Coleman, *A History of Cant and Slang Dictionaries: Volume III: 1859–1936: Volume III: 1859–1936* (Oxford: Oxford University Press, 2008), 243.

[50] Lambert's shifting use of class actually aligned more closely with the way the concept was used in India, shifting across groups to signify practice, race, class, and religion depending on the location. Susan Bayly, *Caste, Society and Politics in India from the Eighteenth Century to the Modern Age* (Cambridge: Cambridge University Press, 2001).

and upper part of their body bare while women wear panteloons [sic]. These are very large but they are so tight round the ankles that it is a mystery how they remove them and some other parts it is the reverse."[51] Lambert, who had entered the country through Bombay, on the western coast, wrote this description from Rawalpindi, far north in the Punjab. He aptly observed the regional differences in Indian dress culture, even if his use of vocabulary was idiosyncratic. He may have heard large pieces of cloth fashioned into garments referred to as saris and assumed this terminology applied across genders.

But Lambert was not content to rely on hearsay alone. He dedicated himself to training in the language of the people around him.[52] While stationed in India, he took and passed exams in Hindustani, Pashtun, and Punjabi.[53] When his regiment moved on to Burma, he began learning Burmese, eventually hiring Moung Poh Win, a police interpreter, as a tutor. In November of 1891, after nine months of instruction, he traveled to Mandalay to take a language exam and "made friends with a wealthy Karen [on the train] who was going to Mandalay for the purpose as myself," who helped quiz Lambert on Burmese for the exam.[54] Language study seems to have provided Lambert with a broader range of acquaintances than he would otherwise have had. He refers to the Karen man as "his friend" multiple times – a companionate designation for a native man unusual among military memoirists. Lambert also forged new friendships at the exam, with another private and a lieutenant colonel from a different regiment. In the days following, Lambert wandered all over Mandalay, sightseeing and buying souvenirs. He met up with his Karen friend again, who introduced him "to some Burman friends, one of them being an interpreter. We discussed the subject of the day for a while."[55] The exam system may have facilitated such cross-class and cross-race encounters, but such sociability does not carry through Lambert's narrative.

[51] Frederick Lambert, "The Golden Penny and My Life in the Army: The Diary of a Soldier," 1889, National Army Museum, London, 9506-75-24, 31.

[52] This habit continued even after Lambert's Indian service ended disappointingly. He reads German while serving as a reactivated reserve soldier in the South African War. Frederick Lambert, "The Golden Penny and My Life in the Army: The Diary of a Soldier," 1889, National Army Museum, London, 9506-75-25/27.

[53] Diaries of Pte F Lambert, 1st Battalion Devonshire Regiment, India and Burma, 1889–1893, and South Africa, 1899–1901, 9506-75-8, National Army Museum, London.

[54] Frederick Lambert, "The Golden Penny and My Life in the Army: The Diary of a Soldier," 1889, National Army Museum, London, 9506-75-24, 87.

[55] Ibid., 87.

In his descriptions of Indian and Burmese dress and caste, Lambert is bemused, but not openly hostile to either native people or native culture, and he is eager to learn from various native teachers. This changes in his poetry. The last twenty pages of "The Golden Penny" are taken up by original poems written in a mélange of Kipling's style and doggerel on the subjects of India and Army life. Perhaps in tribute to his inspiration, Lambert's poetry is far more racist than any of his descriptions of South Asians in the journal or memoirs. In his ironically titled "The Joys of India," Lambert attempted to work through the disjunction between what he saw as Indian women's ugliness and their (he believed) caste-based sexual rejection of him.[56]

Lambert applied this bitter poetic tone to class analysis as well. In "Look Before You Leap," the poem most obviously inspired by Kipling in subject and meter in Lambert's collection, the treatment of British soldiers by their civilian superiors is a betrayal of their service in the Indian Rebellion:

> And then the Europeans when/In their traps they ride/When going past a Soldier they/Turn their heads with pride/But in 1857 when they were so afraid/They flocked around our soldiers/To beseech their friendly aid/And though oft times defended there/The recompense they showed/They asked our General to forbid us/Walking through their private roads … Now when a soldier comes to India/For just about a year/He need not look for luxuries/For that will be his share.[57]

He goes on to lament poor traveling conditions, native beggars, and the high cost of military uniforms.

Lambert is aware of and unhappy about class difference here in ways that are not present in his other writings. Lambert may have been imitating the style of drinking songs and poems that critiqued the lowly conditions of the soldier and sailor. It is possible that the poetic form, rather than confining Lambert to certain themes, gave him the freedom to write honestly about his reactions to his life in India and in the Army. These poems, written after a few years' service in which Lambert's persistent attempts at self-improvement had failed to yield any tangible results, were written in a mood of disappointment. Lambert was attempting to climb several rungs up the social ladder by proving himself competent not only to be a noncommissioned officer but a commissioned officer as well. It is little wonder that his initial enthusiasm for Indian difference resolved itself in disdain for the country that had promised so much potential for social mobility and delivered so little.

[56] Ibid.   [57] Ibid.

Enlisted men received confused messages on the relationship between military service and education. Recruiters held up the opportunity to advance as one of the boons of joining the Army, along with hot meals and a steady income. Regimental libraries stocked classic works of literature and history. And, according to Army regulations, enlisted men had to prove a certain level of educational attainment to be eligible for promotion. In practice, though, educating the troops was a matter of low priority. Few new recruits cited schooling as a motivator in joining up, novels proved far more popular than histories in regimental libraries, and men received promotions first and worried about passing exams second, if at all. Enlisted men could take exams in their native languages and even earn a small bonus for passing, but bounties decreased as fluency increased, discouraging men from proceeding too far in study.[58] Apart from language exams, the British Army offered little in the way of officially sanctioned opportunities for enlisted men to acquire colonial knowledge. And such knowledge was not necessary for navigating the world of the cantonment and the spaces beyond.

A private soldier who proved himself in military campaigns (which were far and few between in India at this time – Lambert mentions no actual fighting in his memoir) might be promoted up the ranks. A man who had a useful manual skill might eventually attain high non-elite status as a sergeant or corporal. These promotions were one of the few means by which working-class men could move up in the Victorian world. But Lambert's autodidacticism had no place in the military hierarchy and so received no encouragement. His discharge papers list his education certificates, medals and decorations, and certificate of character, but make no mention of any of the other language exams he passed, because there was no space on the form to note accomplishments of that sort. The notion of a working-class Orientalist fell far outside the social imaginary of the Raj and so had no place in its institutional structures.

Compare Lambert's voluntary language learning to the state-mandated instruction of Urdu for boys' schools.[59] The regulation applied to schools for European boys in India receiving state funding. By 1906, the government had come around, to a degree, to the necessity of training Indian-born Europeans in the skills they would require to

---

[58] Oriental Languages 1895–96: Hindustani: adoption of a uniform test for all India and revised scale of rewards. New exam in Urdu & a Proficiency Test, British Library, IOR/L/MIL/7/7305 164.6.

[59] Code of Regulations for European Schools in India and Burma 1905 with Explanatory Notes and Instructions Applicable to the Punjab Only, 5th ed. (Lahore: Mufid'I'Am Press, 1906).

remain in India. Part of the military's reluctance to reward autodidacticism in soldiers like Lambert came from a lasting distaste for settlement. Soldiers were intended to return to Britain or, if they did want to stay in India, to work in segregated railway communities purposefully designed to inculcate respectability in their inhabitants.[60] While soldiers could certainly stay on employed in other capacities, the railway colonies provided a means of corralling the population and defining it as if not fully British, then at least Anglo-Indian. Colonial knowledge acquired by British enlisted men undermined British ideas about the permanence of their role in India and the stability of class in their empire, while Urdu education among domiciled boys represented an unwilling capitulation to the realities of a growing creole population in need of skills.

Women's Knowledge

Thus far, I have been discussing men's colonial knowledge without differentiating women's experience and indeed with very little reference to women at all. The imperial institutions through which most British in India experienced empire gendered both the acquisition of colonial knowledge and access to printed resources. Women of working-class origin lived within the military or commercial hierarchies that determined their husbands' status, but had little direct control over how their careers advanced. Following along with the military's obsession with working-class morality, women could remain chaste and perform as close an approximation of middle-class domesticity as they were able. Women's colonial knowledge was not acknowledged as such, but it could help establish their households as respectable. As we have seen, women had to learn how to manage a household in a new environment with a new set of resources – servants, bazaars, and new foodways. For the majority of British working-class women in India, colonial knowledge and imperial culture blended together. Acquiring the skills to run a household involved learning how to manage native Indian servants and interact with shopkeepers in the bazaar. Housekeeping knowledge of this variety necessitated blending information on running a household in India and running a household of any type. These women's colonial knowledge contained within it elements of class mobility. And they had to accomplish this while maintaining the veneer of working-class respectability.

---

[60] Bear, *Lines of the Nation*, 65.

In early March 1890, Pollie Keen was stationed in Sialkot in the Punjab and wrote to her mother about the servants:

It has been a certain caste of the natives Christmas last week and they seem to have enjoyed themselves. We saw some of them drunk. Our cook asked for half the day on Friday. I told him I would cook the dinner so that he could go earlier but he said No memsaib [sic], me cook dinner then go, so we had dinner about a quarter past 12 and he was gone by one o'clock. When he came on Saturday morning his white coat was all red as if he had had a lot of ochre thrown over him tho they were all alike.[61]

Pollie was describing Holi. While the colorful Hindu spring festival would have been familiar to many elite Anglo-Indians, who read accounts of native celebrations in guidebooks and travel narratives, Pollie seemed to have had no prior knowledge of the holiday.[62] What she did know was that she was witnessing a festive occasion, and one that included part, but not all, of the native population of Sialkot. She gleaned this information by chatting with her servant – when writing to her mother, she rendered this conversation in a stereotyped pidgin English ("no Memsahib, me cook dinner, then go"). Their relationship as she described it, though, seems to have been both informal and fairly liberal on her side – possibly a result of Pollie's own time in service before her marriage. To describe the festivities to her mother, Pollie used the vocabulary and concepts to which she had access – and that her mother might have hoped to understand. She wrote of Christmas, caste, and clothing, rather than festival and religion.

While Pollie acquired much of her detail through observation, she did inquire after the Indians with whom she came into regular contact. In August of 1891, she wrote to her mother: "Today has been … quite a carnival. Our milkman came tonight…. On a piece of ribbon round his neck he had 9 gold rings, very thick, worth a hundred and 5 rupees … three gold rings on one hand and gold rings in her [presumably his wife's] ears nearly as thick as my wedding ring. I told him he was both rajah [sic] and he laughed."[63] Pollie's account offered an intriguing mix of mundane and exotic – the milkman dripping in the jewels of a rajah and his wife's adornments surpassing Pollie's own. Pollie seemed at ease

---

[61] Pollie Keen to Mary Holloway, March 9, 1890, IOR MSS Eur. F528/9.
[62] Hobson-Jobson, first published in 1885, lists the festival under "Hooly" and includes multiple printed references to it dating back to the seventeenth century. Henry Yule and Arthur Coke Burnell, *Hobson-JobsonHobson-Jobson: A Glossary of Colloquial Anglo Indian Words and Phrases, and of Kindred Terms, Etymological, Historical, Geographical and Discursive*, New Edition (London), 425.
[63] Pollie Keen to Mary Holloway, August 16, 1891, IOR MSS Eur. F528/10.

exchanging jokes with the milkman and his wife – whether they were likewise amused is another question.

Pollie had not been trained to have servants, nor brought up with the expectation that she would one day be keeping house in India. It is perhaps this unpreparedness that led her to be so open with her Indian staff and learn from them. "There was a native wedding the other night," Pollie wrote, in a letter dated from her first year in the country.

The bride was 6 years and her husband was 7 or 8. Our cook told us that the boys walked round her seven times then she was his wife. There was all sorts of music and they all went to the Bazaar and had a beanoh [celebration]. They keep it up half the night for nearly all the village natives turn out and join in and then the boy and girl go home with their own parents until they get a certain age then they have to get married again before they live together.[64]

This story of an Indian marriage is dropped into the letter between an account of having a clergyman visit for tea and the enlisted men's amateur theatrical. Pollie did not interpret the cook's account for her mother, nor did she make any comment on the ages of the bride and groom. There was no critique of marriage customs or disgust at the youth of the participants – in spite of the letter being written in the midst of debates in both India and Britain on the correct age of consent and marriage for Indian women.[65] For middle-class women, taking a stand on the age of consent could provide a powerful means of engaging in politics – and example of colonial knowledge being put to use. Pollie's main concern, though, as in most of her stories of native Indian life, was with the noise of the celebrations, which invariably, in her descriptions, last well into the early hours of the morning. If her understanding of the festivities was embedded in an awareness of popular criticism of Indian marriage practice, she did not make them explicit.

In spite of Pollie's apparently chatty relationship with her servants, she developed little but a cursory knowledge of Indian life and continued to interpret Indian religion through a Christian framework. Two years after her arrival in India and her first description of Holi, she again referred to it as a "Christmas," though she does embellish her account with add-itional details. "...Have been to the Bazaar tonight to see the fireworks. It amused the children and it is amusing to see the natives in each of their

---

[64] Pollie Keen to Mary Holloway, April 24, 1890, IOR MSS Eur. F528/9.
[65] See Antoinette Burton, *Burdens of History: British Feminists, Indian Women, and Imperial Culture, 1865–1915* (Chapel Hill: University of North Carolina Press, 24). Tanika Sarkar, *Hindu Wife, Hindu Nation: Community, Religion, and Cultural Nationalism* (Charlottesville: University of Virginia, 2001), Ch. 6 & 7.

houses.... They have a chattie or box filled with powder coloured and each one that goes to visit them they throw some over them ... they always get new white things ... all colours here and there about them and the more they get thrown on them the more welcome they seem to be."[66] Pollie's account of her children's pleasure at seeing "the natives in each of their houses" suggests that the family was at least casually familiar with some of the Indian population of Sialkot, even if only as touristic observers of local culture.

Pollie's letters reveal attempts to understand the native world of Sialkot through observation and induction, but with the support of very few facts. A month after Holi, she described another holiday, writing that "some of the natives ... have been passing today in hundreds from the villages round all going down to the city to the big church I think next month is the harvest."[67] Pollie's speculations about the harvest season suggest she is attempting to find some reason for the holiday. Her reference to the "big church" again points to an understanding of Indian religion received solely through Christian symbolism. Pollie's use of Christian comparisons, in contrast to Wonnacott's reliance on Saxon and Nordic ones, suggests a difference in the racial implications of informed and semi-informed Orientalist knowledge. While Wonnacott seemed to have been familiar with the types of texts that would make pagan comparisons, Pollie had only her own knowledge of Christianity to rely upon. As a result, William saw the Indian religious practices as in line with European ones of an earlier time, while Pollie related them to her own use and experience of Christian celebrations.

It is possible that Pollie had developed a deeper knowledge of Indian religion after two years in the country, but chose to use more easily comprehensible terms for the benefit of her correspondent – her mother, who had never left England. Regardless of Pollie's own understanding of Indian religious life, relaying it to her mother in familiar language perpetuated a view of Indian life in which strange customs were rendered manageable by erasing their cultural specificity and reframing them as versions of Christian ceremony. Letter writers like Pollie were essential to bringing knowledge of the imperial world to their working-class communities in Britain, but with only their own ideas about Indian life to work from, they gave their correspondents incomplete views of native India. Elites may have been just as unsuccessful in conveying detail about their subjects, but elite correspondents would usually have had greater access to other information on Indian life.

---

[66] Pollie Keen to Mary Holloway, March 14, 1892, IOR MSS Eur. F528/11.   [67] Ibid.

For working-class correspondents, these first-hand accounts were sometimes the only information they had.

If girls were educated at all for empire, they were educated to be exemplars of British morality and domestic life. One of the few opportunities working-class women had to be directly trained for colonial life (apart from missionary schools) came with the establishment of training academies for girls emigrating abroad with the help of the Girls' Friendly Society (GFS). The GFS operated under the auspices of the Anglican Church, preparing working-class girls for assisted emigration schemes by teaching domestic and nursing skills. These schools were dedicated to creating ideal British workers to establish British domesticity in the settler colonies and providing a class of respectable future wives for British men. India was excluded from these plans when the society was founded in the 1880s, but GFS interest in the Subcontinent grew once the existence of the domiciled population came to its attention in the early years of the twentieth century.[68]

For the GFS, educating girls for India consisted of a combination of moral education and vocational training, which would give the girls the resources to support themselves and avoid falling into immoral employment (anything from working as a barmaid to prostitution).[69] The GFS did disseminate some information on the dangers of life in India in the form of a "friendly letter of warning & advice" to the nurses and governesses who belonged to the society.[70] Nurses and governesses did not quite cover the range of employment that Indian-born GFS members undertook – Indian-born women were also likely to work in shops and in many of the growing business and secretarial roles.[71] GFS also provided training for girls both in Britain and in India. The Indian training was focused on domestic economy.[72] Taken together, GFS education for empire prepared girls to act as respectable, domestic, maternal figures operating under the rubric of British values and norms. Local knowledge was only relevant when it could help the girls avoid the supposedly twinned temptations of easy money and vice. As in the case of the British soldier, education for empire was moral education.

---

[68] "The Girls' Friendly Society in India" (Lahore, 1917) Women's Library 5GFS/01/110.
[69] Lahore Diocesan Leaflet Vol. 1 1911 Women's Library 5/GFS/2/164, 4–8.
[70] Flying Post Friendly Work supplement pub February, June, and October 1906, Women's Library 5/GFS/01/107.
[71] In 1908, the Bombay branch reported that they planned on opening a rest lodge devoted solely to girls being trained in business professions. "Agenda Book Committee of Council for GFS in India," Women's Library 5/GFS/01/107.
[72] "Girls' Friendly Society," Women's Library 5/GFS/01/107.

Conclusion

Certain commonalities exist between men's and women's education for empire and their uses of colonial knowledge and imperial culture. Education for empire, where it did exist, resisted specificity. If a non-elite man or woman wanted to acquire local knowledge, they had to strike out on their own. This hesitation to provide useful colonial knowledge to working-class subjects reflects elite and official British concerns about the permanence of British rule in India in particular, the problems associated with a domiciled population, and the ties between moral and social development. School boards, teachers, and makers of education policy saw little purpose in educating the British working class for India if they were not settling there. With no attempts to promote emigration to the colony, the sort of booster literature that might have tempted working-class Brits to the Australian outback or the Canadian prairies and offered an image (however embellished) of imperial culture to the metropole did not exist for India. Those who attained "too much" colonial knowledge while in the country might choose to stay. And because men and women who sought out colonial knowledge from native informants, personal relationships, and experience of Indian culture appeared to be "going native," they drew derision, rather than praise, from the colonial government and military.

In some ways, working-class men and women received all the preparation they needed to go to India. As part of the British Army, they expected to be shipped anywhere in the world. The hierarchies and regulations of British military service created a confining, but legible, institution. In this lack of preparation, we can see what the British state – through the Army and through its schools – valued in those who worked and fought for them. If non-elite Brits did serve any purpose in India beyond that of a standing army or a reliably loyal labor force, it was as representatives of British respectability. Most attempts at improving conditions for soldiers and their families – which led to reading rooms, improved housing, and education – grew as much out of fears of their misbehaviour showing British rule in a bad light as charitable urges. Thus education for respectability attempted to sustain the British class system in India, while the content of that education forced British non-elites – women in particular – to perform middle-class morality and domesticity. Those who could work within that framework of outward-facing respectability could get ahead – see, for example, Dick Keen, who managed to avoid being demoted multiple times for drunkenness, likely because he had a personable wife and family bolstering his status as a married man.

In the preceding two chapters, we have seen how British institutions – the Army, the education system in both India and Britain, even publishers of advice literature – failed to understand, and in many cases to even acknowledge, working-class experiences of India. To some, like Frederick Lambert, existing in the official imperial imagination as simply a soldier, with no potential for advancement based on learning, rankled. But for others, not being fully known by the power structures of the British India left a great deal of freedom for improvisation and self-fashioning, at least for a time. Women like Pollie Keen and Ada Lee took advantage of the uncertainty around social position to shape their domestic lives in ways that worked for them. Men like Woodruff and Macpherson, in contrast, gained what they could from their military service. For Macpherson, the British Army was a starting point for a life spent in empire – moving from Scotland to India or Australia. Woodruff, who mastered imperial culture and gained what colonial knowledge he could incidentally, rather than concertedly, ended up putting his mastery to use and creating precisely the type of guidebook to military and imperial life that had been lacking. It was only with the popular reimagining of a common soldier as heroic and honorable that came with the advent of the First World War that soldiers' knowledge was recognized to have any value.

6 Fragmented Families
Tracing the Afterlives of Working-Class India

When Sarah Cross went into the hospital to give birth to her son John, she was relieved to see her neighbor Pollie Keen there. The two women supported one another, "groaning one against the other from about 6 in the morning," until their babies were born in the early afternoon.[1] John William Montague Cross was born alongside Marjorie Keen and into a similar sort of family. Sarah's husband, John Thomas Cross, like Dick Keen, had started life as a farm laborer and made his way up to farrier serjeant, which meant that he looked after the hooves of the horses that Dick shod. In spite of these similarities, and John and Marjorie's nearly identical starts in life, the history of the Cross family diverges from that of the Keens, and that of the other families we have met in this book. The Cross family did not leave behind a collection of correspondence like the Keens did, nor did any of their diaries or memoirs, like those written by William Wilkie or Frederick Lambert, make it to an archive. Their history, much like that of the fictional O'Haras in *Kim*, survives in enlistment records, death certificates, census forms, and two mentions in Pollie Keen's letters.

John Thomas married Sarah Lily Collins in the autumn of 1887 without leave. Unlike Pollie, who was supported on the strength of the regiment, Sarah would have spent the first few years of her marriage in unstable housing, scrambling for money. Sarah was brought onto the strength of the regiment in October of 1889, some eight months before John was born, suggesting the Crosses were either very lucky or very good at family planning. Though she left the hospital before Pollie, Sarah had a difficult time recovering from John's birth. She was still unwell when she and Pollie had the two children, who had been born alongside each other, baptized together later that summer.[2]

John Thomas and Sarah moved frequently with the regiment. After John's birth, Sarah had another three children, a son born in Rawalpindi

---

[1] Pollie Keen to Mary Holloway, July 14, 1890, MSS Eur. F528/9.
[2] Pollie Keen to Mary Holloway and sons, July 20, 1890, MSS Eur. F528/9.

and a daughter in the neighboring hill station of Kalabagh. By 1895, John's regiment had been transferred back to England, and a second daughter was born there. John Thomas had initially signed on for one of the shorter six- to seven-year terms of service made available to troops with the Cardwell Reforms in the 1870s. This measure had been intended to prevent marriages like the unsanctioned one John Thomas and Sarah entered into, offering men a shorter enlistment and the possibility of returning to civilian life, marrying, and raising a family while still in their twenties. But, like many other soldiers, John Thomas reenlisted many times over, stretching out a military career to nearly two decades. By 1900, he was among the troops sent to South Africa, and it was on the voyage out that he died of pneumonia while his ship was docked at Las Palmas on the Canary Islands.[3]

John Thomas' death threw the Cross family into a crisis. Back in England with four children under the age of ten, Sarah turned to the help of the Royal Military Asylum. The Asylum, which was founded during the Napoleonic Wars to take in the orphaned children of soldiers, would provide John with an education and, more importantly, food, clothes, and lodging. Run on the monitorial system, students rose through levels of instruction, with the older students teaching the younger ones and the most advanced selected to become pupil teachers and eventually take classes of their own. The majority of students, however, did not rise to this level of scholastic achievement, and at 14, they were given the option to join the military (for boys) or be apprenticed to a trade (for boys and girls). John Cross took that later path. He was apprenticed "to his mother," which is to say that Sarah took him back into her home when he left school, having by this point found work as a cook and been better able to support her children. Sarah settled in Surrey and likely would have used the connections she developed there to find her son work as a gardener. But by 1910, at age 20, John had followed his father's path into the Army. He might have made this choice because he had a hard time supporting himself as a gardener – his medical history at enlistment lists his weight as a scrawny 118 pounds.[4]

Living as a widow in England gave Sarah more control over her fate. She was not dependent on the good graces of the regiment nor on a speedy remarriage. In England, remarriage was not the only respectable way for a widowed white working-class woman to support herself. Service, factory work, and relying on what would likely be larger family networks were all options. Sending her eldest to the Royal Military

[3] Register of Deceased Passengers March 1900, PRO BT 334/22.
[4] John WM Cross, Medical history, August 24, 1910.

Asylum gave Sarah Cross the leeway to go into service, something that would have been far more difficult had she had no one to look after John. Anxieties around class and race did not manifest themselves in the same way as they did in Indian schools for the British working classes. If there were students of mixed parentage in the Asylum, the school did not acknowledge their existence and so did not struggle to create a curriculum that could draw racial and class lines in the same way that Indian charity schools did. Returning to England reestablished Sarah, John, and the other Cross children in the British class system and secured their racial status. Ultimately, John Cross' birth year determined his fate far more conclusively than an early childhood spent in India. He turned twenty-four only weeks before the First World War began and died at Ypres in October of 1914.

A family story like that of the Crosses has not yet appeared in this book, not because the family is unusual but because they are average. It was unusual for working-class family papers to make their way into the archive in the first place. This is not to say that these families did not produce the same love letters and Valentines, passive-aggressive newspaper clippings, and pleas for funds, but that they were unable or disinclined to preserve them or donate them. I have only been able to tell the story of the Cross family in this much detail because of two details in the archives. First, the two mentions of her neighbor Mrs. Cross in Pollie's letters, accompanied by birth dates for both the Keen and Cross children. And second, John's distinctive middle name, William Montague, which made it possible to pick out his birth records from the scores of other John Crosses. Like the Cross family, whose story is visible among thousands of others that remain untold, the stories of working-class empire told in this book so far have been shaped and informed by the letters, journals, memoirs, and ephemera that found their way into the archive. In some cases, like that of the Cole family, these fragments provided a vivid snapshot of a few years in a family's life. In others, like those of the Keen family, remnants collected in the archive stretched across many years and offered a panoramic view of the lives and experiences of multiple generations – and multiple family histories.

This concluding chapter returns to the stories generated by these archival collections. But it also moves past them to investigate what happened to these families once they returned to Britain. In some cases, like that of the Coles, the letters that so brilliantly brought to life a working-class marriage are almost all the traces that remain of the family's story. In others, like the Palmers, the letters of only partially literate correspondents provide the clues to uncover a multigenerational family history. Thus, while the survival or destruction of the paper remnants of family histories cannot tell us whether people succeeded or failed in empire, they can help us understand how a working-class Raj came to be remembered – or forgotten – by subsequent generations. In doing so, we will be able to see how time spent in India shaped – or failed to shape – these peoples' experiences and understandings of themselves as members of an imperial nation and, once again, a working class.

Railway Widows and Working-Class Wives

George Cole and James Palmer died in India. It was only because of their deaths that any of their correspondence survived in the first place – as letters kept in the East Indian Railway files without a return address to send them on to. Lucy and George's letters end abruptly in 1862 with the sole surviving letter from George, likely unsent at the time of his death. According to this missive, he had started questioning his decision to come to India in the first place. He had just seen a friend die and was shaken by the new realization that he might not make it home alive. "This is the country to Bring a man to his sense," he wrote, "expetially when he sees 14 or 16 Buried in a week But Let us hope God will Spare my Life to See you once again."[5] His name disappeared from the annual list of East Indian Railway Company employees in 1862. Lucy Cole appears in the 1871 Census, still living in Stratford and now married to a man named John Dow.[6] But apart from this piece of evidence that Lucy remarried after George's death, the Cole-Dow family disappears from the archives.

Like George, James Palmer disappeared from the annual list of East Indian Railway Company employees in 1862. The last letter in James' possession was dated March 1862. The Palmer mother and daughters were fairly reliable correspondents, writing every few weeks. Given the length of time it took for the mail to reach India, James was likely still alive in the early summer of 1862, but died soon after. Ann would not have learned about this death until months later. Though Ann had not planned for James' death, she had, as we have seen, taken steps to provide some financial security for herself and her children. Moving closer to her father gave her greater access to family support.

Though no letters remain for this period, we can trace Ann's route through the census records and make some educated guesses about her motivations. She moved south along the London Road, from Huntingdon to Hitchin, near her father, and finally to Hoddesdon.

---

[5] George Cole to Lucy Cole, September 8, 1862, MSS Eur. F133/42.
[6] "Lucy Cole," *Census Returns of England and Wales* (The National Archives: Public Record Office RG10/1626/118: 115).

Before James died, Ann's father had suggested she and the children stay with him in Wymondley, an offer she may have taken him up on after her husband's death.[7] Moving closer to family support and moving toward London would both have been likely options for a widow who needed to support young children. But living close to, or with, her father was only a short-term solution. Although employment options for widows were more plentiful in England than India, working-class women in England too relied on remarriage as a survival strategy. Even with employment, women's earning potential would be severely curtailed by low wages and the demands of childcare.[8] Ann met Thomas Guttridge, a man fourteen years her junior who worked as a brewer in Hoddesdon. By 1871, the couple had married and had a daughter named Elizabeth, born in 1869. Young Ann, who had helped her mother with her correspondence, was 19, living away from the family home and working as a servant. Diana, the younger girl, was still living with her mother and new stepfather. Although Thomas had a relatively low-paying job at one of the Hoddesdon breweries, the family had enough money to keep Diana, who would by this time have been sixteen years old, at home.[9] Ann Palmer had mentioned in some of her letters to James that she worried Diana was slower to learn than her sister, which might explain why at sixteen she was still living in the family home, not attending school and with no occupation.

Ann Palmer's persistence in the archive should not be taken as proof of her success and Lucy Cole's failure, but rather as a demonstration of the arbitrary nature of the surviving records of working-class lives. Ann's moves aligned better with the years in which the census was taken, she married a man with a more distinctive last name, and her daughter Diana remained at home longer than was usual for working-class girls. What the Cole and Palmer records can tell us is how different working-class women based in England managed their husband's temporary elevation in income engendered by working in India. Increased income, or expectations thereof, allowed Ann Palmer to set herself up well initially, with a comparatively large home that could be used to generate income and provide for the family. Ultimately, though, with James' death, she relied on remarriage to secure her future and that of her children. Lucy Cole, perpetually short of money, likewise remarried.

---

[7] Ann to James Palmer, September 16, 1861, IOR MSS Eur. F133/112.
[8] Griffin, *Bread Winner*, 4.
[9] The couple might also have kept Diana at home to help look after her new sister, a practice that Emma Griffin identifies as common among working-class families. Griffin, *Bread Winner*, 28.

The gamble that George and James took in seeking out much higher incomes in India ultimately did not pay off; both their families in England went through a period of intense upheaval and eventually settled back into lives similar to the kind they might have lived had their husbands never left.

Army Families and Social (Im)mobility

Neither William Wonnacott nor Dick Keen intended to go to India when they joined the Army. Though both men likely understood a posting on the Subcontinent to be a likelihood upon enlistment, neither joined regiments that were bound to take them there. And neither intended their term of service to be accompanied by such swings in social status – for Dick, a climb up the social ladder for himself and his family, and for William, a descent down it. Both Emily Wonnacott and Pollie Keen had to figure out how to embed themselves and their children in the social and domestic worlds of the troop ships, cantonments, and hill stations they passed through. And the surviving Wonnacott and Keen children all had to readjust to altered social positions upon their return to England. The sheer volume of the Wonnacott and Keen family correspondence makes each family invaluable chroniclers of their respective social alterations.

William Wonnacott sent both Nellie and Willie back to England after Emily died. Remaining in India in spite of several attempts to return home early, he filled his time sketching and studying for a BA. He envied his brothers' success and what he saw as the greater degree of control over their lives that came with it. Robert ran a school, and John was an architect who had been made a fellow of the Royal Society. Even Emily's brother, Tom, had received a university degree. William answered an advertisement in the *Times*, writing to a man in Camden Town who offered to coach him for university examinations at the rate of 5 shillings per communication.[10] These examinations would allow him to receive a degree from the University of London without ever having attended. His mother eagerly joined in this project, sending him various university prospectuses. A degree, William thought, might "give me a standing above my fellows" and qualify him to be a subinspector of schools.[11] A higher level job was attractive not only because of the relative prestige involved but also because it would serve as a buffer against the

---

[10] William Wonnacott to mother, March 9, 1875, IOR MSS Eur. C376.5.
[11] William Wonnacott to mother, December 20, 1874, IOR MSS Eur. C376.5.

geographic instability that had sent William and Emily around the world and separated the family.

William Wonnacott finally left India at the end of 1877. His regiment made its way to Aden, where they expected to be stationed for another year. Though he was impatient to reunite with his children, William was fascinated by the city, writing to his brother about the coffee trade and the camel trains bringing goods to the port. He noted with wry self-knowledge that though "at present I am favorably impressed but daresay I shall grumble my full when the heat sets in."[12] William's activities in Aden were not too different from those in the various Indian cantonments he had lived in over the years. He taught children and adults, stopping the lessons early in the day as the weather grew too hot. He attended concerts in the evening. The mail ran quicker closer to home, and he sent a flurry of letters to his mother about Nellie's schooling and more requests for an up-to-date photograph of his daughter. By the autumn of 1878, his regiment had once again boarded a ship, this time to return to England at last. It was on board the ship that William died of an abscess of the liver, on October 6, 1878, and was buried at sea.

William's colonel wrote to his brother Robert in praise of him. The letter reinstated William as a "gentleman among gentlemen" by virtue of his "education and talents." In his twelve years with the regiment, he "led in glee class & joined in the endeavours of the officers to alleviate the dullness of an Indian station & to dispel the melancholy that drives soldiers to drink in cholera camps & other miserable places."[13] This praise situated William firmly on the side of the officers – as a man who would control the unruly tendencies of the soldiers – though still not among either group. Along with the letter, Woods appended a list of William's belongings, which included boxes of books and diaries, a folio of his watercolors, uniform pieces, the fabric to make a summer cloak for Nellie, and bundles of letters.

The Wonnacott children managed to regain the status their parents had so worried over upon their return to England. Both children lived with their grandparents when they first arrived, but Willie was soon sent to be looked after by his uncle John. When they were old enough, both children were enrolled in school in Cornwall: Willie at the institution his uncle Robert ran and Nellie at a nearby girls' school. For Willie, schooling brought him even closer to family, with his uncle as headmaster and his cousins attending the same institution. Nellie initially was to have been taught by her grandmother, but she was sent to school in

---

[12] William Wonnacott to T.R. Wonnacott, January 19, 1878, IOR MSS Eur. E376.6.
[13] Colonel Woods to T.R. Wonnacott, November 9, 1878, IOR MSS Eur. E376.6.

Cornwall along with Willie. Before he died, William and his mother had a lengthy discussion about Nellie's education. His mother had apologized for sending her away, but William wrote back with the wry understanding of an experienced teacher and father: "I should do the same if I were at home, for I shouldn't trust myself to withstand their cunning."[14] In spite of these early signs of rebellious nature, Nellie followed her parents' path and worked as a teacher, passing qualifying exams in 1886, at eighteen.[15] She taught at a school in Brighton, where she eventually became principal. Nellie did not marry until her late forties. Her husband, Lewis Nathaniel Powell, came from the landed gentry and, apart from a brief stint in a bank in his youth, did not work. Nellie's life trajectory looked similar to that of other girls of her class. Her later marriage might be attributable to her orphaned status – she would have had to spend more time building a career that would insure her financial stability than young women who could rely on the help of living parents. And she, like her father, might have craved the autonomy that came with a stable career. Willie, like his uncle John, became an architect. He married a woman named Jessie Hope in 1896, and they had two children.

Neither Nellie nor Willie took the peripatetic course that their parents had. Both stayed close to home, Nellie staying in the south of England and Wales and Willie settling in the suburbs of London. While Nellie's late marriage marks her life course as unconventional, both Wonnacott siblings found respectable occupations for themselves that ensured class and geographic stability. Willie and Nellie's teenage and adult years demonstrate the success of the Wonnacotts' strategy of sending their children home. The children did regain and maintain the status that their parents felt the family had lost in their years in India. But this success was dependent not solely on returning to Britain but on the presence and support of their family once they got there.

The reams of letters Emily and William wrote to their families helped to solidify the family ties that would ultimately aid Nellie and Willie. William's stable relationship with his mother and with the Short family and his correspondence with his brothers and with his own children all worked to keep the Wonnacott children within the family circle. William was conscious and careful about this. Though he missed his children very much, he allowed them to set the terms of the relationship and correspondence. When his mother wrote to him in Aden, complaining that Willie, at school in Cornwall, was an infrequent correspondent, William defended his son, writing, "I have asked his uncle not to compel him to

---

[14] William Wonnacott to mother, February 3, 1878, IOR MSS Eur. C376.6.
[15] "Class List," *The Educational Times*, August 1, 1886, 277–78.

write against his will, as I am afraid he will grow to detest letter writing, and those to whom he would have to write."[16] By sensitively managing his family's correspondence from afar, William was able to nurture relationships that lasted beyond his death. This type of affective work was essential to ensuring his children's futures. Had the small-scale spats Emily had with her own family festered, or had William been a less reliable correspondent, his England-based relatives would have been far less likely to provide the education and mentoring that were necessary to secure his children's place back among the British middle class. The Wonnacott family maintains a sense of itself and its history to this day, managing a website devoted to genealogists interested in learning more about their Wonnacott ancestors.

The fate of the Keen family upon their return from India offers a useful contrast to the Wonnacotts. Pollie and Dick Keen experienced as great a change in social status as Emily and William Wonnacott did. Pollie's Indian upward mobility mirrored the fears of British officials that lower-class Europeans in India would see the Subcontinent as an attractive place for settlement, disrupting the unique relationship between England and India. But the Keen family letters express little anxiety or celebration of the changes in their fortunes. Like the Wonnacott children, who, with family help, regained their class status upon return to England, the Keens resumed a working-class life, with some alterations. The Keens returned to England in the spring of 1894. Dick and Pollie and their surviving children, Dorothy, Eva, and Marjorie, moved into the Royal Artillery Barracks in St. John's Wood. Pollie was pregnant on board the ship as the family returned to England and gave birth to a son, Arthur, in the autumn of 1894. Fewer letters survive from this period, though it seems that Pollie wrote with relative frequency even when separated from her mother by a dozen, rather than thousands, of miles. In the winter of 1894–1895, she wrote to Mary, first berating her for not writing and then describing a series of outings the family had gone on. Pollie and Dick had taken the children to watch what she described as "thousands" of ice skaters in Regents Park.[17] She did not seem to regret her loss of status or relative prosperity upon returning to England. But Pollie did describe a few incidents that might give us a sense of the family's change in status and her own indifference to it.

Pollie had always considered her relationship with her employers as more familial than that of servant and employer. Soon after his birth, Pollie brought baby Arthur to visit the Lewes family, for whom she had

---

[16] William Wonnacott to mother, January 27, 1878, IOR MSS Eur. C376.6.

[17] Pollie Keen to Mary Holloway, Winter 1895, IOR MSS Eur. F528/15.

worked as a servant in her teens. She admired the Lewes daughter, who had surpassed Pollie in height since they had last seen each other. This type of familiarity, along with the letters Pollie wrote the family from India, suggest that at least from Pollie's perspective, the hierarchies that did exist made little difference in the relationship. Pollie also reported on some outings sponsored by the regiment. "The Major paid for all the women and children to go to the circus and the Friday after gave us all a tea in Barracks and everybody a present."[18] These excursions were similar to the picnics in that Dick and Pollie kept up their social life, attending the second guards' ball. This type of socializing was not too different from what they had experienced in India, though Pollie noted that she had a friend mind her children, rather than relying on the presence of servants. She described these outings as having "had a little life hear."[19] It is only in her diminutive invocation of "a little life" that Pollie's English letters make any indication that she might be bored or disappointed with her life back home. With the exception of the above examples, Pollie remained silent as to the effect of the enormous change in condition the family experienced as they left life in England for India and returned once more. Back in England, Pollie would still be an NCO's wife, but she would no longer enjoy the material benefits of the Indian service. Nor would she enjoy the boost in status afforded by her position as a white woman in a country defined by racial hierarchies. The same quality of cheerfulness that makes Pollie's letters such a pleasure to read makes them difficult to parse for evidence of her emotional responses to the family's changing circumstances.

The comfortable world of Army balls and picnics did not last long for the Keens. Dick's bouts of illness recurred in England, and he was discharged in 1895 as medically unfit. This could be a challenging time for military families, especially those who had been stationed far from friends and family. As an NCO, Dick was left with a pension, but it would not have been enough to support a family of five. The family moved to Egham, near Pollie's mother, and Dick found work as a builder. The work would have been difficult for someone discharged for medical reasons, and Dick died in 1910 at 50. There are no letters from this later period of the Keens' life, likely because Pollie now lived within walking distance of her mother. The family papers contain reproductions of photographs from this period, showing Dolly in a fur collar, Pollie posing in a garden, and Eva in a studio, holding a feathered fan. The Keen children remained in school for a time, but went out to work

---

[18] Ibid.   [19] Ibid.

by their mid-teens. Dolly went into domestic service, just as Pollie had. Arthur, who was born just after the family returned to England, found work in a bootmaker's shop by the age of sixteen. The girls married working-class men. There is some indication, though, that the children thought of their time in India – or at least as children of the Royal Horse Artillery – as definitional. When she married in 1914, Eva listed her father's occupation not as laborer, but as saddler. The Keen family donated Pollie's letters and some family photographs to the British Library in 2005. This donation suggests that family memory persisted for over a century.

The Wonnacotts and Keens each returned to their social positions once they returned to England. Though William Wonnacott did not make it back alive, he did ensure that his children regained their position within his family of origin. The Keens likewise went back to living as a working-class family upon their return. William did not survive to record his thoughts on this return to what he would have perceived as normalcy, and Pollie provided little insight into her own reactions. The best measure, then, of each family's relative success in the years following their return is the fact that their papers were donated to the archives. Enough of the Keen and Wonnacott descendants lived, retained family connections, and developed a sense of family memory to make such a donation possible.

Single Men, Family, and Work

Working-class single men formed by far the largest proportion of British inhabitants of the Raj. This book has sought to understand these men as part of families and larger social networks. The single men whose stories are featured in Chapter 1 – John Brand and Ned Crawford – did not live long past the period of their correspondence. William Wilkie, whose accounts of domestic military life shaped Chapter 3 of this book, returned to Scotland, married, wrote his memoir, and lived into the twentieth century. Wilkie, whose adult life stretched across the second half of the nineteenth century; John Brand, who experienced imperial war and imperial stasis; and the Crawford brothers, who took advantage of the disparate options available to working-class men, give us a sense of the opportunities afforded by empire and its limitations.

Wilkie's regiment returned to Britain in 1865, and he started to make his way back to Scotland. Upon docking in Portsmouth, Wilkie temporarily abandoned some aspects of his newfound piety. He sheepishly admitted to his daughter that "he forgot himself" amid the excitement of shore leave and "lost a badge & strips which he now is deprived of a penny a day of the pension."[20] After this, the regiment continued on to Scotland, and he was discharged at Stirling on September 8, 1865. Though Wilkie joined the reserves, he considered his service to be over. After his discharge, he reinstated his religious networks – visiting the church recommended to him in India by the preacher who had given him religious tracts.

Wilkie was able to draw on both his connections made in India and those maintained in Scotland for work. He contacted a former employer about taking a job in Edinburgh, but ultimately decided to return to Dundee and lodge with "an old comrade soldier" and his wife.[21] Wilkie readjusted to Scottish life, leaving the parrot he had brought back with him to be looked after by the neighborhood washerwoman and noting that "things did seem strange to me for a good while after being so long under military restrain."[22] He found work as a weaver in Dundee (likely in the Baxter Brothers linen works) and met up with former soldiers from time to time. The men he kept in touch with had followed similar life paths to his own, leaving weaving jobs to join the Army, spending years in India, and returning to take up the work once again.

As he settled into post-Army life, Wilkie noted that "not a few of my old comrades and companions were taking unto themselves wives I thought I could not do better than to follow their example." His time in the Army had given him ample opportunity to observe a variety of marriages and develop his own taxonomy of success and failure. He did so in the environment of a cantonment and camp – with its large propor- tion of unmarried men and marriage practices that ran against the middle-class ideal. "I did not wish to have [a wife] unsuitable for there is many of them for that act [marriage] was not like the act I had just conformed to, the ten year act but it was for life."[23] While in the earlier sections of his memoir set in India Wilkie filtered his Indian reminis- cences through a Scottish lens, at the end of his tale he used military metaphors and comparisons to understand his experiences back in Scotland.

He met Jane, the woman he would marry, in the fall of 1865. "I can give you the date of that important question, it was on the first of November I asked her to have a walk." This was quickly followed by a Hogmanay engagement (which he compared, again in military terms, to "a Highland sortie") and a February wedding.[24] The couple had five children, two of whom survived to adulthood – Martha, to whom

---

[20] William Wilkie's Reminiscences, British Library, IOR MSS Eur. B221, 112.
[21] Ibid., 116.   [22] Ibid., 119.   [23] Ibid., 119.
[24] William Wilkie's Reminiscences, 121.

Wilkie's memoir was dedicated, and Peter. Martha married a man named Robert Ogilvie two decades her senior. Robert was employed as a machine fitter, and the family occupied a two-up two-down house in a respectable working-class neighborhood.[25] Peter moved up the social ladder slightly, working as an assurance agent and living with his wife Margaret on the high street in Perth.[26]

Though Wilkie had little trouble finding work when he first arrived back in Britain, he cycled through a series of jobs in the decades that followed. From the 1870s into the 1890s, he worked in a jute mill, first in the warehouse and later as a night watchman. This was the job he held while writing his memoirs, in which he noted that "work was not so difficult to get then [1865] as it is now 24 years afterwards."[27] By the 1891 Census, he was listed as a draper and finally in his will as a "pedlar." These shifts in employment, especially those in his later years, track the changing fortunes of Dundee, shifting from linen to jute production and a skilled to a less skilled labor force. In their will, William and Jane Wilkie left their children little more than their personal effects and some small amounts of money – William specifically mentioned his Lucknow medal and silver watch, and Jane her clothing.[28] Wilkie's moves – to the Army, to India, back again, and through varied forms of employment until his last years – are emblematic of the moves made by working men who turned to India in the latter years of the nineteenth century for opportunity that seemed increasingly scarce in their regions of Britain.

The afterlives of John Brand and the Crawford brothers survive in much less detail. John Brand, who spent most of his time in India ill or convalescing, saw enough action to merit an Afghan War Medal. By 1880, he had returned to Britain and was living in the troop depot in Canterbury and considering whether or not to apply for a discharge on grounds of ill health.[29] He wrote to his friend Peter Gardiner that he hoped neither his boys nor the sons of their friend Will Brown would ever enlist in the military.[30] In England, he remained engaged in the political conversations that had punctuated his experience in India. He worried alongside Peter, who was working as an engine driver, whether the North British Railway workers would go out on strike and celebrate the

[25] "Martha Ogilvie," *Census of Scotland 1901* (National Records of Scotland: Census 56/21/11).

[26] "Peter Wilkie," *Census of Scotland 1901* (National Records of Scotland: Census 30/114/13).

[27] Ibid.   [28] Scotlands People NAS Holograph Settlement of William Wilkie.

[29] John Brand to Peter Gardiner, April 14, 1880, Papers of John Brand, NLS Acc. 6386.

[30] John Brand to Peter Gardiner, May 23, 1880, Papers of John Brand, NLS Acc. 6386.

Liberals' victory in the general election.[31] Relying on his own Indian experience of stasis, he predicted that the Liberals would do little to change the course of the war in Afghanistan – he compared the new government to "Mr McCawber in Pickwick waiting for something to turn up day after day, which something never did turn up."[32] Brand was ultimately not discharged until 1883, when the medical board at Canterbury finally diagnosed him with tuberculosis after years of lung infections.[33] Brand's correspondence wound up in the Scottish archives through donation, suggesting that Peter thought enough of the letters and the friendship to preserve them, and his descendants noted their significance.

Edward Crawford likely died in India. Like most of the men whose papers are found in the F133 file, his effects made their way to the archive because there was no one to easily pass them along to when their owners died. Perhaps because of Ned's early death, his brother Martin never followed up on his thoughts of signing on with the East Indian Railway in his turn. By 1900, he was still unmarried and still employed as an engine driver in the same coal fields he had worked when Edward went to India. But Martin did eventually take up another of the options available to a working-class man looking for opportunity, and in 1907 he sailed to the United States.[34] He ultimately found work as a rail car inspector and settled in East St. Louis.[35] It is possible that Ned's Indian experience shaped Martin's choice to emigrate and settle in a location outside the British Empire.

Other Choices and Imperial Memory

None of the men or families discussed thus far in this book made the choice to stay in India or to move on to other parts of the empire. This is in part an artifact of the archives consulted – people who moved on to Australia were far more likely to leave their papers in the Australian archives than return them to Britain. But working-class men did pass through India and move on to settler colonies. Tom Lloyd, for example,

---

[31] John Brand to Peter Gardiner, March 13 and April 14, 1880, Papers of John Brand, NLS Acc. 6386.

[32] John Brank to Peter Gardiner, April 14, 1880, Papers of John Brand, NLS Acc. 6386.

[33] Royal Hospital Chelsea: Soldiers Service Documents, WO 97, Piece 2352, National Archives UK.

[34] "New York Passenger Arrival Lists (Ellis Island), 1892–1924." Microfilm Serial: *T715, 1897–1957*; Line: *21*; Page Number: *62*.

[35] "Martin Crawford." *US Census 1910*. East St Louis Ward 5, Saint Clair, Illinois; Roll: T624_322; Page: 4B; Enumeration District: 0121; FHL microfilm: 1374335.

had much in common with the soldiers and railway workers we have followed thus far. Born in Wales in 1857 to an itinerant farm laborer and a charwoman, Lloyd joined the Royal Fusiliers at twenty.[36] He was stationed first in Ireland and later in India, and he fought in the Second Anglo-Afghan War. At the end of his service, he returned briefly to England and then emigrated to New Zealand, where his brother was managing a mining company. Lloyd married an Irish emigrant named Annie Bradley in 1887. The couple briefly managed a hotel, but Lloyd returned to the mines in the 1890s as an engine driver. Though Lloyd is only one example of service followed by settlement, his experience of movement between imperial sites, occupations, and social positions is not unusual.[37] His experience points to the utility of thinking about global movements of people and their historiographies through families – Lloyd went to New Zealand to join a brother in business, who might have sponsored him to settle and certainly offered him a job. While the Army could provide opportunities to move away from a family of birth or delay starting a family of one's own, once military service ended, former soldiers had limited options and little institutional aid in starting a life outside of the Army.

As we have seen, a "second generation" of people of British descent born in India remained. The luckiest boys among them found employment with the railways or in low-level clerkships. The fortunate girls married or, later in the nineteenth century, took advantage of new opportunities for shop or clerical work. We find the histories of the unluckiest among them in the Report of the Pauperism Commission.[38] The so-called indigent Europeans recorded within its pages provided a reminder of the failures of British moral vision and claims to racial superiority in the colonies. Alongside this indigent population and the larger domiciled population, the mixed-race population that had been a source of anxiety since the late-eighteenth century persisted and grew, though it resisted categorization. As the 1883 Report on the Census of British India regretfully noted, "there [was] great confusion between this class [Eurasians] and the European," with census respondents misrepresenting their heritage and census takers recording guesses or sometimes

---

[36] Thomas Lloyd, Karachi to Kandahar. The Diary of 1709 Private Thomas Phillips Lloyd, 2nd Battalion, 7th Royal Fusiliers (City of London Regiment), February 9, 1880 to December 31, 1880 being a record of his service in the 2nd Afghan War of 1878–1880, National Army Museum 9404–86.

[37] David Hackett Fischer, *Fairness and Freedom: A History of Two Open Societies: New Zealand and the United States* (Oxford University Press, 2012), 217–220.

[38] Report of the Pauperism Committee, IOR/L/PJ/6/331, File 1809 and 1892.

nothing at all for lack of space.[39] The colonial and military policies aimed at clarifying, categorizing, and maintaining class and racial distinctions between British non-elites and racial others ultimately collapsed in on themselves.

It is among these domiciled families that we can see the histories of British men and women who remained in India. Eleanor May Boult was born in Mhow in 1916 to a British-born father and a mother with deep roots in India. Boult's father had joined the Army as a private and left as a sergeant, going on to work as a driver on the railway. She considered herself to be fully British, though it is likely that her mother had some Indian antecedents; Boult noted that her mother never talked about her childhood or family.[40] Stephen Turner, who was Eurasian, was barred from the Indian Civil Service, bluffed his way into the Political Department in Baluchistan under Indianization, and lived as a domiciled European.[41] These families enjoyed the material advantages of living in India, including servants, managerial status, and (much improved by the second and third decades of the twentieth century) boarding school education for their children. The Turners and Boults successfully turned India into a hybrid colony, living functionally as settlers in a nonsettler colony – accomplishing at a familial level the feat that British policy had tried to prevent. It was only with Independence that both families resettled permanently in Britain. And with this resettlement, they purposefully characterized themselves as British, not Indian, erasing to some extent both their Indian heritage and their older working-class roots.

For men and women whose time in India could be measured in years, rather than generations, return to Britain offered fewer opportunities for reinvention. Instead, those who came back worked to reintegrate themselves into their communities of origin. Frederick Lambert returned to England and found employment as a postman in Essex.[42] Pollie Keen came back to Egham in Surrey with her family, and some of her children went into service.[43] William Wilkie returned to his position as a weaver in Dundee.[44] For those who did not return, families and friends preserved

---

[39] *Report on the Census of British India*, vol. 1 (London: Eyre and Spottiswoode, 1883), 53.
[40] Eleanor May Boult Papers, Interview with David Blake, IOR MSS Eur. R/183.
[41] Dorothy (Turner) Westlake, *"It wasn't really disobedience,"* IOR MSS Eur. C354. The catalog description of Stephen Turner refers to him as a domiciled European, not Eurasian, though Dorothy's texts make it clear that he was mixed race.
[42] Diaries of Private Frederick Lambert, National Army Museum 9506-75.
[43] Keen Family Tree, IOR MSS Eur. F528/20.
[44] William Wilkie's Reminiscences during his sojourn in the Crimea and during the Indian Mutiny was written from memory while night watchman in the Angus Jute works Dundee 1890–91, IOR MSS Eur. B221.

letters and mementos where they could, as the Wonnacotts and Peter Gardiner did. They did what was needed to survive the loss of family and income, as in the cases of Lucy Cole and Ann Palmer. Through these attempts at managing emotion, finance, and memory, these moves can be seen as both efforts at reintegration and efforts to create a separation between Indian and British periods of life.

★★★★

Contained within these stories of life after India is the key to understanding why the working-class Raj has been overlooked in the scholarship of modern Britain and has faded in the historical memory of the British working class. To conclude, I want to consider why this elision has occurred and what it can tell us about the afterlife of imperial experience. Thinking about the forces that compelled families and individuals to make the choice of whether to return, to stay or to move on can help provide some answers to the question of what happened to the memory of the working-class Raj. Those who had nurtured family relationships while in India might turn to relatives for help in establishing themselves. The relative strength of familial relationships sustained or created in India correlated imperfectly with the next steps taken. These choices were shaped by individual subjectivity, the quality of ties to home, and the nature of friendships and familial relationships.

Maintaining and reestablishing Britishness once back in Britain was just as important, if not more so, than it had been in India. Men and women who returned with stories of Indian servants, managerial responsibility, or elevated social status might have found it difficult to reintegrate into their communities of origin. Tales of the good old days would quickly become tedious. Historians and contemporaries alike identified this social dynamic among the elite Indian civil servants and military officers who returned to reduced circumstances in Britain. Those who had emphasized their ties to family in their letters home might do the same back in Britain, reinforcing conformity with their communities rather than difference.

For families who returned, the same epistolary forms that transmitted imperial culture from India to Britain contributed to its decline at home. Written communication became increasingly unnecessary as people returned to their communities of origin and shared memories of Indian life that would be kept within nuclear families, greatly lessening the need for letter writing. As we have seen throughout, correspondents prized maintaining relationships and shared bases of experience over unfamiliar tales. Reintegration into working-class life in Britain did not require people to be silent about their time in India, but instead to make those experiences peripheral to an understanding of their own lives. And just as Frederick Lambert learned in India, working-class Britons derived little benefit from claiming colonial knowledge, in either India or Britain.

Workingmen's stories of empire in their own right proved of little interest to the public at large. Those that did get told and published tended to be wrapped up in accounts of military service more generally. The book has been framed between the Indian Rebellion and the First World War, and this framing too helps to explain the absence of Indian stories from working-class life histories. Though the British successfully suppressed the Indian Rebellion, that conflict was not remembered as a victory, but as an all-too-close defeat. The iconic working-class figure of the Rebellion for the British was not in fact a soldier at all, but a soldier's wife. Jessie Brown's sighting of the Highlanders at the relief of Lucknow, depicted in song, painting, and on stage in the years following the Rebellion, memorialized the figure of the suffering white woman as much as the triumph of British military and imperial power.[45] This inauspicious beginning, followed by decades of "little wars" and military service more characterized by passive waiting than action, did not lend itself to narrative. The First World War inaugurated a whole new form of military memoir, concerned less with the details of campaigns and more with the trials of trench warfare and the absurdity of war. It was in this context that Frank Richards' account of his own wartime experiences as an enlisted man was first published. He was only asked to write *Old Soldier Sahib* about his time in India after the success of his first book.

While Indian service was not an unusual part of working-class lives, neither was it something that people could plan for over generations. Sons of men who had gone into the Army might talk about joining up themselves, but they had no control over where they went. Among the families studied here, there is little evidence of sons or daughters following their parents to India. Had Ned Crawford, James Palmer, or George Cole survived their time in India, their sons would not have naturally turned to work on the Indian Railways for employment. And indeed, having a family working or soldiering in India could prove a deterrent – as might have been the case with Ned Crawford's brother and John Brand's friends – rather than an inducement to follow the same path. The institutions of empire that employed working-class men saw no benefit, and indeed feared a great deal of possible harm, from creating generations of working-class families with ties to India. For working-class families, then, military service

[45] Dion Boucicault, *Jessie Brown; or, The Relief of Lucknow, a Drama in Three Acts* (Samuel French: 1858), Brantlinger, *Rule of Darkness*, 206.

or employment in India was undertaken as an economic move, rather than as part of a family tradition. Much as British schools saw little need to prepare students for the realities of life in empire, so did parents see little need to pass down knowledge to the next generation.

Efforts to manage family relations had significant effects on the ways in which people communicated and remembered imperial service. Indian experiences, and the fluid nature of status in India, were buried in forgotten letters home, little-read memoirs, and memories. If people did share their experiences after the fact, they largely survived as oral traditions, available only to those who bothered to ask. The stories in the *Family Life and Work Experience before 1918* oral history collection provide a useful example of this phenomenon. Tellingly, the interview questions are focused on working-class experience in Britain, but imperial service comes up time and time again. Subjects recall their parents' time in India and their own childhood memories. Frederick Hanrahan, a Liverpool man born in 1903, recalled that his father had spent 12 years in India before settling back in England and working as a tram driver. Rosemary Nash recalled that her parents had courted for the eight years her father was posted in India with the Royal Horse Artillery. Upon his return, they married and her mother occasionally took in washing to supplement the family income. Rosemary herself went into service at eighteen, living in, just as her mother had. In these interviews, parental service in India is spoken of as an unremarkable part of a life history, as normal as the birth of a sibling or leaving school.

While I was researching this book, I rented a room from a woman whose family were working-class Londoners who had lived in the East End for generations. One Sunday afternoon, she brought her grandmother over for lunch, and we all got to talking about what I did in the library all day. The grandmother recalled that, for part of his military service in the 1920s and 1930s, her father had been stationed in India. She had not mentioned this fact to her granddaughter before, and this story had formed no part of the family lore. She was not hiding this bit of family history nor purposefully forgetting it; it simply had not come up without prompting. This category of family story – not unmentionable, but unmentioned – has helped to shape the memory and forgetting of the working-class Raj. It is the very ordinariness of accounts like these that matters. British working-class life in the nineteenth and early twentieth centuries included the experiences of living abroad, filling ample leisure time, managing servants, exploring foreign landscapes, and observing different cultures. These working-class experiences of empire have been little remembered not because they were unusual or incidental to working-class life in Britain but because they were so common a part of it as to be unremarkable.

Bibliography

Archival Collections

British Library

General Collections
Family Life and Work Experience before 1918
Report of Her Majesty's Civil Service Commissioners, Great Britain
   Civil Service Commission

India Office Records
Alphabetical List of European and East-Indians in the Company's
   Service East Indian Railway Company 1862
Annual Report of the Ootacamund Lawrence Asylum for the Year
   Ending 1859
Code of Regulations for European Schools in India and Burma
   1905 with Explanatory Notes and Instructions Applicable to the
   Punjab Only
Final Report of the Revised Settlement of the Rawalpindi District in the
   Punjab, 1893
Fort William Military Proceedings for October 1863 no. 384
Henry Lawrence Collection, Military Department
House of Commons Question on the Lawrence Press, 1890
Imperial Gazetteer of India, 1881–1905
Railway Home Correspondence
Report and Returns of the Abu Lawrence School, 1907
Report of La Martinière College Lucknow, for the Year Ending 31st
   March, 1883
Report of the Commission Appointed to Enquire into the Constitution
   and Working of the Lawrence Military Asylums in India; with
   Reports by a Deputation Directed to Visit the Several Asylums, 1872
Report of the Lawrence Military Asylum [Sanawur], for the Orphan and
   Other Children of European Soldiers, Serving or Having Served in
   India, for the Financial Year Ending 30th April, 1858–68
Report of the Outram Institute to Which Is Added a Report on the
   Women's Sewing Class

Report of the Pauperism Committee, Proceedings of the Lieutenant-Governor of Bengal General Department Miscellaneous Calcutta
Report of the Sir Henry Lawrence Memorial Asylum at Murree, for the Year 1902–3 for Orphans and Other Children of European Soldiers Serving, or Having Served, in India
Report on the Census of British India, 1883
Statement Exhibiting the Moral and Material Progress and Condition of India during the Year 1910–11

India Office European Manuscripts

Dorothy Westlake Papers
Eleanor May Boult Papers
James Jones Collection
Keen Family Papers
Letters of Gunner Luck
Mauger Monk Papers
Maynard, H.J. "A Day in the Life of a Civilian Officer," lectured delivered Rawalpindi, 1913
Macnabb Papers
Papers forming part of the estates of Indian Army officers, surgeons and men; and of personnel of the East Indian Railway Company who died in India
Print Catalogue Advertisement for clothing, furniture, etc. from Wrenn, Bennett, &co, Madras c 1900
William Wilkie's Reminiscences during his sojourn in the Crimea & during the Indian Mutiny was written from memory while Nightwatchman in the Angus Jute works Dundee
William Wonnacott Papers

London Metropolitan Archive

London School Board Library Report
School Board of London Records

National Archives Kew

Census Returns of England and Wales
Home Office Materials Submitted by Schools
Public Elementary School Files
Register of Courts Martial for NCO in India
Royal Hospital Chelsea: Soldiers Service Documents

National Archives of India

Home Dept Medical Proceedings
Military Collection

National Archives Scotland

Census of Scotland
Diary of a Journey to South India, Alex Hamilton Papers
Robert Shirra Collection
ScotlandsPeople Wills

National Army Museum

Frederick Lambert, "The Golden Penny My Life in the Army The Diary of a Soldier" 1889/1902
Private William Randall Papers
Private G Bryan 4 Hussars, "My Experiences on the March from Bangalore to Secunderabad" September 1903
Private Thomas Phillips Lloyd 2nd Battalion 7th Royal Fusiliers City of London Regiment "Karachi to Kandahar the Diary of 1709 9 February 1880 to 31 December 1880 being a Record of his service in the 2nd Afghan War of 1878–1880"
Private Robert Austin Whiting, 1st Bn 3rd (The East Kent) Regiment of Foot (The Buffs) "Battles Long Ago. A Veteran's Memories. Private of The Buffs', from 'The Dragon', April 1940; relates the history of, 1870–1885"

National Library Ireland

Little Family Letters
Soldiers' Estate Letters

National Library Scotland

Diary of ES Grey, Veterinary Surgeon
Edward Fraser Papers
Isabella Plumb Correspondence/Letter Book
Medical Notebook of Surgeon Lt Col Douglas Blair Brown
Minto Papers
Papers of Private John Brand
Papers of William Marwick
Punjab Letter Books
Scottish Decolonization Project Oral Histories
Rev JC Matthew, Army Chaplain, Letters

Wellcome Library

Lillias Anna Hamilton Collection
Records of the Army Medical Department

Women's Library

Girls' Friendly Society Records
Henry J Wilson Correspondence

Hyslop Bell's Report
Josephine Butler Letter Collection
Records of the Association for Moral and Social Hygiene
Records of the British Committee of the Continental and General
    Federation for the Abolition of State Regulation of Vice
Records of the International Bureau for the Suppression of Traffic
    in Persons

Newspapers and Periodicals

The Army and Navy Magazine
The British Army and Navy Review
The Calcutta Review
The Civil and Military Gazette
The Englishman
Indian Annals of Medical Science
Journal of the Military Service Institution of the United States
The Pioneer
The Scotsman
The Times
The Times of India
Turnovers from the Civil and Military Gazette

Primary Sources

Andrew, Elizabeth and Katharine Caroline Bushnell. *The Queen's Daughters in India*. London: Morgan and Scott, 1899.
Army School of Cooking. *Handbook for Travellers in Indian Burma and Ceylon Including the Provinces of Bengal, Bombay, and Madras the Punjab, North-West Provinces, Rajputana, Central Provinces, Mysore, Etc. the Native States, Assam and Cashmere*. 4th ed. London: John Murray, 1903.
Baines, Jervoise Athelstane. *Census of India, 1891: General Report*. London: 1893.
Bentley, R., ed. "The Council of Military Education on Army Schools, &c., &c." *The British Army and Navy Review* IV (1866): 154–55.
Boucicault, Dion. *Jessie Brown; or, the Relief of Lucknow: A Drama in Three Acts*. Samuel French, 1858.
Mrs. Beeton (Isabella Mary). *The Book of Household Management*. Farrar, Straus, and Giroux, 1861, 8.
British Association for Cemeteries in South Asia Website. "About BACSA." www.bacsa.org.uk/?page_id=11. Accessed July 20, 2015.
Chota Mem. *The English Bride in India: Hints on Indian Housekeeping*. 2nd ed. Madras: 1909.
Chota Sahib. *Camp Recipes for Camp People*. Madras: 1890.
Cocker, Max. *Lovedale: The Lawrence Memorial Royal Military School South India: A Personal Account*. London: c.1988.
Cotton, James Sutherland, Sir Richard Burn, and Sir William Stevenson Meyer, *Imperial Gazetteer of India*. London: 1908.
Cotton, Sophia Anne, ed. *Memoir of George Edward Lynch Cotton, D.D.* London: 1871.

Danvers, Frederick Charles. *The Portuguese in India: Being a History of the Rise and Decline of Their Eastern Empire*. London: 1894.

Dawe, W. H. *The Wife's Help to Indian Cookery: Being a Practical Manual for Housekeepers*. London: 1888.

Duke, Joshua. *Ince's Kashmir Handbook and Guide to Visitors Appendix*. Calcutta: Thacker, Spink & Co., 1892.

The Englishwoman in India: Containing Information for the Use of Ladies Proceeding To, or Residing In, the East Indies, on the Subjects of Their Outfit, Furniture, Housekeeping, the Rearing of Children, Duties and Wages of Servants, Management of the Stables, and Arrangements for Travelling to Which Are Added Receipts for Indian Cookery by a Lady Resident. London: Smith, Elder and Co., 1865, 11.

Ewart, Joseph. *A Digest of the Vital Statistics of the European and Native Armies in India: Interspersed with Suggestions for the Eradication and Mitigation of the Preventable and Avoidable Causes of Sickness and Mortality amongst Imported and Indigenous Troops*. London: 1859.

"Family Life and Work Experience before 1918, 1870–1973." *Colchester, Essex: UK Data Archive*, 2009. http://dx.doi.org/10.5255/UKDA-SN-2000-1.

Forster, E. M. *A Passage to India* (1924 reprint). New York: Harcourt Brace Jovanovich, 1984.

Garrett, Elizabeth. *Morning Hours in India: Practical Hints on Household Management, the Care and Training of Children, &c.* London: Trübner & Co., 1887.

Indian Manual of Military Cooking. Calcutta: 1906.

Kipling, Rudyard. *Kim*. New York: Doubleday, 1901.

Lawrance, Harriet and Jessie Stirling Coyne. *Cookery for the Million, with Useful Hints to Houewives*. Montreal: 1877.

Lawrance, Harriet and Jessie Stirling Stirling. *Cookery for the Million Being 202 Practical, Economical, Recipes in Indian Cookery*. 2nd ed. Bangalore: Daily Post and Examine Press, 1886.

Marryat, Florence. *GUP*. London: Richard Bentley, 1868.

Middleton, Viscount. *Army and Militia Pamphlets Showing the Conditions of Service in the Army and Militia Respectively*. London: 1898.

Moore, W.H. *The Asylum Press Almanac and Compendium of Intelligence for 1883*, vol. LXXXII. Madras: 1882.

Moore, W.J. *A Manual of Family Medicine for India*. London: J&A Churchill, 1874.

Moore, W. "The Contagious Diseases Acts: Worthlessness of These Measures Both in England and India Demonstrated by an Important Memorandum of the Army Sanitary Commission: Together with a Reprint of Professor Stuart's Reply to Sir William Moore, and of the Speech of the Secretary of State for War on the Army Estimates." 1 January 1895, www.jstor.org/stable/60240702.

New York Passenger Arrival Lists (Ellis Island), 1892–1924." Microfilm Serial: T715, 1897–1957; Line: 21; Page Number: 62

Nightingale, Florence. *How People May Live and Not Die in India*. London: Longman, Roberts, & Green, 1864.

Ootacamund Lawrence Asylum. *The First Annual Report of the Ootacamund Lawrence Asylum, for the Year Ending 1859.* Madras: Adelphi Press, 1859.

Paterson, T. V. and W.H. Elliott. *The Art of Living, Or, Good Advice for Old and Young.* London: 1885.

Peacock, E.B. *A Guide to Murree and Its Neighbourhood.* Lahore: W. Ball, Printer, 1883.

Plowden, William Chichele. *Report on the Census of British India,* vol. 1. London: Eyre and Spottiswoode, 1883, 38.

Report of the Commission Appointed to Enquire into the Constitution and Working of the Lawrence Military Asylums in India; with Reports by a Deputation Directed to Visit the Several Asylums. Simla: Government Central Press, 1872, 42.

Report of the Lawrence Military Asylum, for the Orphan and Other Children of European Soldiers, Serving of Having Served in India, for the Financial Year Ending 30th April, 1863. Sanawar: Lawrence Asylum Press, 1863, 23.

Report of the Lawrence Military Asylum, for the Orphan and Other Children of European Soldiers, Serving of Having Served in India, for the Financial Year Ending 30th April, 1864. Sanawar: Lawrence Asylum Press, 1864, 4.

Report of the Lawrence Military Asylum, for the Orphan and Other Children of European Soldiers, Serving of Having Served in India, for the Financial Year Ending 30th April, 1868. Sanawar: Lawrence Asylum Press, 1870, 22.

Report of the Outram Institute to Which Is Added a Report on the Women's Sewing Class. Dum-Dum: Outram Institute Press, 1861, 2.

Richards, Frank. [Francis Philip Woodruff]. *Old-Soldier Sahib.* London: Faber & Faber, 1936.

Robertson, F. A. *Final Report of the Revised Settlement of the Rawalpindi District in the Punjab.* Lahore: The "Civil and Military Gazette" Press, 1893, 172.

Sarkar, Tanika. *Hindu Wife, Hindu Nation: Community, Religion, and Cultural Nationalism.* Charlottesville, NC: University of Virginia, 2001.

Scott, Paul. *The Raj Quartet.* London: Penguin Books, 1966–1975.

Shadwell, L.J. *Notes on the Internal Economy of Chummery, Home, Mess and Club.* Bombay: Thacker & Co. Ld., 1904.

Statistical Abstract Relating to British India No. 23. *Digital South Asia Library.* http://dsal.uchicago.edu/statistics/.

Steel, Flora Annie and Grace Gardner. *The Complete Indian Housekeeper & Cook: Giving the Duties of Mistress and Servants the General Management of the House and Practical Recipes for Cooking in All Its Branches,* 7th ed. London: William Heinemann, 1909.

Thackeray, William. *Vanity Fair.* 1848. New York: Penguin, 1984.

Tilt, Edward John. *Health in India for British Women and the Prevention of Disease in Tropical Climates.* 4th ed. London: J&A Churchill, 1875.

Wilson, Anne Campbell. *Letters from India.* Edinburgh: Blackwood, 1911, 10.

Wyvern, Kenney-Herbert. *Culinary Jottings for Madras: A Treatise in Thirty Chapters on Reformed Cookery for Anglo-Indian Exiles, Based upon Modern English & Continental Principles.* Madras: 1878.

Yule, Henry and Arthur Coke Burnell. *Hobson-Jobson: A Glossary of Colloquial Anglo Indian Words and Phrases, and of Kindred Terms, Etymological, Historical, Geographical and Discursive.* New ed. London: 1903.

Yule, Henry, A. C. Burnell, and Kate Teltscher, eds. *Hobson-Jobson: The Definitive Glossary of British India*, Oxford World's Classics. New York, NY: Oxford University Press, 2015.

Secondary Sources

Amato, Sarah. *Beastly Possessions: Animals in Victorian Consumer Culture*. Toronto: University of Toronto Press, 2015.

Anderson, Clare. *Legible Bodies: Race, Criminality, and Colonialism in South Asia*. Oxford: Oxford University Press, 2004.

Subaltern Lives: Biographies of Colonialism in the Indian Ocean World, 1790–1920. Cambridge: Cambridge University Press, 2012.

Anderson, Valerie. *Race and Power in British India: Anglo-Indians, Class and Identity in the Nineteenth Century*. London: Tauris, 2015.

Arnold, David. *Colonizing the Body: State Medicine and Epidemic Disease in Nineteenth-Century India*. Berkeley: University of California Press, 1993.

"European Orphans and Vagrants in India in the Nineteenth Century." *The Journal of Imperial and Commonwealth History* 7, no. 2 (1979): 104–27.

"Poor Europeans in India, 1750–1947." *Current Anthropology* 20, no. 2 (1979): 454–55.

"Race, Place and Bodily Difference in Early Nineteenth-Century India." *Historical Research* 77 (May 2004): 254–73.

Auerbach, Jeffrey A. *Imperial Boredom: Monotony and the British Empire*. Oxford: Oxford University Press, 2018.

Bailey, Peter. *Leisure and Class in Victorian England: Rational Recreation and the Contest for Control, 1830–1885*. London: Methuen, 1987.

Ballantyne, Tony and Antoinette M. Burton, eds. *Moving Subjects: Gender, Mobility, and Intimacy in an Age of Global Empire*. Urbana: University of Illinois Press, 2009.

Ballhatchet, Kenneth. *Race, Sex, and Class under the Raj: Imperial Attitudes and Policies and Their Critics, 1793–1905*. London: Weidenfeld & Nicolson, 1980.

Barton, David, and Nigel Hall, eds. *Letter Writing as a Social Practice*. Philadelphia: John Benjamins, 1999.

Baylies, Carolyn. *The History of the Yorkshire Miners: 1881–1918*. London: Routledge, 1993.

Bayly, C. A. *Empire and Information: Intelligence Gathering and Social Communication in India, 1780–1870*. Cambridge: Cambridge University Press, 1996.

Bayly, Susan. *Caste, Society and Politics in India from the Eighteenth Century to the Modern Age*. Cambridge: Cambridge University Press, 2001.

Bear, Laura. *Lines of the Nation: Indian Railway Workers, Bureaucracy, and the Intimate Historical Self*. New York: Columbia University Press, 2007.

Bellich, James. *Replenishing the Earth: The Settler Revolution and the Rise of the Anglo World, 1783–1939*. Oxford: Oxford University Press, 2009.

Benson, John. *The Working Class in Britain, 1850–1939*. Rev. ed. London: I. B. Tauris, 2003.

Bickers, Robert A. *Empire Made Me: An Englishman Adrift in Shanghai.* New York: Columbia University Press, 2003.

Blunt, Alison. "Embodying War: British Women and Domestic Defilement in the Indian "Mutiny," 1857–8." *Journal of Historical Geography* 26, no. 3 (July 2000): 403–28.

Domicile and Diaspora: Anglo-Indian Women and the Spatial Politics of Home. Malden, MA: Wiley-Blackwell, 2005.

Boucher, Ellen. *"Empire's Children: Child Emigration, Welfare, and the Decline of the British World" 1869–1967.* Cambridge: Cambridge University Press, 2014.

Bourke, Joanna. *Working Class Cultures in Britain, 1890–1960: Gender, Class, and Ethnicity.* London: Routledge, 1994.

Bowley, Arthur Lyon. *Wages in the United Kingdom in the Nineteenth Century* Cambridge: Cambridge University Press, 1900.

Brantlinger, Patrick. *Rule of Darkness: British Literature and Imperialism, 1830–1914.* Ithaca, NY: Cornell University Press, 1988.

Brief Account of Past Ten Years of the Institution Established in the Himalayas by Sir H.M. Lawrence for the Orphan and Other Children of European Soldiers Serving, Or Having Served in India. Lawrence Military Asylum Press, 1858, 81.

Briggs, Asa. *Victorian Things.* Rev. ed, 1988. Stroud, Gloucestershire: Sutton, 2003.

Bryder, Linda. "Sex, Race, and Colonialism: An Historiographical Review." *The International History Review* 20, no. 4 (1998): 806–22.

Buckley, K. D. and E. L. Wheelwright, *False Paradise: Australian Capitalism Revisited, 1915–1955.* Melbourne: Oxford University Press, 1998.

Buettner, Elizabeth. "Cemeteries, Public Memory and Raj Nostalgia in Postcolonial Britain and India," *History & Memory* 18, no. 1 (Spring/Summer 2006): 5–42.

Empire Families: Britons and Late Imperial India. Oxford: Oxford, 2004.

"Problematic Spaces, Problematic Races: Defining 'Europeans' in Late Colonial India." *Women's History Review* 9, no. 2 (2000): 277–98.

Burnett, John, David Vincent, and David Mayal. *Autobiography of the Working Class: An Annotated Critical Bibliography.* Brighton, Sussex: Harvester Press, 1984.

Burton, Antoinette. *Archive Stories: Facts, Fictions, and the Writing of History.* Durham, NC: Duke University Press, 2005.

Burdens of History: British Feminists, Indian Women, and Imperial Culture, 1865–1915. Chapel Hill: University of North Carolina Press, 1994.

Dwelling in the Archive: Women Writing House, Home, and History in Late Colonial India. New York: Oxford University Press, 2003.

Burton, David. *The Raj at Table: A Culinary History of the British in India.* London: Faber & Faber, 1993.

Bushnell, Katharine and Elizabeth Andrew. *Summary of Evidence Records of the Association for Moral and Social Hygiene.* Women's Library. London Metropolitan University, 3BGF.

Cain, P.J. and A. G. Hopkins. *British Imperialism, 1688–1990.* London: Longman, 1993.

Cannadine, David. *Ornamentalism: How the British Saw Their Empire*. Oxford: Oxford University Press, 2002.

The Rise and Fall of Class in Britain. Rev. ed. New York: Columbia University Press, 2000.

Caplan, Jane. *Written on the Body: The Tattoo in European and American History*. Princeton: Princeton University Press, 2000.

Caplan, Lionel. "Iconographies of Anglo-Indian Women: Gender Constructs and Contrasts in a Changing Society." *Modern Asian Studies* 34, no. 4 (2000): 863–92.

Carter, Marina. *Voices from Indenture: Experiences of Indian Migrants in the British Empire*. London: Leicester University Press, 1996.

Chakrabarty, Dipesh. *Rethinking Working-Class History*. Princeton: Princeton University Press, 2000.

Chatterjee, Indrani, ed. *Unfamiliar Relations: Family and History in South Asia*. New Brunswick, NJ: Rutgers University Press, 2004.

Clapson, Mark. *The Routledge Companion to Britain in the Twentieth Century*. London: Routledge, 2009.

Clark, Anna. *The Struggle for the Breeches: Gender and the Making of the British Working Class*. Berkeley: University of California Press, 1995.

Cleall, Esme. *Missionary Discourse: Negotiating Difference in the British Empire, c. 1840–1895*. London: Palgrave Macmillan, 2012.

Code of Regulations for European Schools in India and Burma 1905 with Explanatory Notes and Instructions Applicable to the Punjab Only, 5th ed. Lahore: Mufid'I'Am Press, 1906.

Cohen, Deborah. *Family Secrets: Shame and Privacy in Modern Britain*. Oxford: Oxford University Press, 2013.

Cohn, Bernard S. *Colonialism and Its Forms of Knowledge: The British in India*. Princeton, NJ: Princeton University Press, 1996.

Coleman, Julie *A History of Cant and Slang Dictionaries: Volume III: 1859–1936: Volume III: 1859–1936*. Oxford: Oxford University Press, 2008.

Colley, Linda. *Britons: Forging the Nation*. New Haven: Yale University Press, 1992.

Captives: Britain, Empire, and the World, 1600–1850. New York: Knopf Doubleday Publishing Group, 2007.

The Ordeal of Elizabeth Marsh: A Woman in World History. 1st Anchor Books ed. New York: Anchor Books, 2008.

Collingham, E.M. *Curry: A Tale of Cooks and Conquerors*. Oxford: Oxford University Press, 2007.

Imperial Bodies: The Physical Experience of the Raj, c.1800–1947. Malden, MA: Polity, 2001.

Cooper, Frederick and Ann Laura Stoler, eds. *Tensions of Empire: Colonial Cultures in a Bourgeois World*. Berkeley: University of California Press, 1997.

Cox, Anthony. Empire, *Industry and Class: The Imperial Nexus of Jute, 1840–1940*. London: Routledge, 2012.

Croll, Andy. "Starving Strikers and the Limits of the 'Humanitarian Discovery of Hunger' in Late Victorian Britain." *International Review of Social History* 56, no. 1 (April 2011): 103–31.

Cunningham, Hugh. *The Invention of Childhood*. London: BBC Books, 2006.

Leisure in the Industrial Revolution c1780–c1880. London: Croom Helm, 1980.

Dalrymple, William *White Mughals: Love and Betrayal in Eighteenth-Century India*. Reprint ed. New York: Penguin Books, 2004.

Daly, Suzanne. *The Empire Inside: Indian Commodities in Victorian Domestic Novels*. Ann Arbor: University of Michigan Press, 2011.

Darwin, John. *The Empire Project: The Rise and Fall of the British World-System, 1830–1970*. Cambridge: Cambridge University Press, 2013.

Datta, Arunima. "Becoming Visible: Travel Documents and Travelling Ayahs in the British Empire," *South Asian Studies* 38, no. 2 (July 3, 2022): 141–60.

Davidoff, Leonore and Catherine Hall. *Family Fortunes: Men and Women of the English Middle Class 1780–1850*. Rev. ed. London: Routledge, 2002.

Delap, Lucy. *Knowing Their Place: Domestic Service in Twentieth-Century Britain*. Oxford: Oxford University Press, 2011, 56.

Dewey, Clive. *Anglo-Indian Attitudes: The Mind of the Indian Civil Service*. London: Bloomsbury Academic, 2003.

Dirks, Nicholas. *Castes of Mind: Colonialism and the Making of Modern India*. Princeton: Princeton University Press, 2001.

The Scandal of Empire: India and the Creation of Imperial Britain. Cambridge, MA: Belknap Press, 2008.

Dussart, Fae Ceridwen. "'That Unit of Civilisation' and 'the Talent Peculiar to Women': British Employers and Their Servants in the Nineteenth-Century Indian Empire." *Identities* 22, no. 6 (November 2, 2015): 710–11.

Earle, Rebecca, ed. *Epistolary Selves: Letters and Letter-Writers, 1600–1945*. Aldershot, Hampshire: Ashgate Publishing Ltd, 1999.

Edney, Matthew. *Mapping an Empire: The Geographical Construction of British India, 1765–1843*. Chicago: University of Chicago Press, 1997.

Eley, Geoff. *The Future of Class in History: What's Left of the Social?* Ann Arbor: University of Michigan Press, 2007.

Elliott, Bruce David Gerber and Suzanne Sinke. *Letters Across Borders: The Epistolary Practices of International Migrants*. Basingstoke, Hampshire: Palgrave Macmillan, 2006.

Finn, Margot. "Anglo-Indian Lives in the Later Eighteenth and Early Nineteenth Centuries." *Journal for Eighteenth-Century Studies* 33, no. 1 (2010): 49–65.

"The Barlow Bastards: Romance Comes Home from the Empire," in Margot Finn, Michael Lobban, and Jenny Bourne Taylor, eds. *Legitimacy and Illegitimacy in Nineteenth-Century Law, Literature and History*. Basingstoke: Palgrave Macmillan, 2010.

"Colonial Gifts: Family Politics and the Exchange of Goods in British India, C. 1780–1820." *Modern Asian Studies* 40, no. 01 (March 9, 2006): 203–31.

Fischer, David Hackett. *Fairness and Freedom: A History of Two Open Societies: New Zealand and the United States*. Oxford: Oxford University Press, 2012.

Fischer-Tiné, Harald. *Low and Licentious Europeans: Race, Class, and White 'Subalternity' in Colonial India*. New Delhi: Orient BlackSwan, 2009.

Fischer-Tiné, Harald and Jana Tschurenev. *A History of Alcohol and Drugs in Modern South Asia: Intoxicating Affairs*. London: Routledge, 2013.

Fisher, Michael Herbert. *The Inordinately Strange Life of Dyce Sombre: Victorian Anglo Indian MP and a "Chancery Lunatic."* New York: Columbia University Press, 2010.

Forth, Aidan. *Barbed-Wire Imperialism: Britain's Empire of Camps, 1876–1903.* Berkeley: University of California Press, 2017.

Frawley, Maria H. *Invalidism and Identity in Nineteenth-Century Britain.* Chicago: University of Chicago Press, 2010.

French, David. *Military Identities: The Regimental System, the British Army, and the British People, c. 1870–2000.* Oxford: Oxford University Press, 2005.

Frost, Ginger S. *Illegitimacy in English Law and Society, 1860–1930.* Oxford: Oxford University Press, 2016.

Victorian Childhoods. Westport, CT: Praeger, 2009, 14.

Frost, Mark R. "Pandora's Post Box: Empire and Information in India, 1854–1914," *The English Historical Review* 131, no. 552 (October 1, 2016): 1043–73.

Furneaux, Holly. *Military Men of Feeling: Emotion, Touch, and Masculinity in the Crimean War.* Oxford: Oxford University Press, 2016.

Furneaux, Holly and Sue Prichard. "Contested Objects: Curating Soldier Art." *Museum and Society* 13, no. 4 (2015): 447–61.

Gerber, David. *Authors of Their Lives: The Personal Correspondence of British Immigrants to North America in the Nineteenth Century.* New York: New York University Press, 2006.

Ghose, Indira ed. *Memsahibs Abroad: Writings by Women Travellers in Nineteenth Century India.* Delhi: Oxford University Press, 1998.

Ghosh, Durba. *Sex and the Family in Colonial India: The Making of Empire.* Cambridge: Cambridge University Press, 2006.

Gilroy, Paul. *There Ain't No Black in the Union Jack.* 2nd ed. London: Routledge, 2002.

Goodman, Sam. "Spaces of Intemperance & the British Raj 1860–1920," *The Journal of Imperial and Commonwealth History* 48, no. 4 (July 3, 2020): 591–618.

Great Britain Civil Service Commission. *Report of Her Majesty's Civil Service Commissioners.* H.M. Stationery Office, 1884, xxv.

Griffin, Emma. *Bread Winner: An Intimate History of the Victorian Economy.* New Haven: Yale University Press, 2020.

Gullace, Nicoletta. *The Blood of Our Sons: Men, Women, and the Renegotiation of British Citizenship during the Great War.* New York: Palgrave Macmillan, 2002.

Hagerman, Christopher. *Britain's Imperial Muse: The Classics, Imperialism, and the Indian Empire, 1784–1914.* Basingstoke, Hampshire: Palgrave Macmillan, 2013.

Hall, Catherine. *Civilising Subjects: Metropole and Colony in the English Imagination 1830–1867.* Cambridge: Polity Press, 2002.

Macaulay and Son: Architects of Imperial Britain. New Haven: Yale University Press, 2012.

Hall, Catherine and Sonya O. Rose, eds. *At Home with the Empire: Metropolitan Culture and the Imperial World.* Cambridge: Cambridge University Press, 2006.

Hall, Nigel. "The Materiality of Letter Writing," in David Barton and Nigel Hall, eds. *Letter Writing as a Social Practice*. Philadelphia: John Benjamins, 1999, 88.

Hanna, Martha. "A Republic of Letters: The Epistolary Tradition in France during World War I." *AHR* 108, no 5 (2003): 1338–61.

Harper, Marjory. *Emigrant Homecomings: The Return Movements of Emigrants, 1600–2000*. Manchester: Manchester University Press, 2005.

Harper, Marjory and Stephen Constantine, *Migration and Empire*. Oxford: Oxford University Press, 2010.

Harrison, Brian. *Drink and the Victorians: The Temperance Question in England 1815–1872*. 2nd ed. 1971. London: Faber. ACLS Humanities E-Book, 2012.

Hawes, Christopher. *Poor Relations: The Making of a Eurasian Community in British India 1773–1833*. Richmond, Surrey: Curzon, 1996.

Hawkins, T.H. and L.J.F. Brimble. *Adult Education: The Record of the British Army*. London: Macmillan & Co. Ltd, 1947.

Heathcote, T.A. *The Military in British India: The Development of British Land Forces in South Asia, 1600–1947*. Manchester: Manchester University Press, 1995.

Herbert, Christopher. *War of No Pity: The Indian Mutiny and Victorian Trauma*. Princeton, NJ: Princeton University Press, 2008.

Holmes, Martha Stoddard. *Fictions of Affliction: Physical Disability in Victorian Culture*. Ann Arbor: University of Michigan Press, 2009.

Holmes, Vicky. *In Bed with the Victorians: The Life-Cycle of Working-Class Marriage*. London: Springer, 2017.

Hopkins, Eric. *Childhood Transformed: Working-Class Children in Nineteenth-Century England*. Manchester: Manchester University Press, 1994.

Hubel, Teresa. "In Search of the British Indian in British India: White Orphans, Kipling's Kim, and Class in Colonial India." *Modern Asian Studies* 38, no. 1 (2004): 227–51.

Huddleston, George. *History of the East Indian Railway*. Calcutta: Thacker, Spink & Co., 1906.

Hyam, Ronald. *Empire and Sexuality*. Manchester: Manchester University Press, 1991.

Imy, Kate. "Queering the Martial Races: Masculinity, Sex and Circumcision in the Twentieth-Century British Indian Army," *Gender & History* 27, no. 2 (August 2015): 374–96

Ishiguro, Laura. *Nothing to Write Home about: British Family Correspondence and the Settler Colonial Everyday in British Columbia*. Vancouver: University of British Columbia Press, 2019.

"Relative Distances: Family and Empire between Britain, British Columbia and India, 1858–1901." PhD diss., University College London, 2011.

Jalland, Pat. *Death in the Victorian Family*. Oxford: Oxford University Press, 2000.

Kaushik, Roy. *The Army in British India: From Colonial Warfare to Total War 1857–1947*. London: Bloomsbury Academic, 2013.

Kennedy, Dane. *The Magic Mountains: Hill Stations and the British Raj*. Berkeley: University of California Press, 1996.

Kriegel, Lara. *The Crimean War and Its Afterlife*. Cambridge: Cambridge University Press, 2022.

Lambert, David and Alan Lester, eds. *Colonial Lives across the British Empire: Imperial Careering in the Long Nineteenth Century*. Cambridge: Cambridge University Press, 2006.

Lambert, Frederick. *The Golden Penny and My Life in the Army: The Diary of a Soldier*. London: National Army Museum, 1889, 31–32.

Lawrence, Jon and Miles Taylor. "The Poverty of Protest: Gareth Stedman Jones and the Politics of Language: A Reply." *Social History* 18, no. 1 (1993): 1–15.

Lee, Ying S. *Masculinity and the English Working Class: Studies in Victorian Autobiography and Fiction*. New York: Routledge, 2007.

Lethbridge, Lucy. *Servants: A Downstairs View of Twentieth-Century Britain*. London: Bloomsbury, 2013, 78.

Levine, Philippa. *Prostitution, Race, and Politics: Policing Venereal Disease in the British Empire*. New York: Routledge, 2003.

Light, Alison, *Common People: In Pursuit of My Ancestors*. Chicago: University of Chicago Press, 2015.

Mrs. Woolf and the Servants: An Intimate History of Domestic Life in Bloomsbury. New York: Bloomsbury Press, 2008.

Linch, Kevin and Matthew Lord, eds. *Redcoats to Tommies: The Experience of the British Soldier from the Eighteenth Century*. Woodbridge, Suffolk: Boydell & Brewer, 2021.

Lutz, Deborah. *Relics of Death in Victorian Literature and Culture*. New York: Cambridge University Press, 2015.

Lyons, Martyn. "New Readers in the Nineteenth Century: Women, Children, Workers," in Guglielmo Cavallo and Roger Chartier, eds. *A History of Reading in the West*. Cambridge: Polity Press, 1999.

MacMillan, Margaret. *Women of the Raj: The Mothers, Wives, and Daughters of the British Empire in India*. New York: Random House Trade Paperback, 1988.

Mansfield, Nick. *Soldiers as Workers: Class, Employment, Conflict and the Nineteenth-Century Military*. Oxford: Oxford University Press, 2016.

May, Andrew J. "Exiles from the Children's City: Archives, Imperial Identities and the Juvenile Emigration of Anglo-Indians from Kalimpong to Australasia." *Journal of Colonialism and Colonial History* 14, no. 1 (2013), doi:10.1353/cch.2013.0016.

Mayhew, Henry. *London Labour and the London Poor*. David England and Rosemary O'Day, ed. Ware, Hertfordshire: Wordsworth Editions Ltd., 2008.

MacKenzie, John M. *Propaganda and Empire: The Manipulation of British Public Opinion, 1880–1960*, Manchester: Manchester University Press, 1986. Reprinted 2003.

MacKenzie, John M. and Tom Devine, eds. *Scotland and the British Empire*. Oxford: Oxford University Press, 2011.

McCabe, Jane. *Race, Tea and Colonial Resettlement: Imperial Families, Interrupted*. London: Bloomsbury Academic, 2017.

McClintock, Anne. *Imperial Leather: Race, Gender and Sexuality in the Colonial Contest*. Routledge: London, 1995.

McKibbin, Ross. *The Ideologies of Class: Social Relations in Britain 1880–1950.* London: Clarendon Press, 1990.

Metcalf, Thomas. *Ideologies of the Raj the New Cambridge History of India.* Cambridge: Cambridge University Press, 1997.

Mizutani, Satoshi. *The Meaning of White: Race, Class, and the "Domiciled Community" in British India 1858–1930.* Oxford: Oxford University Press, 2011.

Moir, Martin and Lynn Zastoupil. *The Great Indian Education Debate: Documents Relating to the Orientalist-Anglicist Controversy, 1781–1843.* New York: Routledge, 2013.

Moorhouse, Geoffrey. *To the Frontier.* London: Hodder and Stoughton Ltd, 1984.

Murphy, Sharon. *The British Soldier and His Libraries, c. 1822–1901.* London: Palgrave Macmillan, 2016.

Neill, Jeremy. "'This Is a Most Disgusting Case': Imperial Policy, Class and Gender in the 'Rangoon Outrage' of 1899." *Journal of Colonialism and Colonial History* 12, no. 1, (2011).

Oddy, Derek J. "Gone for a Soldier: The Anatomy of a Nineteenth-Century Army Family." *Journal of Family History* 25, no. 1 (2000): 39–62.

Omissi, David. *The Sepoy and the Raj: The Indian Army, 1860–1940.* Basingstoke, Hampshire: Palgrave, 1993.

Pati, Biswamoy, ed. *The 1857 Rebellion.* New Delhi: Oxford University Press, 2007.

Pearsall, Sarah. *Atlantic Families: Lives and Letters in the Later Eighteenth Century.* Oxford: Oxford University Press, 2008.

Pearson, M. N. *The Portuguese in India.* Cambridge: Cambridge University Press, 1988.

Peterson, Audrey C. "Brain Fever in Nineteenth-Century Literature: Fact and Fiction," *Victorian Studies* 19, no. 4 (1976): 445–64.

Poovey, Mary. *Uneven Developments: The Ideological Work of Gender in Mid-Victorian England.* Chicago: University of Chicago Press, 1988.

Porter, Bernard. *The Absent-Minded Imperialists: Empire, Society, and Culture in Britain.* Oxford: Oxford University Press, 2004.

Porter, Dale H. *The Thames Embankment: Environment, Technology, and Society in Victorian London.* Akron, Ohio: University of Akron Press, 1998.

Pradhan, Queeny. *Empire in the Hills: Simla, Darjeeling, Ootacamund, and Mount Abu, 1820–1920.* Oxford: Oxford University Press, 2017.

Prendergast, Christopher. *Cultural Materialism: On Raymond Williams.* Minneapolis: University of Minnesota Press, 1995.

Procida, Mary A. *Married to the Empire: Gender, Politics and Imperialism in India, 1883–1947.* Manchester University Press, 2002.

Ramusack, Barbara. *The Indian Princes and Their States, the New Cambridge History of India,* Vol. 3, Part 6. Cambridge: Cambridge University Press, 2004.

Rand, Gavin and Kim A. Wagner. "Recruiting the 'Martial Races': Identities and Military Service in Colonial India." *Patterns of Prejudice* 46, no. 3–4 (July 1, 2012): 232–54.

Rappaport, Erika. "'The Bombay Debt': Letter Writing, Domestic Economies and Family Conflict in Colonial India." *Gender & History* 16, no. 2 (2004): 246–48.

Rappaport, Erika, Sandra Trudgen Dawson, and Mark J. Crowley, eds. *Consuming Behaviours: Identity, Politics and Pleasure in Twentieth-Century Britain.* London: Bloomsbury Publishing, 2015.

Ray, Utsa. *Culinary Culture in Colonial India: A Cosmopolitan Platter and the Middle Class.* Cambridge: Cambridge University Press, 2015.

Reddy, William M. *The Navigation of Feeling a Framework for the History of Emotions.* New York: Cambridge University Press, 2001.

Richardson, Ruth. *Death, Dissection and the Destitute.* 2nd ed. Chicago: University of Chicago Press, 2001.

Riedi, Eliza. "Assisting Mrs. Tommy Atkins: Gender, Class, Philanthropy, and the Domestic Impact of the South African War, 1899–1902." *Historical Journal* 60, no. 3 (2017), 745–69.

Riello, Giorgio. *How India Clothed the World: The World of South Asian Textiles, 1500 1850.* Boston: Brill Academic Publishers, 2009.

Rock, David. "The British of Argentina," in Robert Bickers, ed. *Settlers and Expatriates: Britons over the Seas.* Oxford: Oxford University Press, 2010.

Roque, Ricardo and Kim Wagner. *Engaging Colonial Knowledge: Reading European Archives in World History.* London: Springer, 2011.

Rose, Jonathan. *The Intellectual Life of the British Working Classes.* 2nd ed. New Haven: Yale University Press, 2010.

Ross, Ellen. *Love and Toil: Motherhood in Outcast London, 1870–1918.* New York: Oxford University Press, 1993.

Rothschild, Emma. *The Inner Life of Empires: An Eighteenth-Century History.* Princeton: Princeton University Press, 2011.

Said, Edward W. *Orientalism.* New York: Vintage Books, 1979.

Scott, Joan Wallach. *Gender and the Politics of History.* Rev. ed. New York: Columbia University Press, 1999.

Scott, Joan, Bryan D. Palmer, Christine Stansell. "Scholarly Controversy." *International Labour and Working Class History.* 31 (1987): 24–49.

Sen, Satadru. *Colonial Childhoods: The Juvenile Periphery of India, 1850–1945.* London: Anthem Press, 2005.

"The Orphaned Colony: Orphanage, Child and Authority in British India." *Indian Economic and Social History Review.* 44 (2007): 463–88.

Sengupta, I. and D. Ali. *Knowledge Production, Pedagogy, and Institutions in Colonial India.* London: Springer, 2011.

Sharpe, Jenny. *Allegories of Empire: The Figure of Woman in the Colonial Text.* Minneapolis: University of Minnesota Press, 1993.

Sinha, Mrinalini. *Colonial Masculinity: The 'Many Englishman' and the 'Effeminate Bengali' in the Late Nineteenth Century.* Manchester: Manchester University Press, 1995.

Spear, Thomas George Percival. *The Nabobs: A Study of the Social Life of the English in Eighteenth Century India, by Percival Spear.* Rev. ed. 1932. London: Oxford University Press, 1963.

Stanley, Peter. *White Mutiny: British Military Culture in India.* New York: New York University Press, 1998.

Stedman Jones, Gareth. *Languages of Class: Studies in English Working Class History, 1832–1982.* Cambridge: Cambridge University Press, 1984.

Outcast London: A Study in the Relationship between Classes in Victorian Society. 2nd ed. 1984. London: Verso, 2013.

"Working-Class Culture and Working-Class Politics in London, 1870–1900; Notes on the Remaking of a Working Class." *Journal of Social History* 7, no. 4 (1974): 460–508.

Steedman, Carolyn. *Dust: The Archive and Cultural History.* New Brunswick, NJ: Rutgers University Press, 2002.

Labours Lost: Domestic Service and the Making of Modern England. Cambridge: Cambridge University Press, 2009.

The Radical Soldier's Tale John Pearman 1819–1908. London: Routledge, 1988.

The Tidy House: Little Girls Writing. London: Virago, 1982.

Stewart, Gordon T. *Jute and Empire: The Calcutta Jute Wallahs and the Landscapes of Empire.* Manchester: Manchester University Press, 1998.

Stoler, Ann Laura. *Along the Archival Grain: Epistemic Anxieties and Colonial Common Sense.* Princeton, NJ: Princeton University Press, 2009.

Carnal Knowledge and Imperial Power: Race and the Intimate in Colonial Rule. Berkeley: University of California Press, 2002.

Race and the Education of Desire: Foucault's History of Sexuality and the Colonial Order of Things. Durham, NC: Duke University Press, 1995.

Strange, Julie-Marie. *Fatherhood and the British Working Class, 1865–1914.* Cambridge: Cambridge University Press, 2015.

Streets-Salter, Heather. *Martial Races: The Military, Race, and Masculinity in British Imperial Culture, 1857–1914.* Manchester: Manchester University Press, 2004.

Subrahmanyam, Sanjay. *The Portuguese Empire in Asia, 1500–1700: A Political and Economic History.* 2nd ed. Chichester, West Sussex, UK: Wiley-Blackwell, 2012.

Thompson, Andrew S. *The Empire Strikes Back?: The Impact of Imperialism on Britain from the Mid-Nineteenth Century.* London: Routledge, 2014.

Thompson, E. P. *Customs in Common: Studies in Traditional Popular Culture.* New York: W.W. Norton, 1991.

The Making of the English Working Class. 1963, New York: Vintage, 1966.

"Time, Work-Discipline, and Industrial Capitalism." *Past & Present* 38 (1967): 56–97.

Tomlinson, Jim. *Dundee and the Empire: "Juteopolis" 1850–1939.* Edinburgh: Edinburgh University Press, 2014.

Trustram, Myrna. *Women of the Regiment: Marriage in the Victorian Army.* Cambridge: Cambridge University Press, 1984.

Van Onselen, Charles. *New Babylon, New Nineveh: Everyday Life on the Witwatersrand 1886–1914.* Rev. ed. 1982. Johannesburg: Jonathan Ball Publishers, 2001.

Vincent, David. *Literacy and Popular Culture: England 1750–1914.* Cambridge: Cambridge University Press, 1993.

Wahrman, Dror. *Imagining the Middle Class: The Political Representation of Class in Britain, c.1780–1840.* Cambridge: Cambridge University Press, 1995.

Wald, Erica. *Vice in the Barracks: Medicine, the Military and the Making of Colonial India, 1780–1868.* London: Palgrave Macmillan, 2014.

Walkowitz, Judith R. *Prostitution and Victorian Society: Women, Class, and the State.* Cambridge: Cambridge University Press, 1991.

Walvin, James. *Fruits of Empire: Exotic Produce and British Taste, 1660–1800.* NewYork: New York University Press, 1997.

Williamson, Jeffrey G. "Earnings Inequality in Nineteenth-Century Britain." *The Journal of Economic History* 40, no. 03 (1980): 457–75.

Woods, Robert. *The Demography of Victorian England and Wales.* Cambridge: Cambridge University Press, 2000.

Index

Milton Keynes UK
Ingram Content Group UK Ltd.
UKHW051844190124
436231UK00007B/8

9 781009 356589